DAYS OF WRATH

ALSO BY ROBERT KATZ

DEATH IN ROME
(1967)

BLACK SABBATH
(1969)

THE FALL OF THE HOUSE OF SAVOY
(1971)

A GIANT IN THE EARTH
(1973)

THE CASSANDRA CROSSING
(1977)

ZIGGURAT
(1977)

THE SPOILS OF ARARAT
(1978)

ROBERT KATZ

DAYS
OF
WRATH

The Ordeal of Aldo Moro:

The Kidnapping

The Execution

The Aftermath

DOUBLEDAY & COMPANY, INC.
GARDEN CITY, NEW YORK
1980

LIBRARY OF CONGRESS CATALOGING IN PUBLICATION DATA

Katz, Robert, 1933–
Days of wrath.

Includes bibliographical references and index.
1. Moro, Aldo, 1916–1978—Kidnapping, 1978
(March 16)   2. Italy—Politics and government—
1976–   3. Brigate rosse.   4. Terrorism—
Italy.   I. Title.
DG579.M63K37   364.1′54′0924
ISBN: 0-385-14910-7
Library of Congress Catalog Card Number 79–7050

FIRST EDITION

To my parents and to my family

CONTENTS

DRAMATIS PERSONAE

The Family

ALDO MORO, president of Christian Democracy, the nation's ruling party; five times Prime Minister; university professor; Italy's leading statesman; uncontested candidate for the presidency of the republic.

ELEONORA MORO, his wife of thirty-three years.

MARIA FIDA, their married eldest daughter, and a journalist.

ANNA, married daughter, and a pediatrician.

AGNESE, unmarried daughter still living at home, a student at the University of Rome.

GIOVANNI, unmarried son still living at home, a student at the University of Rome.

LUCA, "the little one," the Moros' two-year-old grandson (by Maria Fida).

The Family Friends

NICOLA RANA, Moro's private secretary.

CORRADO GUERZONI, his press secretary.

SERENO FREATO, his long-time aide and confidant.

FRANCO TRITTO, his university assistant.

DON ANTONELLO MENNINI, a young parish priest.

GIANCARLO QUARANTA, head of the February '74 Movement.

The Christian Democrats

The Chief of State:

GIOVANNI LEONE, President of the republic, nearing the end of his term of office.

The Government:

GIULIO ANDREOTTI, Prime Minister.

FRANCESCO COSSIGA, Minister of Interior.

NICOLA LETTIERI, Under Secretary of the Interior.

FRANCESCO BONIFACIO, Minister of Justice.

TINA ANSELMI, Minister of Health.

The Party:

BENIGNO ZACCAGNINI, secretary general.

GIOVANNI GALLONI, vice secretary.

REMO GASPARI, vice secretary.

FLAMINIO PICCOLI, president of the party's delegation to the Chamber of Deputies (lower house of parliament).

GIUSEPPE BARTOLOMEI, president of the party's delegation to the Senate.

RICCARDO MISASI, a grass-roots leader.

The Senators

AMINTORE FANFANI (Christian Democrat), president of the Senate.

GIOVANNI GRONCHI (Christian Democrat), ex-President of the republic.

GIUSEPPE SARAGAT (Social Democrat), ex-President of the republic.

The Communists

ENRICO BERLINGUER, secretary general of the party.

UGO PECCHIOLI, party shadow Minister of Interior.

The Socialists

BETTINO CRAXI, secretary general of the party.

CLAUDIO SIGNORILE, vice secretary.

GIULIANO VASSALLI, a prominent Roman lawyer.

The Church

POPE PAUL VI.

UGO CARDINAL POLETTI, Vicar of Rome.

MSGR. GIOVANNI CAPRIO, an official of the Roman Curia.

MSGR. REMO PANCIROLI, Vatican spokesman.

MSGR. PASQUALE MACCHI, the Pope's private secretary.

DON ANGELO CURIONE, a secret papal envoy.

The Consultant

DR. STEVE R. PIECZENIK, Deputy Assistant Secretary of State for Management, United States Department of State.

The Red Brigades' Lawyers

GIANNINO GUISO, the Socialists' *gola profonda* (deep throat).

SERGIO SPAZZALI, "the pessimist."

EDUARDO DI GIOVANNI, the Rome connection.

The Red Brigades

RENATO CURCIO, "the historic chief" (imprisoned).

MARGHERITA CAGOL, his wife, and the only person recognized by the Red Brigades (after her death in a 1975 shootout) as their founder.

"DR. NIKOLAI," a courier between Aldo Moro and the family.

PAOLA BESUSCHIO, a candidate for a prisoner exchange with Moro.

ALBERTO BUONCONTO, a non-*brigatista* terrorist and prisoner-exchange candidate.

ORGANIZATIONAL CHART OF TWO OF THE FOUR EXISTING COLUMNS OF THE RED BRIGADES (ROME, MILAN, TURIN, GENOA)

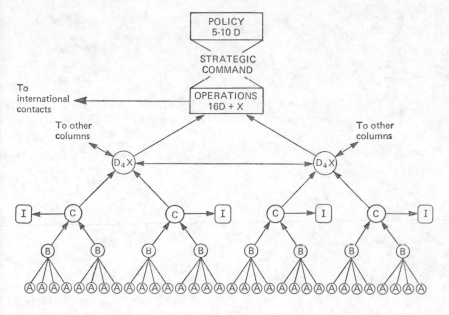

A = Cell operative (simple brigatista) D = Column command (four-man directorate)

B = Cell commander X = Unknown number

C = Brigade chief I = "Irregulars" (sympathizers/above-suspicion secret operatives)

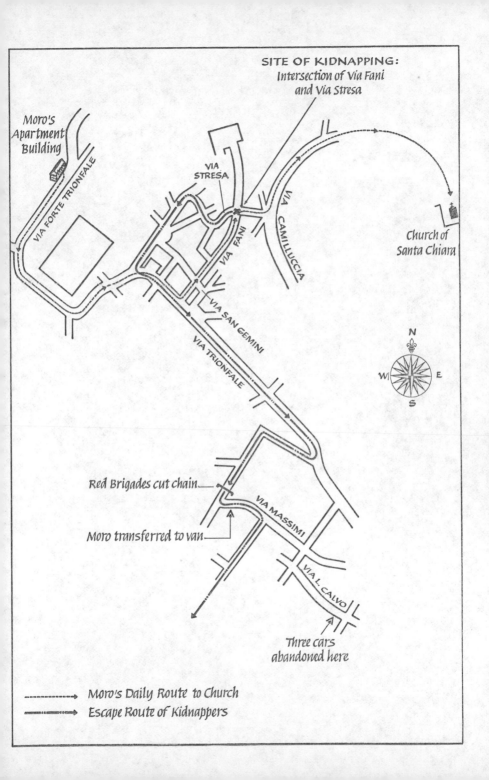

SITE OF KIDNAPPING:
Intersection of Via Fani
and Via Stresa

Moro's Apartment Building

VIA FORTE TRIONFALE

VIA STRESA

VIA FANI

VIA CAMILLUCCIA

Church of Santa Chiara

VIA SAN GEMINI

VIA TRIONFALE

N
W   E
S

Red Brigades cut chain

VIA MASSIMI

Moro transferred to van

VIA L. CALVO

Three cars abandoned here

⟶ Moro's Daily Route to Church
⟹ Escape Route of Kidnappers

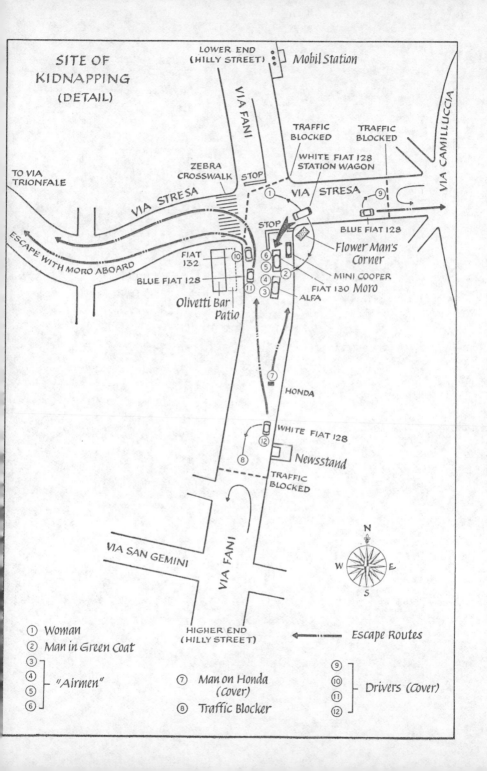

FOREWORD

Aldo Moro was kidnapped in an urban guerrilla ambush on the morning of March 16, 1978, by the Red Brigades. He was murdered on the morning of May 9 looking into the eyes of two particularly cold-blooded killers of the Red Brigades. In the intervening fifty-four days he was annihilated by a community of men of power of which he was one.

He was annihilated—in the strictest sense of the word: to remove the force of; to reduce to nothing—by a government of his own creation, by the political party over which he presided, by the first parliamentary majority in the Atlantic alliance hinged to Eurocommunist power, by an aggregate of mass media looting truth in a news grayout, and finally, by an astonishingly uncritical consensus of world opinion led to believe that some Great Principle of Democracy was the price of the prisoner's freedom.

The reasons for his annihilation were wholly impersonal. To be sure, there were indications that he might be forced by his captors to "talk." Apart from the fear this generated among his fellow politicians in a country unpurged of many scandals, the intelligence services of this and other member nations of NATO were concerned about what the five-time Prime Minister might reveal. But the custodianship of state and supranational secrets was only a small factor in the decision-making process aimed at neutralizing the threat posed by Moro's capture—namely the will of the most powerful man in Italy to survive.

The actual Deciders, including those publicly accused by Mrs. Moro of having by acts of omission ratified her husband's death sentence, behaved certainly without malice, and in most cases, they went against the deepest wishes of their heart. The making of a nonperson of Aldo Moro, his physical and moral abandonment by society's forced withdrawal of his integrity, was determined by a curious conjunction of time and the vicissitudes of power. From the moment the Red Brigades laid their hands upon his substance as a human being, he began to be transformed into the statue that will one day stand in some Roman piazza bearing his name.

Moro's power, however formidable were the forces arrayed against it, was not easily recalled. From his cell in an elusive, desolate "people's prison," he waged a complex, highly articulate, and ingenious battle for his life. He succeeded in engaging not only the fullest energies of his family and friends who did not conform to the way of the juggernaut (notably the Pope, two ex-Presidents of the republic, and the UN Secretary General), but also, as will be seen, a part of the Red Brigades themselves.

He refused the stage-managed martyr's role proffered by his peers. There could be no glory in dying for the pastiche of special interests that held sway in Rome. There was only the dignity of campaigning well for life in his own intensely political style, and when he understood that he had lost—in advance of those who were fighting on his side—he damned his false mourners, absolved no one of responsibility, and said a simple last farewell. He died an antihero, a hero of his time.

This is a report on his struggle and his death. It is a story—as much as a series of bloodletting truths can resemble a story—of how a powerful man and his family were moved by the locking together of a combination of circumstances into direct conflict with a political force of his own making, and how that man and his family responded. What began, in terms of a story, as high melodrama—a startling *coup de main* on a sunstruck street in Rome—was turned by the wrench of dramatic irony into a pure tragedy worthy of a bardic pen.

I have no such pen, but I was drawn into taking a more than passing interest in these events by the repeated observation that the aspects of the case referred to above were being missed. Moreover, after it was all over, the whole world applauded a hitherto untried strategy of confrontation with political terrorism, which in fact had been totally misunderstood. Thus, when the Washington *Post,* for example, wrote while commending the new strategy that Moro's kidnappers deliberately forced him "deeper and deeper into psychological breakdown, advertising the stages of their progress by publishing his increasingly distraught and desperate letters,"[1] it was revealing how extraneous it was to what had gone on in Rome, as well as how successfully Rome had covered up. A grave injustice was being compounded into a historical error, and a dangerous precedent had been set on an international scale.

I was in Rome for all of Aldo Moro's fifty-four days. Not that I am one who believes that those who are present and involved in events are better placed than others to judge. On the contrary, the exact opposite is closer to the truth, which is why the administration of justice and the writing of history, for instance, are the natural dominions of disinterested parties only. Indeed, my only claim to objectivity is the alien eye through which I followed the case at close hand.

Normally, the only events I "cover" are those that happened long ago or have never happened at all. On the day Aldo Moro was kidnapped, though I like everyone else in Rome became aware of the news almost instantly in multiple, tangible ways, I was on my way to a quiet corner of the city to work on a story that took place in Rome four hundred years ago. I was in a different time frame, and after being momentarily shaken by the present, I was more content than ever to return there. In the years I had lived in Italy, I had had only two relatively close encounters with Aldo Moro, neither of which had altered my prejudice that he was precisely as he had been portrayed with devastating wit by the great Italian actor Gian Maria Volonté in a film called *Todo Modo.* In that film, the Moro character, the symbol of a decadent Christian Democracy, is eliminated in the end by his party's corruptors, the CIA. Had I not been retransported to the days of the Counter-Reformation, I might have wondered how much truth there was in what many Romans were saying about *Todo Modo* having been prophecy in the can. That, as I said, was my prejudice; I, like the distinguished author of the novel on which the film was based, Leonardo Sciascia, was yet to discover who Aldo Moro really was.

For a time, it was only on my brief but daily trips to the frantic present that I took notice of something amiss in Rome, but when Aldo Moro's letters began to arrive from the people's prison, I knew by the response of the men of power that a wicked fear had grabbed the Italian boot, and someone was bound to fall.

Little happens in Italy that is not linked to the aims of one or another political party, and here was a situation, I was perhaps last to realize, where the principal aims of *all* the main parties coincided. This was especially true for the superparties—the ruling Christian Democrats and the most powerful Communist Party in the West.

On the day Moro was kidnapped a new government was to be empowered, and the parliamentary majority on which it was to be based was the broadest in the history of postwar Italy. It included, after thirty years of ostracism, the Communists, who by a few percentage points were second only to the Christian Democrats in clout at the polls. The Communists' entry on March 16 into the majority was the result of a delicate work of statecraft of which Moro himself was the author. Thus had he become the target of the Red Brigades, who had timed his capture to his twenty-minute drive to Parliament to give his blessing to the new government's accession.

The Communists, who had gained access to state power on promises of defending democracy, now sought with a frenzy to disassociate itself from the communism of the Red Brigades. The Communists rushed to the forefront to proclaim themselves the staunchest protector of the state, its institutions, and law and order. The Christian Democrats, whatever their individual sentiments toward their captured leader, could do no less, and so the race to the hard line was on.

Indeed, the heartless, intractable stance that was to dominate the entire range of events leading (inexorably, one sees now) to Moro's slaying emerged almost at once. Backed internationally, especially by the United States and West Germany (for reasons, I was later to discover, that had little to do with Italy and the case in question), it left no margin of flexibility. From the beginning, one was either a hawk or a dupe of the Red Brigades. All criticism of the official line was trampled down, and the biggest critic of all, Aldo Moro, was said to be pathologically mad.

Giorgio Bocca, an independently minded Italian journalist, painted this picture shortly after Moro's death:

On March 16, the façade [of a free press] came down and one could see how the transmission of information really worked. The political parties, the owners or the patrons of the newspapers and television made the decisions and the editors carried them out. Hypocrisy, lies, exaggerations, and outright inventions, which a few days earlier would have been considered unacceptable, were sent to the composing room and printed without the slightest protest. The dissidents, rather than be marginalized, fell into line; the columnists, rather than be censored, censored themselves. The majority view, everyone knew, was inspired by the interests of the two great parties of power: the Christian Democrats and the Communists. . . . the general tenor was, "He who is not with us is either a scoundrel or a friend of the enemy."[2]

I had personally witnessed this sort of thing in other countries, in India and Bangladesh, in Eastern Europe, and in my own country during the Vietnam War and in the fifties. But Italy after Mussolini had lost its taste for intolerance. As this was the first time such a reaction had been engendered by modern political terrorism, from which no country appears to be immune, it seemed worthy of attention. Foreigners, I think, tend to hone the sense that sniffs out freedom in trouble.

Early in April, I put my rummagings of the sixteenth century in the kind of foot-long cardboard box writers use to store their work, and I began to watch the events in Rome more carefully than before. In those days, however, it was quite difficult to learn anything that was not in the newspapers, and like the atmosphere, the newspapers were exactly as Bocca described them. Nevertheless, there was an information underground of sorts. It had its origins in the Moro family's need to communicate what the mass media refused to convey. The more the affair hurtled toward its climax, the more elaborate and accessible was the counternews. I will speak of all this in its proper place, but it was not until the terrible end, or weeks later, when tensions even for those who truly grieved began to subside, that I was able to really begin the work of sorting fact from fancy.

My task was made easier by a number of factors. The first was the onset of contrition. Many people were suddenly taken with sorrow for having sowed the hard line to reap nothing, and some, though far from all, were now quite willing to talk. In the same vein was the conduct of the press, which, among other amends, assigned some of its best investigative reporters to retrace the fifty-four days in an unjaundiced way.

Second was the slight shift in the political balance of power caused by local elections in May. This brought about a certain infighting in the capital, which would have been of little interest to outsiders had not its internal logic forced the steady leakage of almost all the known secret documents in the Moro case.

Finally, I was in a somewhat privileged position. Over the years I had developed my own sources of information in Rome, which is nothing unusual for a person of my profession, except that many of these sources had been and still were in touch with the protagonists in the Moro case. A small number had themselves been protagonists. As a result, I was favored with much unpublished material and was able to make contact with circles still completely closed, particularly the Moro family and the Red Brigades.

This is not to say, however, that the reader has in his or her hands anything resembling a definitive work on the case of Aldo Moro. Unfortunately, that book will be a long time coming. Many circles or inner circles remain more than closed; they are sealed hiding places from justice and shame. What has been attempted here is an initial effort to straighten the doctored record of events that weighed so heavily in those days and seem now more than ever in need of review. This hardly ensures that in trying to do so I have managed to entirely avoid adding new errors to old, but my work is based exclusively on all that is known and what I have come to know in the course of my research. I have given no space to my imagination nor credit to anybody's fiction.

My purposes notwithstanding, I, too, am obligated to keep certain confidences. The Moro case is hot. His killers are at large. The fortunes of men and women are still in play. Wounds of mind, body, and soul have yet to heal. Blood matters of life or death are real in the most literal sense. Let the reader be assured, however, that nothing of what I am not at liberty to disclose would alter the substance of this report. For reasons of prudence, requests for anonymity, and, above all, due respect for the Moro family's self-imposed reserve, I ask the reader's indulgence wherever I fail to satisfy a natural curiosity about certain intimate details. As for my sources, I have, in the customary fashion and within the limits cited, indicated the origins of everything that follows.

What follows is a narrative of the world's second experience with a universal Confusion of Tongues.

R.K.

Rome, March 16, 1979

DAYS OF WRATH

I

ARREST

You will see,
they will make us pay
for our political line. . . .[1]

I.

Some cities never rest, but Rome sleeps hard and awakens leadenly. When night deepens, even the traffic signals relent, the reds and the greens giving way to a more sensible flashing amber. The tide of public transportation ebbs. Street lamps burn with a halo. For long periods, whole minutes, sometimes, Rome sounds as it did in the beginning; you can hear the Tiber. The night before the Red Brigades kidnapped Aldo Moro, as the city slept in this fashion, somebody slashed all four tires of an itinerant flower vendor's van.

At about seven-fifteen on the morning of March 16, 1978,[1] Antonio Spiriticchio, dressed in work clothes and a rumpled red smock, stepped out of his apartment building behind the Piazza del Popolo and discovered the damage. For years he had been leaving regularly at that hour to make his way to the flower market on the right bank of the Tiber and then on to his sidewalk vending place on the northeast corner of Via Mario Fani. Via Fani, situated in a modern, high-rent residential district on Monte Mario, was miles from the flower man's home. Today, he knew, was a losing day. He was staring at $350 worth of crime and there was no hope at all he would get it fixed in time to buy and sell his wares.

By now Rome was wide awake, and though the flower man would be absent from his Via Fani corner, at least eighteen other men and women were moving about the city in one manner or another so that an ungodly appointment might be kept in that space made empty for this day.

One of them was a noncommissioned officer in the Carabinieri named Domenico Ricci. He was in plainclothes, a pinstripe suit, driving toward Monte Mario in a dark-blue, executive-type Fiat sedan. He had set out from the extreme opposite end of the city, where he lived with his wife and two young children. At forty-three, Ricci for the past eighteen years had been Aldo Moro's personal driver.

In 1964, when Moro formed his first government, Ricci became part of the five-man bodyguard assigned to protect Italy's most re-nowned statesman. In those years, he drove a car very much like the present one except that it was bulletproof. It was also very heavy due to the steel plating and as a consequence sluggish and troublesome. It had fallen happily into disuse, and at the moment, he was awaiting one of the newer, more sophisticated armored models, which Moro had officially requested.

Ricci was unaware that the president's request would never be acknowledged, but it is doubtful that he worried. On the contrary, he felt sublimely secure in the presence of Aldo Moro. In Italy there is an old peasant saying that no one ever touches the truly mighty, and Ricci, like everyone else in the guard, came from a family of peasants. In any event, they were armed to the teeth, down to the very latest Beretta M-12. The M-12 fires at the rate of five hundred rounds per minute, and they had a small arsenal of them. They were kept in the escort car, locked in the trunk.

It was a glorious morning, the Thursday before the arrival of spring. But spring was weeks in the air. The newspapers, days ago, had reported that the beaches were already crowded; the Virginia creepers—that ubiquitous "Roman" plant—had buds as thick and as long as a baby's thumb. Via Fani was particularly lush. The stone walls and iron gates that separated the terraced buildings from the street were laden with undulant folds of ivy. Cypress, pine, and cedar rose tall in many gardens. Newly planted mimosa trees, pregnant with the beginnings of fragrant life, lined the side-walks.

There was little activity on the street. Here and there, if the observed routine be the guide, people in well-cut business dress got into their cars and drove off to work. The No. 48 bus, which linked the northern hills of the city to the center, passed most infrequently; it only stopped in Via Fani on its return route, coming back from downtown in the opposite direction of the morning traffic. At this hour, it was almost always empty, and when it stopped at all, one or two housekeepers alit. There was a newsstand on the southeast corner, but it was rarely busy, and the proprietor's young son was tending it now.

Life in the Via Fani, which hardly ever rose above the decibels of the upper middle class, had changed somewhat in recent months. Many of the residents who at this moment were taking their first coffee in the confines of a Hollywood kitchen used to gather instead at the Olivetti Bar, directly across the street from the flower man's corner. Olivetti's was, or had aspired to be, one of those throbbing, multifariously stocked pastry-shop-ice-cream-parlor-outdoor Roman cafés that delight more people than does the Colosseum. It was as glossy and as neat as a fresh deck of cards and had a sidewalk patio rendered secluded from pedestrians and passing cars by a border of huge potted plants. But Olivetti's had failed, and now the shutters were down like buttoned lips and the patio was bare. Only the potted plants continued to flourish, affording even more seclusion.

At about eight-twenty a dark-blue, four-door Fiat 132, one of the largest models made by the Turin automobile plant, turned into Via Sangemini, a street perpendicular to the high end of Via Fani (see diagrams on pages xvii and xix). It was heading southeast, but it stopped to discharge two passengers, then continued, turning left into Via Fani. The two who had debarked walked in the opposite direction. They were youthful-looking men dressed in light-blue uniforms with stripes on their sleeves and braiding on their caps. One of them continually tugged at his collar. The other held his cap in one hand. When they got back to Via Stresa, they descended toward the low end of Via Fani, and were joined by two other men wearing the same sort of clothing. They all carried bulging briefcases, at least one of which had an Alitalia decal on it. They talked soberly among themselves. They looked like Alitalia flight officers heading for a limousine stop to take them to the airport.

Up ahead, a small white car with diplomatic number plates was

parked on the flower man's corner.[2] A woman wearing large round
glasses was at the steering wheel, a man in a green loden coat sat
beside her. The 132 with the driver who had carried two of the
uniformed men was parked by the Olivetti, facing in the wrong direction.

By then, Aldo Moro's bodyguards had assembled in the small
courtyard below his penthouse apartment in Via Forte Trionfale,
79, about a third of a mile from Via Fani. Alongside the president's
car stood an unmarked, cream-colored police Alfa Romeo. It had
brought the three police officers who would form the escort. Their
names were Giulio Rivera, Raffaele Jozzino, and Francesco Zizzi.
They were all from the impoverished South. Rivera and Jozzino
were twenty-four and twenty-five years old, respectively. Zizzi was
thirty. It was his first day on this overly prized job.

The fifth and senior man was Oreste Leonardi. He was fifty-two,
a warrant officer in the Carabinieri, an affable old warhorse who
had been with Moro for fifteen years. He was known as "the president's shadow." He was chief of the guard and looked it. His
friends, of which he had many, called him Judo.

As they waited, the Moro household began to empty out one by
one with a morning salute for all. Giovanni, Moro's twenty-year-old
son, had an early appointment with the family dentist. He came out
on the street dressed in jeans and sped off on his motorcycle. The
youngest of his three sisters, Agnese, left for her classes at the University of Rome, a long haul to another part of town, and Mrs.
Moro, a former schoolteacher, went by chauffeured car to the
neighborhood church, where she was engaged in a youth-education
program. The Moros' two other daughters were married and lived
elsewhere, so in the few minutes remaining before Aldo Moro's
punctual descent at nine, the president was alone with his only
grandson, Luca, "the little one," who often stayed with his grand-
parents.

The fifth-story apartment was showered with sunlight pouring
through the loosely woven drapes on the windows. It was a large
duplex, occupying the entire top floor of the building. They had
moved there years ago, when the children were small and they
needed many bedrooms. Moro was secretary general of the Christian Democrats then, and spacious quarters and reception rooms

seemed an obvious necessity for the chief executive of the nation's ruling party, but it had been the bedrooms that had mattered. The truth was that the Moros rarely received anyone outside the strictest circle of family friends, and even when he was head of government their solitude was unbreachable. ("Consider my husband a widower," said Mrs. Moro, rejecting the role of First Lady.)[3] At the office, depending on which office, it was *signor segretario*, or *signor presidente*, or simply *professore*, but at home he was always *papà*, even to *mamma* and the family friends, and on weekends and vacations he took the children to the sea.

Two rare, album-type photographs survive from one day in the summer of 1961. In both of them, Moro is alone on the beach at Terracina with his daughter Anna, about whom he seemed always to worry so much. Anna, in pinafore and pigtails, is twelve, and her father, who in three years will be Prime Minister, is not yet forty-five. He is seated on a canvas folding chair, an open book resting on his lap. We are supposed to believe, it seems, that he is looking up from reading to Anna, who is crouched on the sand by his side. But they both seem strained. Moro is wearing a suit and a tie, and not a grain of sand is on his shoes. He looks as though he were only passing through, surrendering one moment in a busy politician's day to get the kind of publicity shots that go down so well in this country where the concept of family is holier than the Pope. Anna, pouting, her eyes a defiant stare into the camera lens, appears to be saying that this is all sham. But the second photograph reveals that something quite different might be nearer the truth. It was taken many hours later, for the shadows in the first are stark and noonish while those of the second are long, made by the softer light of a late-afternoon sun. Now Moro and daughter are walking along the shoreline, unaware or unconscious of the camera, which is at their backs, capturing them barely in profile. Anna holds the book now, and she moves a few paces behind her father, somewhat closer to water's edge, as they head into the sun. Anna is turned wholly to the open sea, her free arm extended in an embrace that reaches out to the horizon, and if there were a way to look into her face we are sure it would be shining. Moro, his collar no looser than before, his suit none the worse for this time of day, peers straight ahead, inscrutably, except that we sense that he has been with her all day, and suddenly we *know* that the uneasiness in the first photo had been caused by an intrusion into a time meant for a man and his child only. He *does* read to his daughter, and when he goes to the beach he *really* wears a suit and a white shirt and a tie, and that's nobody's business but his own.[4]

Anna's golden pigtails were long unraveled now, and she was married and six months pregnant, but he still worried about her, and not only her. There were intimate family problems that he felt he alone knew how to handle. Only the very closest were aware of what they were.

It was, then, a man deeply attached to his family and his personal privacy who promptly at nine that morning left his apartment for the last time. He was sixty-one years old, still extremely vigorous, but he had gone gaunt of late, and the famous streak of white hair was lost as he had turned completely gray. His briefcase was stuffed with pills of one sort or another, and though he was taller than most men, he was stooped. There were rumors that he was seriously ill, but they were as false as they were perennial, for Aldo Moro, *papà par excellence,* was nevertheless by far the most powerful political figure in Italy, and he had enemies at home and abroad. They were a thousandfold more numerous than his friends, and they were a majority even among those considered his friends, much more so than he suspected on this day.

Shortly after Moro, carrying his medicine-chest briefcase and a gray homburg, moved from his elevator to the back seat of his car, a man wearing a woolen ski cap arrived at the top of Via Fani on a Honda motorcycle. He made a slow approach to the low end and looped back again. This was a signal that the president was on his way.

The man on the Honda took up a position by the newsstand beside a white four-door Fiat 128. Two men were in that car. The kidnap team of eleven men and one woman was at the ready.

In addition to the two vehicles by the newsstand, it was deployed as follows (diagram on page xix):

The white 128 with the diplomatic plates and the blue 132 remained parked as before on the northeast and northwest corners of Via Fani and Via Stresa. The woman, a slender, long-haired figure in jeans, was still at the wheel of the first car beside the man in the green loden coat; she, and the driver of the second car, had their engines idling. Farther east along Via Stresa, near the main artery Via Camilluccia, was a blue 128 with one man at the wheel, and another blue 128 stood alongside the Olivetti bar in Via Fani. Like the 132, it was parked against the flow of traffic. Directly across the street, where the flower man's truck would have been, was a Mini Cooper station wagon. Both of these two cars were empty, but the 128 had the key in the ignition. The four men dressed as pilots lingered behind the potted plants on the Olivetti patio.

Some minutes before, they had been seen by a woman making a full stop at the intersection, and she had taken them for employees of the bus company, but when one of them waved her on brusquely, she was convinced that they were police. Another witness thought they were in the Air Force and a third was certain that they were musicians in a martial band. The truth was that the uniforms had been designed by themselves for convenience, for swift disposal. The only thing uniform about them were the caps, which had been purchased in a shop in downtown Rome. The men were otherwise dressed in ordinary light-blue business clothes covered by ordinary blue lightweight raincoats, on the sleeves of which one of their comrades had sewn the stripes of a second lieutenant in the Italian Air Force. Officers in the Italian Air Force wear no markings on their outer coat sleeves, and any airline pilot—commercial or military—as well as busmen, musicians, and policemen would have immediately recognized them as being not of their own kind, but that, and the fact of the stolen cars and the many strange movements around Via Fani, mattered nothing now; only three or four minutes remained.

Three or four minutes was the amount of time it took to go from Aldo Moro's pine-shaded driveway to the full-stop sign at the low end of Via Fani. He had been taking the same route daily for about fifteen years regardless of where his final destination might be. He had, in fact, four separate offices in different parts of the city, and depending on whether he was going to Parliament, or to teach at the university, or elsewhere, there were several ways of getting there, not one of them necessarily requiring passage through Via Fani. The reason for the invariable use of that faceless street of scarce connections was that although Moro's days were unpredicta-

bly varied, he began them all with a few silent moments in one particular church, the Church of Santa Chiara. A circular, modern,
brick building, it stands at the bottom of the Camilluccia in a busy
piazza with excellent access to all parts of town. From the Moro
residence high above it, the speediest, if not the only way to Santa
Chiara's, is through Via Fani.*

Twelve years before, the threat Moro faced was singled out in a
satirical article that appeared in a rightist magazine. "The most
dangerous moment in Honorable Moro's day," it said, writing when
Moro was head of government, "is when he goes out in the morning."⁵ It then went on to trace his route through Via Fani to the
Church of Santa Chiara, showing how and where an enterprising
assassin might act in a variety of ways along the journey, down to
placing a tack poisoned with curare on Moro's seat in the pew. It
was supposed to be funny, a political "cartoon" against what was
for those times said to be an absurdly exaggerated security guard
for Italy. This was Rome, not Dallas, the magazine commented
wryly. Today, it was Dallas and then some.

Even before Moro's car turned into the top of Via Fani at a few
minutes past nine that morning, it was already a historic day for
Italy in which Moro, even had he stayed home in bed, would rank
first among all others. The president was on his way to attend the
ceremonial embodiment of the greatest triumph of his political career.

After months of political warfare, a new, unprecedented form of
government in Italy was to present itself to Parliament at ten
o'clock that morning. It would ask for a vote of confidence, and everyone knew it would get it. Based on a five-party parliamentary
majority that included the Communists, it had gathered the support

---

* Nevertheless it was an ideal site for an urban guerrilla ambush. Indeed, it is
doubtful that a kidnap assault, given Moro's movements, could have been
carried out in any other place *but* Via Fani. Apart from the cover of the
Olivetti patio, it was the only street on Moro's itinerary with a full stop. To be
sure, few motorists obey the unenforced traffic laws in Rome (which explains
why the kidnap squad took no precautions about parking their cars in the
wrong direction), but the abundance of foliage blinding the Via Fani-Via
Stresa intersection, as well as the downhill slope, would persuade even the
most reckless driver to proceed prudently. There were other ways to Santa
Chiara Church, slightly longer, but infinitely safer.

of the representatives of more than 90 per cent of the nation's electorate.

This towering unity had been constructed, in many ways like a
house of cards, as the only viable alternative to full-fledged Communist executive power in a strategic country of the Western alliance. As it stood, it could function only with Communist co-operation. It was the beginning of the world's first experiment with
"Eurocommunism"—which was communism that had proclaimed
itself nonrevolutionary, independent of Soviet or any other foreign
controls, and, above all, tolerant and democratic. Many foreign capitals were watching Rome, reserving their opinions.

All this, with the cutting edge of personal power and the muscle
of prestige, Aldo Moro had built. It was a fragile masterwork of
statecraft only he could have fashioned, and as its maker, he more
than anyone else understood the fundamental flaw in its structure:
It would leave Italy without any significant opposition.

History had taught with a cudgel how wicked governments
might come to be in the absence of opposition, and that lesson was
uppermost in his mind.[6] But these were times pressing with emergency. There was talk of economic collapse, and the flares of civil
strife were in the air. The new majority, guided by a careful hand,
would be a salutary measure for his country, Moro believed, a temporary expedient in what he foresaw as a process from which a government with a truly "sacred and interchangeable" opposition
would emerge.[7]

There would be a time and a place to exercise that guiding hand.
Five times Prime Minister, and more unique, a man of vision, he
had risen above the day-to-day affairs of politics. In the coming December, when both houses of Parliament were due to elect a new
Chief of State, as is the septennial custom in Rome, it was a
foregone conclusion, a virtual promise, that he would win by accla-
mation. He would be President of the republic, President of Presidents.[8]

The guiding hand was leafing through the morning newspapers
as the president's car went down Via Fani. Invariably, a packet of
the nation's ten or twelve most important dailies was left for him on
the back seat, and with no less regularity he sat directly behind
Ricci, his driver, and read them.

The big story of the day, apart from the presentation of the new government to Parliament, was a large-scale Israeli offensive against the Palestinians in retaliation for a terrorist raid some days earlier. Moro's own party paper, *Il Popolo,* gave prominence to Italy's and the Vatican's disapproval of Israel's response, which was considered to be excessive. The Italians appealed for "responsibility and balance."[9]

The president, who could not but approve of Rome's position, had an open briefcase on his lap, but not the one with the medicines. His car was a mobile fifth office, and at the moment it contained five briefcases filled with papers and books. Two were in the locked trunk and the others were with him on the back seat.

Leonardi, the head of the guard, was in the right front seat, and the other three men were in the escort Alfa Romeo close behind him. All the windows were up. The view ahead from, say, the height of the newsstand was normal, except for the absence of the flower man. The street was quiet. The newsstand vendor's son was reading. He looked up when the small motorcade went by, saw Aldo Moro, and returned to his reading. A man and a woman were walking their dog. At the low end a man on a motorbike was heading past the Mobil station into the Via Fani-Via Stresa intersection coming from the opposite direction. Life was going on.

As Ricci approached the full-stop sign, the white car with the diplomatic plates began an illegal maneuver, though that was neither strange nor alarming. The woman driver was backing into Via Fani from the corner of Via Stresa, positioning her car on the white stop line. It appeared as though she had made a wrong turn and now wished to go straight through the intersection. It was not the most practical way to do so, but the trespasses of drivers in Rome are apt to be taken lightly with a woman at the wheel—an advantage the kidnappers could count on.

Ricci was braking for the full stop now behind the woman driver. Although he and Rivera, who was driving the Alfa, were about to turn right, both cars were forced to remain in the left lane because of the Mini Cooper that was parked by the curb. Thus, per plan, they were lining up behind the woman driver. Before Ricci could come to a halt, the woman, instead of going forward now, continued to come at him in reverse like a driving-school tyro who had gotten her gears crossed. Ricci tried to avoid her and almost did.

He cut sharply to the right, but the parked Mini left little space for jockeying, and he clipped her right rear end, stopping. Rivera, in the Alfa, braked hard but rammed Moro's car straight on at low impact. There was hardly any damage.

The woman driver and the man in the green loden coat sprung from both sides of their car—a natural reaction, it seemed, but here all pretense ended.

The woman arched into the middle of the street, facing Ricci. The man went to the right side of Moro's car, toward Leonardi. The four men in uniform had bolted from the Olivetti patio and were fanning out alongside the two cars carrying Italian- and Danish-made submachine guns.

All in the same instant, one of the men in the white 128 by the newsstand got out, and flashing an automatic weapon, blocked all traffic entering Via Fani, and the driver in Via Stresa cut off the Camilluccia, from where the No. 48 bus was due to arrive.

By now, the woman and the man in the loden coat were riddling Ricci and Leonardi in a studied crossfire angled to reduce the risk of injuring Moro, while two of the "airmen" were firing at the escort Alfa. When the woman was satisfied that her man, Ricci, was dead, she backed into the intersection to hold off traffic, and from that vantage point, where she could observe all aspects of the operation, she assumed the function of commander. The other two uniformed men had opened the back door of Moro's car and were swiftly ushering the president to the 132 across the street.

"Let me go! What do you want from me?" he was heard to say. But he offered little resistance and he spoke in the polite form of speech. He carried his open briefcase part of the way, then dropped it at the curb by the Olivetti bar. His abductors seized the other two briefcases. They left his hat behind.

There was a great deal of shouting among the attackers, the woman directing the others. One of them cried out at the man and the woman with the dog. They did not hear what he said; neither did they ask him to repeat it, and they fled.

The man on the motorbike froze as he got to the intersection and heard the shooting. "I saw people diving for cover," he said later. "The ones in the uniforms were screaming like madmen."

There was a burned smell in the air.

The newsboy thought he had heard a pneumatic hammer. He

went out from his kiosk to see what was happening and the man on the Honda pointed a gun at him. He leaped behind a parked car, hearing another burst of fire from the low end.

Some eighty bullets had been spent at this point, which was no more than fifteen or twenty seconds since the first salvo had been fired. Many of them had gone wild, pockmarking the nearest buildings, shattering window panes, and ricocheting inside some apartments. The man on the motorbike had taken a spray of fire, as he leaped unharmed for cover. But more than enough bullets—thirty-six—had found their mark. Ricci and Leonardi were dead, fallen one upon another, leaking blood from fourteen wounds. Rivera, flung back at the wheel of the Alfa, was dead, too, one hand clutching the unlifted radiotelephone. Zizzi, the man on the job for the first time, was still alive but unconscious. He would die that way at noon. None of them had had a chance to even draw their service pistols, but Officer Jozzino, though wounded, had his in hand and had crawled out of the back right seat. He fired twice. Someone who had been in a cover position, the man on the Honda, it seems, fired once and killed him.

The woman at the intersection command post waved her hand in a wide circle. Witnesses said she seemed to be signaling someone on a roof or by a high window, but in any case, gunfire stopped in Via Fani.

The kidnappers now had more passengers and less vehicles than they had begun with, but the getaway had been well choreographed. The white 128 by the newsstand picked up the man who had held back the traffic at the high end and one or two of the uniformed killers at the low end. The man on the Honda escaped alone, turning right on Via Stresa and into the Camilluccia. This was the route taken by the man who cut off the Camilluccia. The remaining two cars, the 132 and the blue 128, took Via Stresa in the opposite direction, and they were followed by the white 128. But between the lead car, containing Moro, and the blue 128 was an Alfa Romeo. It was being driven by an ex-police officer who had been an eyewitness to part of what had happened, and he was attempting to pursue them.

Unaware that the kidnap victim was Aldo Moro, he could see a man seated in the rear between two of the uniformed men. One of them was dabbing the president's face with a cloth while pressing firmly on the back of his skull to keep his head lowered and looking straight on. Almost immediately, however, the pursuit car was overtaken and cut off sharply by the blue 128, forcing it to slow down, but the ex-officer continued the chase.

The end of Via Stresa gave onto the wide Via Trionfale, and the three-car convoy began to speed away, but a traffic light at a pedestrian crosswalk brought them all, including the pursuit car, to a full stop just outside the Church of San Francesco, where Eleonora Moro was holding her class. The Moros would never be that close again.

At the light, the ex-officer watched the driver of the 132 cursing the interminable red signal, while one of his comrades in a car alongside gestured at him to be calm. About two hundred yards up ahead was a parked police car, and after the light changed, the ex-officer called the alert when he got there, as the getaway cars continued to weave through downtown rush-hour traffic. The men in the squad car took up the chase, but the kidnappers were inexplicably gone.

The cry of squealing tires in Via Fani had been replaced by an awful silence. The street was a bed of litter. Chips of glass and ammunition shells lay in puddles of human blood. Moro's briefcase stood beside a magazine of unused bullets. One of the "pilots" had dropped his cap and the bogus Alitalia bag. Dead men slumped in two windowless cars. Officer Jozzino, who had taken a final bullet in the head, was stretched out on his back, his arms spread and his legs crossed in a way only a man hurled by a final violence can lie. The newspapers Moro had been reading were scattered; they fluttered in a breeze, some of them batting like moth wings against Jozzino's body. His gun had been thrown far from the reach of his right hand. It sat in a crack in the pavement.

At first people stared. They stared from the street and from windows. Dazed, the man who had been on the motorbike began to cover Jozzino's body with sheets of newspaper. Then someone saw that Zizzi was breathing. The alarm had to be sounded. Many rushed to their phones and found the lines dead. Service in some parts of the district was completely blacked out, sabotaged, it was later determined, to give the kidnappers another edge. Additional failure was due to an overload—which was predictable. Nevertheless, some residents did get through to Rome's emergency number, 113, and at nine minutes past nine, the first blue-and-white "panthers"—the symbol of the Flying Squad—were on the scene.

Within minutes roadblocks were set up in the vicinity, but by that time, the kidnappers were beyond them and had already delivered Aldo Moro to another team. The sudden disappearance of the three-car getaway group, last seen heading southeast on the Trionfale, was explained later. They had taken planned refuge in a little-known sharp turnoff after a stretch of sparsely populated area. This was a private street with a gate at the end chained and padlocked, preventing access to Via Massimi, where the second unit was waiting. When all three cars had entered the dead-end street, the woman who had driven the car with the diplomatic plates got out of the blue 128. She had a pair of heavy-duty wire cutters and an identical replacement chain, but after she forced the gate open, it was left that way.

On the other side, in Via Massimi, was a van, probably a German Ford "Transit," which resembled a VW microbus. It had windows only in the forward section, however, as well as rear-loading doors. It was white, unmarked, and had been modified after it had been stolen, equipped with a dashboard-activated siren. Moro was put aboard here, and the van took off on a westerly route, screaming with false authority. The assault group abandoned the 132 in another dead-end street nearby. Some of the kidnappers left the scene on foot.

The blaring white van was seen for the last time making for the Via Aurelia, the road built by the Romans to carry their legions to sea. Moro was in the rear of the van. He had either been blindfolded or in some other way thrown into darkness. The sight of faces, things, and places from now on would be the surest sign he was going to die.

2.

The rest of the world did not know whether the president was alive, wounded, or dead, but the news that he had vanished traveled at the speed of light. Only moments after the flight from Via Fani, even before what had happened was known, there was something in the morning air of the city that breathed ominously. Walking through the baroque *centro storico*, miles from Monte Mario, one had an instant tactile and visual sensation of fear whipping through the streets. Perhaps it was because it suddenly seemed that every car in Rome had been an unmarked police car, as every one of them that actually had been was radioed into service. Sirens went on like floodlights, and all models of cars tore at high speed from almost every direction. Young men inside wearing sweaters and jeans were unmasking their guns from leather shoulder bags. This surprisingly large undercover and Rome's two hundred Panthers drove the rest of the traffic off the streets and discouraged the use of cars. Shutters closed, and shops that were about to open kept their doors locked in abeyance. People went indoors or didn't come out. Romans are not always as gregarious as they appear.

At nine twenty-five one of the nation's three radio networks broke the news to all of Italy. The speaker's voice was shaking. He said:

Dear Listeners. This is the GR2 newsroom. We interrupt this broadcast to bring you a dramatic announcement that seems almost unbelievable, and though there is no official confirmation as yet, unfortunately it appears to be true.

The president of Christian Democracy, the Honorable Aldo Moro, was kidnapped in Rome a short while ago by terrorist commandos.

This unheard-of, we repeat, unbelievable episode happened almost in front of the Parliament member's house in the Camilluccia district.

The terrorists are said to have attacked the escort that was accompanying the Christian Democratic president and then forced him into a car that drove off leaving no trace behind.

We do not know anything further at this moment. During the course of the morning, naturally, we will interrupt our broadcasts to keep you informed.

The only thing to add is that Honorable Moro's escort was composed of five police officers. It is said that they are all dead.[1]

"Terrorist commandos." No one knew for certain who they were, but "educated guesses" among the men of power were already in the making. There is in Italy a self-flagellating myth (but in the end part of a larger, self-complimentary myth) that anything punctual, efficient, or carried out with precision cannot be Italian, and from the very outset it began to be said that something darkly international had visited Via Fani.

Someone rushed forward who had "witnessed" tall, blond men cry, *"Achtung! Achtung!"*; someone else was willing to swear that one of the terrorists called another, "Hans." The striking resemblance of the operation to the 1977 kidnapping of German industrialist Hanns-Martin Schleyer by the Red Army Fraction was highly suggestive. That very morning, investigators found "evidence" of Russian, Bulgarian, Czechoslovakian, and Chinese weapons, and it was an indisputable fact that the counterfeit Alitalia bag left behind bore a label that read, "Made in Germany." The CIA would make its entry later* but now, in the absence of hard intelli-

---

* For a discussion of the "international plot" theories in which the U.S. embassy in Rome and the CIA would come under serious suspicion and open criticism at extremely high levels of Italian society, see pp. 263–65.

gence, preventive measures had to be taken. No one could know at this stage whether the surprise attack was not but a prelude to a larger offensive, a *coup d'état,* or a civil war. Political and social tensions, grating since January, had been rawest in recent days, and the timing of the Moro abduction seemed to be ushering in the crisis of crises.

Every government has its contingency plans, and Italy was no exception. At ten o'clock a coded alert went out by teletype from the communications center in the Ministry of Interior to all police forces on the mainland and the islands. It was classified, quaintly, PAPA ("absolute precedence over absolute precedence"), and it ordered the immediate institution of a plan that had never yet been used—the most massive response to terrorism this country had ever seen: Plan Zero.

Such top-secret plans were stored in the vaults of police headquarters and prefectures, and as might be expected, only the highest authorities had access to them. But they were kept in sealed packets, and until the order was given to execute them, these officials had no knowledge of their contents, which is wisdom in any country and all the more so in one where state secrets are difficult to keep. The trouble was that when police authorities from the Alps to the waters of North Africa shuffled through the secret packets not one of them could find Plan Zero, and when finally the fault was presumed to lie elsewhere, Rome was asked to clarify.

Plan Zero was known in minutest detail to its devisers in the Interior Ministry, but someone had forgotten to have it typed clearly and copied for packing, sealing, and dispatch. All this was done now, though no one cared much about the typing and the packing.[2]

Such was the poor beginning of what did turn out to be the largest and most penetrating police operation in Italian history in which almost 20 per cent of the entire population of fifty-five million were in one way or another searched or checked by the police. Blunders would inevitably occur in any country, and they did here, repeatedly.

For their part, the kidnappers had better luck in maintaining an image of Teutonic preparedness. Between ten-ten and ten-fifteen, local telephone calls were received at newsrooms in Rome, Milan, and Turin, and somewhat later in Genoa. The message recorded in Rome declared:

> This morning we captured the president of Christian Democracy Moro and eliminated his bodyguards, Cossiga's "leatherheads."† A communiqué follows. Signed: the Red Brigades.[3]

"One of ours, a hundred of theirs," the Prime Minister's chief of staff was reported to have said on hearing what had happened. Whether or not he actually did so, the mood among the men of power—which so determined the fate of Aldo Moro—certainly began with Old Testament anger.

The Prime Minister himself, Christian Democrat Giulio Andreotti, had been preparing to open the parliamentary session with a presentation of the government's program. In spite of the guaranteed vote of confidence, he had been expecting a bad-tempered and protracted debate among the parties of the new majority. Seated in the Chamber of Deputies that morning would be a formidable coalition of forces in his own party hostile to Moro's acceptance of the Communists, and they had the authority of NATO and the United States behind them.‡ As for the Communists, they looked upon the whole of the others in the new majority, particularly the Christian Democrats, with deep suspicion. Many of the party's highest leaders had not yet grown accustomed to sleeping in their own beds every night. The winding road to Eurocommunism had been uphill all the way, to say the least, and the latest authenticated conspiracy for a Fascist-military takeover was uncovered only a few years back.

The news had been brought to Andreotti before it had reached

† The reference to Minister of Interior Francesco Cossiga alludes to the West German antiterrorist task force, *Grenzschutzgruppe-9*, known also as GSG-9 or "the leatherheads."

‡ With clear reference to Italy, the State Department on January 12, 1978, had issued an official policy statement saying that it would like to see the Communists have less not more power,[4] and on February 6, NATO Commander Alexander Haig declared that the "highly sensitive military information within the framework of the alliance" would be endangered if the Communists gained power in Italy.[5] This was the sort of "noncomprehension" of Moro's design that had recently induced him to remark privately to a close associate, "You will see, they will make us pay for our political line." Who "they" were, really were, would now become the biggest ponderable in the exquisitely elaborated Italian political mind.

the Chamber. A journalist who by chance had been listening to police calls had burst into the Hall of Frescos in the Prime Minister's palace, where a swearing-in ceremony was taking place. Andreotti's reaction was described as one of "incredulity, alarm, and anger."[6] He took physically ill and was forced to lie down. Soon, he would draft a formal statement, but his sentiments caught fire as the word was passed along.

In the Transatlantico—a lounge in the Chamber of Deputies that in function approximates Washington's Capitol Cloakroom—turmoil erupted. There were shouts that this deed meant war, calls for martial law, a curfew, and the institution of capital punishment, which is constitutionally outlawed in Italy. Rumors of new attacks began to take wing. The president of the Chamber ordered that confidential parliamentary papers be moved into safes.[7] Men and women had tears in their eyes, and wet eyes, some perhaps more sincere than others, would be the leitmotif of the days ahead, but all the tears and bile seemed the necessary venting of emotion now. There was ample support for the belief that reason would prevail. This was Italy, the land where reason was reborn.

In the Street of the Dark Shops,* site of the national headquarters of the Communist Party, members of the Central Committee were gathered at a meeting when the news arrived. Not without reason, the party leaders believed that apart from the unfortunate victims, the capture of Aldo Moro was directed primarily at them.

They, or at least one among them that morning, knew more about the Red Brigades than anyone else outside the "Movement," but they would never forgo the notion that behind it all lay one, perhaps both, of the superpowers. Aldo Moro had led them one step out of long and bitter isolation but that had also brought them be-

* Normally, translations of Italian place and street names (in this case, Via delle Botteghe Oscure) are misleading in that they do not sound at all picturesque in the original, just as in English we never think of, say, Hollywood as a grove of holly or of Pennsylvania Avenue as having any reference to its eclectic etymology. Sometimes, however, by pure (or not so pure) chance the literal coincides with cultural readings that do not escape even the jaded ear, as in this instance, and as in the location of the central offices of the Christian Democrats: Piazza del Gesu, which as any Roman knows because of its Jesuit associations reads as, "the square of [the Society of] Jesus." The irony of it all, as will be seen, grew to a stunning climax in the case of Aldo Moro.

tween the pincers of Washington and Moscow. The party that had
been shaken to the core and transformed by the CIA-backed overthrow of Salvador Allende—the world's first and only demo-
cratically elected Marxist government—now detected every sign of
what it was to call "obscure maneuvers from afar." There was a remarkable coincidence of opposites. Eurocommunism, the so-called
"Third Way"—neither the American nor Soviet way to the New,
Great, or Name-it-yourself Society—was an anathema to the White
House, the Kremlin, and the infinitely less imposing symbols of the
Red Brigades. The Communists, unlike many Christian Democrats,
would never publicly accuse the CIA, and never, never the KGB,
but they proceeded prudently from the assumption that the Red
Brigades were being "manipulated."[8]

Nevertheless, without any help at all, the Red Brigades were a
whole bramble in the side of the Communist Party. Ever since
party chief Enrico Berlinguer had announced the Third Way,
Italian Eurocommunism had claimed to be the most faithful
champion of the democratic state and its institutions. Citing the
scandals upon scandals that had characterized thirty years of
Christian Democratic rule, the Communists presented themselves
as "the party with clean hands," and compared to their adversaries
that was certainly true. But the Red Brigades called themselves
Communists, too, and while few people knew who they were or
what they wished to accomplish by the letting of blood if need be,
many of their captured leaders had grown up in the ranks of the
party, breaking with it when the revolutionary bridges were
burned. Moreover, there was a mighty nostalgia for the Old Way
in the party itself at the grass roots. Those souvenir busts of Comrade Stalin, those brilliantly righteous socialist realist posters,
and the thousand other little red fetishes carried home on rowdy
group flights to the workers' state in the fifties and well into
the sixties were not all lost or even taken down and stored away.
The Central Committee had tried without respite to bury the Old
Way, but the clenched fist of Lenin would always break through. It
was no wonder, then, that they suspected that hands longer than
those of the Red Brigades had plucked Aldo Moro from the streets
of Rome.

Least convinced of the conspiracy theory, without however

rejecting it, was Ugo Pecchioli, whose presence at that early-morn-
ing meeting suddenly became crucial.

Pecchioli, a youthful- and athletic-looking Turinese of fifty-three,
was the party's shadow Minister of Interior. In the Resistance, he
had been a commander of the Garibaldi Brigades, the structure of
which had been amply studied and partially adopted by the Red
Brigades. Now a senator from Piedmont, Pecchioli was vice president of the parliamentary committee on intelligence services, a
member of the defense committee, and in the party hierarchy he
was in charge of the section called "Problems of the State." Lately,
the largest problems of the state had been those of combating political terrorism, manifested on the left by urban guerrilla warfare,
and Pecchioli, who in wartime had helped organize and lead a
Communist insurrection, found himself in these times in the curious
position as the party's, if not the entire nation's, leading expert on
counterintelligence, counterrevolution, and counterinsurgency.

It was Pecchioli who formulated party policy in all matters of
law and order, and at the meeting in the Dark Shops he outlined
what he believed the Red Brigades hoped to achieve in seizing
Aldo Moro.

"We recognized immediately," he said later, "that it was their intention to bring the state to its knees, obstruct the process by which
we were entering the majority, and obtain the release of their
fellow terrorists."[9]

Thus, while less disciplined men and women of power had yet to
get a rein on their sentiments, the Communists were articulating
their response to the threat posed by the morning raid of the Red
Brigades.

"We decided at once," said Pecchioli, "to prevent negotiations."[10]

Since under the Moro design the Andreotti government could not
operate without Communist consent, it would either have to accept
this decision or there could be no Andreotti government.

Even the most categorical decisions, however, are not immune to
erosion and replacement despite the resoluteness with which they
are taken. The nation's political forces could be aligned in other
combinations, returning the Communists to loathed isolation. That
might not "bring the state to its knees" or, necessarily, "obtain the
release" of imprisoned terrorists, but it surely would "obstruct the
process" on which the current Communist leadership had gambled

their all. For now, they expected Andreotti to back their position, but what of Aldo Moro? The power that had made the new majority could be used once more to dismantle it. Dead or in captivity, Moro had yet to be heard from, and the Communists knew a struggle was at hand.

In the Church of San Francesco, just behind Via Fani, Eleonora Moro's class was interrupted by the parish priest.

"Something bad has happened in Via Fani," he told her. "There was shooting."

She read her own misfortune in his eyes. "Call the house," she said. "Don't let them take the baby out." She asked to be taken to Via Fani.

To the world that lay beyond the perimeter of her family, she was a taciturn woman as solemn as cypress on a far-off Tuscan hill. She had shunned all contact with public life as though it might contain the germs of her undoing. On the few, formal occasions she was seen in Rome, her narrow, downcast eyes, looking out from a moonish forehead, seemed to foreshadow the trial that was only now beginning. Other than having shown herself eminently successful in excluding probing strangers from her domains, her qualities were unknown, and in Italian political life, which never relented until every phenomenon was "explained," it was said that being a woman of Ancona, she was reserved, like all the good people from the region of the Marches. The politicians and the pundits would learn a great deal about Eleonora Moro in the days that were coming.

For a while she went unrecognized in Via Fani. Hundreds, perhaps a thousand police and Carabinieri had blocked off the street. The scene of the crime was being swept for clues. The dead men were being absolved of sin and removed.

"I knew them all," Mrs. Moro was heard to murmur as she watched. "They were fine boys. Why take it out on them?"[11]

At about ten-thirty police recovered the 132 that had carried Moro away from Via Fani. It was parked in nearby Via Calvo, a nonthrough street that gave onto a flight of steps and the streets below. On the roof of the blue sedan, in the chrome gutter above the rear door, were flakes of blood. They were still sticky. The interior, however, showed no sign that the president or anyone else had been wounded.

The Vicar of Rome, Cardinal Poletti, was in Via Fani, too. He was there while the bodies were being taken away. He stood, one hand clutched in the other, and of what he saw before him he said later that there was "no possibility of describing such a horrendous crime."[12] Mrs. Moro had already withdrawn, but he would visit her shortly. The cardinal did not always share Aldo Moro's political beliefs, and he had adamantly opposed any concessions to the Communists, but he, like the Holy Father himself, was very close to the family.

The aged Pope, Paul VI, at this moment was in his apartment in the Vatican, stricken with influenza. A day ago, he had had to cancel his weekly general audience, though he had gone to his window of his study to bless the five thousand pilgrims who had come to see him. He had spoken in a tired voice and had sought to excuse his "indisposition." Holy Week would begin on Sunday. He was trying to conserve what little energies remained.

Yesterday, at his window, he had refused to stand behind the external plate of bulletproof glass urged upon him; today, the concern for his safety was clearer. "Once," he said after receiving the news from Via Fani, "this city was the teacher to civilization; now it is an impotent witness to the rebirth of barbarity."[13]

Their senior by twenty years, the Holy Father had known Aldo and Eleonora since their student days. At times, he, too, had disagreed with the Christian Democratic president, most acutely in political circumstances similar to those of today. That was in 1963, when Moro had proposed the very first "opening to the left," which was to give the Socialist Party a taste of state power.† More often, he had stood as an inspiration at Aldo Moro's side.

The Vatican was as eternal as the city in which it stood, and its policies, like those that were now being formed wherever there was power in Rome, would emerge by the careful weighing of alternatives. But Paul was eighty and dying. To Cardinal Poletti he would say privately, "Let us forget about protocol. What can we, as two

† This was some months before Paul's pontificate. As archbishop of Milan, he wrote a confidential letter to the clergy under his jurisdiction in which he said that because of incomprehension among Catholics, "priests must not encourage the so-called 'opening to the left.' "[14]

priests, do for Aldo Moro?"[15] The last battle fought by Paul VI would thus be fought alone and to the Vatican's displeasure.

Throughout the day the world's reaction flowed into Rome—a unanimity of shock and dismay. Because of the time difference, the United States was only opening its morning eyes when everyone else had long been fretting. In Washington, one of the first chores of those in the government concerned with foreign affairs is the ritual reading of the telegrams from U.S. diplomatic missions abroad that wax during the night; the telegrams are distributed in both the State Department and the White House. Now, while officials in the latter drafted a shock-and-dismay statement on the Moro kidnapping for Jimmy Carter's approval, officials in the former elaborated the longer-range view. This was set down in the daily guidance sheets prepared by State to articulate just what the United States is thinking on any given topic of currency.

Today, the United States, pursuing its relatively new policy toward Italy of noninterference but nonindifference, would consider the Moro case as a purely domestic matter. If requested, however, it would gladly lend assistance.[16] That request was already in the making.

In the Square of Jesus, the Christian Democrats decided that the party directorate would remain in "permanent session"—not that anyone feared that the leadership would go off to play by the sea. "This kidnapping," Secretary-General Benigno Zaccagnini declared, "is clearly linked to a plan that aims at upsetting the [new majority]."[17]

Official statements such as this one were interpreted as auguring well just about a hundred yards away by the men in the Street of the Dark Shops. Moreover, the Communists had already had private assurances from the government and the Christian Democrats of a united front against any demands made by the Red Brigades.[18] But public opinion would be watched and evaluated by all before any promises could be redeemed. It would also have to be "guided," to use a word then in vogue with all political parties in Rome. Thus the Communists in their second major decision of the day ordered the mobilization of the entire party apparatus. For now, that meant that a general strike "in protest against terrorism" was called, and the apparatus was able to guarantee that hundreds of thousands of workers, with banners and shouted slogans, would fill the piazzas of the principal cities of Italy, not to mention its front pages and television screens.

Reinforced by workers marched into the streets by other political apparatuses, Italy's instant response to the Red Brigades was a resounding *Terrorismo no, Aldo Moro sì!* But just as Jimmy Carter's prompt message to Rome, in which he said, "I know that millions of Americans join me in praying" for Moro,[19] may have overestimated the actual number of prayers, Italian sentiment from the outset was less than unanimous.

The general strike, which began before noon and was to last until midnight, was real. "The city was literally shut down," wrote the Rome *Il Messaggero* the following morning, and it was the same throughout the nation. But it was also bad for business and all the worse the smaller the business. A local reporter in search of man-on-the-street reactions in Rome found irritation in an open market by the Tiber and a larger sample of indifference.

"Poor Moro?" a fishmonger asked in familiar Roman rhetorical fashion. "I haven't heard anyone say that all morning. The ones who got killed are the poor ones. He's in good shape."

At the Visconti high school of classic studies in the center of town, where 50 out of 350 students had refused to sign a condemnation of the attack, the newsman interviewed a group gathered around.

"Emotionally, I'm in agreement with the action [of the Red Brigades]," one of them said. "But now they [the police] are going to stick it up *our* ass. Either you step up this kind of action, or you pay the consequences. I'm sorry about those five dead men, but they were in the political police, and therefore turds. Moro is the symbol of the Christian Democrats and he's getting what he asked for."

"These acts don't make any sense," said someone else. "They're the sign of total ruin."

Another school, another student: "We were all happy."[20]

In the end it wouldn't matter what *anyone* said.

3.

In the anxious stillness of that afternoon, 588 members of Parliament rose to their feet in the palace built by Bernini that was now the Chamber of Deputies. They paid silent tribute to the men slain in Via Fani. They expressed "impassioned and affectionate solidarity" with Aldo Moro, and when they sat, they listened to Giulio Andreotti's request that his government be approved.

Andreotti, a cool-tempered man with the carriage of one who bears too many of society's burdens, promised a "close, day-to-day relationship" between his government and the new majority, and turning slightly to his left, he recognized the historic import of the Communist Party partnership in the Moro design without actually saying so. The fashion in Rome, among men of high responsibilities, was to speak in a tortuous way, opening many alleys for later retreat or escape if called for (Andreotti: "Let no one think that we are not before a political event."), and the measure of refinement was how ambiguously one conveyed what was tacit.*

Never in Italian history had a government been given a vote of confidence before days, sometimes weeks, of raucous debate. Even this one, prior to the events of this morning, did not expect to be empowered until the Easter holiday, ten days away, though considering the size of the majority, there would be less debate than

* Moro was the acknowledged master of this kind of language by osmosis. His characterization of the center-left formula as "parallel convergences" has become a classic. "I know it makes no sense mathematically," he once said, "but it does politically."[1]

admonitions. Under the circumstances, however, apart from some vulgar antics by the neo-Fascist Party, the approbation came on like a train. The "opposition" retained 5 per cent of the voting power, and that was divided among four irascible splinter parties on the extreme right and left.[2]

The kidnappers, it would later be calculated, had had forty-seven minutes in which their flight could proceed more or less freely. After that all movement in and out of the city was under surveillance, as were the frontiers, airports, and territorial waters. Roadblocks that within a few days would number in the tens of thousands rippled outward from Rome faster than the speed of any form of ground transportation. The transfer of the prisoner in Via Massimi, a description of the new getaway van, and the direction in which it had started off were already known, and while a second switch was possible after the last sighting, it was far more likely that Aldo Moro had reached his destination—the so-called "people's prison"—long before forty-seven minutes had elapsed. The investigators in fact concluded at once that the president was being held somewhere in or very near the city.

The first zone of police operations was thus concentrated within a few square miles radiating from Via Fani, though they were not limited to that area alone. Five thousand men in bulletproof vests began a house-to-house search. It seemed a good, if all too logical beginning. The minds that had plotted the capture of Aldo Moro, it had to be assumed, would have given even more consideration to the security of the people's prison.

As the details of the complexity of the assault began to be assembled—principally by the political section of police headquarters and the Interior Ministry—it became increasingly clear to the authorities that they were up against an escalation in the capability of the Red Brigades for which they were totally unprepared. Not twelve, they estimated, but between fifty and sixty *brigatisti* had to have been directly involved in today's attack if one considered the support logistics required to maintain the operation now. Not that anyone had a notion of what was coming next.

On the contrary, the police had been caught with a current file of intelligence on the Red Brigades that was barely three-dimensional. Their computer knew less. Its Red Brigades program printed out the data and likenesses of twenty suspects, and this material was transmitted at once to the media. A special telephone was installed and the public was asked to feel free to call. It looked good, but it turned out to be the day's second "Plan Zero."

Of the twenty wanted men and women, two had long been out of the country, two were already in prison, two were different photographs of the same person, and one was a "blown" police informer who had infiltrated the Red Brigades; only eight or nine were known members of the organization, and their photographs dated back to another decade.[3]

All this was yet to be revealed. For now it seemed that the state was on the move and that the men of power knew more than they would allow. In the days ahead a recovery effort would in fact be launched, but the authorities on this day could do no more than pretend to be in touch with the knowledge of the gods.

The family, gathered in the penthouse in Via Forte Trionfale, knew much that was true and pertinent but unknown to the world outside, and most of it was infuriating. The Moros' married daughters had come to stay, and the president's brother and sister were there, too, along with some close family friends. There were several nerve-rasping reports that *Papà* had been found dead; fortunately, these were too wildly contradictory to credit. On the plus side was a laboratory analysis that the blood on the abandoned 132 was not of the same type as Moro's. No one was absolutely certain at this hour that the prisoner had actually been in the 132, but further confirmation that he was uninjured would arrive quite soon.† He was, it seemed, alive and physically sound, but Eleonora Moro was aware that his absence from home was due in large measure to objectionable behavior on the part of the authorities in Rome. She had in her possession a copy of a police report filed about twenty days earlier by the dead chief of the bodyguard, "Judo" Leonardi. In it, Leonardi had cited suspicious movements in both the Via Forte Trionfale and around the president's private office across town in Via Savoia. It was in this document that the request had been made for a bulletproof car.

† At four in the morning the white 128 was found—mysteriously, considering the heavy police presence—in the same place as the 132. Blood traces in this car would also test negatively as far as the president was concerned.

Now the family learned from Moro's private secretary, Nicola Rana, that Leonardi's suspicions had in fact been investigated, and on the afternoon of March 15—one day ago—the nation's highest police official had called Moro's office to reassure him that there was no cause for alarm. No mention was made of the armored car.[4]

Eleonora Moro shared with her husband a general skepticism of the authorities in Rome, and there were only a few exceptions. She did not expect that they would handle the present case in a way that would change her opinion for the better. It was, as usual, the movement of power that would count for all, and the family decided that the best way to nurture what power it had without *Papà* was to maintain a silent watch on the motions of others.

In the evening, while the smaller and slightly less representative Senate was repeating the voting pattern of the Chamber, Andreotti addressed the nation, or as he put it, "the families."

Appearing on television after the second chapter of an Italian TV-film version of *Jane Eyre* and before the popular quiz show "Do You Want to Bet?" he seemed more out of place than the programming. Time and Machiavelli had taught the Italians much about politicians, and most recently they had seen the postwar world bared of their last illusions. They had scarce faith in their leaders, many of whom seemed to pass as much time in the courts as in office fighting to stay out of prison. Their Chief of State, Giovanni Leone, had lately been accused of multiple breaches of the public trust, and Andreotti's three previous governments were suspect of acts well below the threshold of law.[5]

An able observer of the contemporary political scene, and particularly of Christian Democracy, had recently described the Prime Minister as "one of the most jaded and cynical" among those at the summit of his party.[6] That was perhaps only partially true, since in interrupting this evening's entertainment Andreotti certainly showed a sensitivity to the low esteem in which the men of power were held and how difficult it was for him to follow Charlotte Brontë. He went before the families with many hats in hand.

"In past decades," he said, "the political class was able to take pride in having guaranteed a normal, peaceful life to all the families. For some time now, things have changed. . . ."

To a people who had known twenty years of fascism and thus

had something to compare with Christian Democratic rule, he said, "Do not be misled by the false conception that a democratic state is weak. In the long run, democracy is never weak." The trouble lay in the short run. The institutions of the democratic state—precious though they were, he said—were in a confrontation "with pitiless hostilities that erupt in diverse forms." This explanation, it was imagined, would help prepare public opinion for the not-so-democratic decree-laws that were at the moment being drafted. Finally, to justify why all this bother now, after innumerable common and political kidnappings of less illustrious Italians, Andreotti spoke as follows:

> We politicians, even those at the highest levels, do not enjoy a status any different from the rest of our citizens, and if I speak to you now, it is not because I did not consider extremely grave the kidnappings suffered by no small number of other families. But today's criminal act, which was timed to coincide with the debate in Parliament has a particular significance, and that needs to be pointed out and told to you firmly, while imploring you to remain calm.[7]

Just what that "particular significance" might be Andreotti left to the great Italian imagination, but in the sidespeak of the day, he appeared to be saying to the families to let the matter rest with him, which, when there is trouble, is always a mighty invitation.

That night the Senate overwhelmingly confirmed the new majority. The fourth Andreotti government had risen like the phoenix from the ashes of this day. To the extent that the Grand Design would hold together, Prime Minister Andreotti could now administer the fate of the Grand Designer any way he saw fit.

II

PRISON

*I, like many others, entered Christian De-
mocracy with the spontaneity and enthusiasm of a religious more than a political
choice. . . . Apart from this origin, which I
insist on claiming because without it I
wouldn't have been a Christian Democrat—I
would have been who knows what or nothing—I cannot deny that I exercised a function of some importance.*[1]

4.

Lonely, restless people stayed awake all night telephoning the police to say that Aldo Moro was with them; others with troubled minds spewed evil over the wires.

There was little more to do now than listen and wait. The Red Brigades had promised a communiqué, without saying when. The manhunt, which would engage thirty-eight thousand men, was indispensable, if only in political terms, but seasoned law-enforcement officers knew that the most difficult time to catch the thief is immediately after the theft, when he enjoys the best of his survival arrangements. Only as the quarry is heard from can the vectors begin to be plotted.

There was no intelligent way of surmising what the Red Brigades would do with Aldo Moro. They had kidnapped only nine men since they made their ethereal debut at the start of the decade. Five of those, after being tried and convicted by a rolling "people's tribunal" in the back of a stolen truck, had been released the very same day that they had been seized. Another had been freed in a police raid, and still another had been ransomed by his family. None of the nine had been killed, and apart from some rough treatment, all had been returned unharmed. One man, held eight days, even claimed that he had benefited ("This experience will help me to meditate and to work for a better future.").[1]

All this meant almost nothing, however. The previous abductions were ancient history in the skeletal annals of the Red Brigades—primitive works of the founding fathers at the expense of men low in the ranks of power. In 1975, following a series of arrests, Italy's top antiterrorist, General Carlo Alberto Dalla Chiesa, of the Carabinieri, had declared that the Red Brigades no longer existed, and for a while it looked that way. The "historic chiefs" were either dead in combat or captured, and on the day Aldo Moro was taken, fifteen of them were standing trial in Turin for all kinds of urban warfare. To be sure, a second generation of *brigatisti* had been heard from. They had blasted their way on the scene in mid-1976 with a political assassination full of vengeance, and before long, assassination seemed the style of the new wave. Continual homage was rendered to their fallen, and for almost two years they had succeeded in disrupting and postponing the trial of their heroes by intimidating would-be jurors and lawyers. This gave heart to the heroes, but there appeared to be a break in continuity from the old school, which had its roots in that year of the great nonrevolution, 1968.

The "new" Red Brigades, as they began to be called by an only slightly less-new breed of terrorologists, showed, they said, two distinct departures from the old: a discipline of steel and a range of objectives cast much higher than before. Whether this proved that the new organization was substantially different from its predecessor or was simply battle-hardened remained an open topic in terrorology, however; in human terms it only added to the uncertainties of the fate of Aldo Moro.

So they waited—the family, the state, and everyone else who had something to gain or regain, attending, like all who wait in the anterooms of things unknown, to their dignity. Rome began to squeeze the face of the nation into a pasteboard mask of unity. At first it would play convincingly, at least to the gallery of the outside world, but it was grotesque and ill-fitting from the start and in the end would crumble.

Behind the mask, Giulio Andreotti began to fulfill his promise of a "day-to-day relationship" with the new majority. On the very first full day of his Administration, he called into council the secretaries general of the five parties that formed the majority. With great secrecy and an air of high emergency, the meeting was held that afternoon in the Palazzo Chigi, the sixteenth-century palace of the Prime Minister, which shares a busy downtown intersection with the city's largest department store, a shopping arcade, and the wondrously worked Roman column of Marcus Aurelius.

In the morning, Andreotti had met with his Interministerial Committee on Security (CIS), an admixture of diplomatic, military, police, and intelligence officials, and now he reported to the new majority. The minutes of that meeting, leaked months later, are revealing of what was important to each of the principal figures managing the set of problems that had sprung from the Pandora's box of the Red Brigades. Outside, as the Easter tourist season resumed with a flourish, the overwhelming sensation was one of benign indifference to yesterday's events, but at the seat of government men of quite another temperament seem to have imagined that their own feelings were being shared by all.

The CIS, Andreotti began, was "very worried about the public's state of mind." The people needed "help," he went on, "in overcoming the widespread sense of fear." The idea was "to avoid the spread of panic." To aid this endeavor along, the CIS had asked that the press be urged to be more "co-operative." Since the two national television networks were owned by the state, they could be told, not urged.

Next came the CIS's evaluation of the Red Brigades. They were few in number, Andreotti reported, but linked to professional killers and supported by the *autonomi* (a loose term meaning "autonomous" that fit almost everyone to the left of the Communist Party). About two hundred *autonomi* were in prison and many more were at the moment being arrested. They would all be interrogated immediately, Andreotti assured.

At this point, the Prime Minister made four of his own proposals, three of which were illegal. They would therefore require legitimization by decreeing "special laws." Andreotti recommended (a) preventive arrests; (b) the use of information obtained in legal wiretaps for purposes other than those for which the original authorization had been given; and (c) the bugging of the prison cells of the defendants in the trial of the Red Brigades in Turin. The fourth proposal concerned the traditionally rival forces of the police and the Carabinieri: the unification of their data banks, which were hitherto kept separate and secret from one another.

Andreotti asked for the secretaries' best counsel, and there was more or less all-around agreement, but in view of the lethal schism that was coming, it is interesting to note where each of these men stood at the beginning.

Speaking for the Christian Democrats was Benigno Zaccagnini. He was known for a trait rare in his party, and that had given him the name "Honest Zac." He was the only man at the meeting whom Aldo Moro might then have included among those he considered his friends, though he did not regard Zaccagnini as a person of special talents. Zaccagnini, like Andreotti (a nonfriend, to say the least), owed his present position to Moro, who had moved both men into place like big guns in the new political strategy. For now, Zaccagnini limited his observations to mere repetitions of Andreotti, saying that the public was frightened, that the media exaggerated, and that tapping telephones "would help a lot."

Enrico Berlinguer, the sad-eyed Sardinian nobleman who had led the Communists since 1972, and had led them to triumph upon triumph, was against the idea of "special laws." The author of the historic compromise, he had been cultivating the image of his party as *the* guarantor of civil rights and liberties, and as the Penal Code was the same one in force since Fascist times, there were already enough laws on the books to carry out what Berlinguer was to call "a scorched-earth policy against subversives."

The best way to do this, he believed, was by increasing the number, efficiency, and salaries of the police and Carabinieri. In the meantime, he was all for tapping telephones, and moreover, deploying the armed forces to augment the police operations and, if necessary, for rounding up the subversives. Who would be considered a subversive and who would pass the test was a point that appears to have gone undiscussed, though Berlinguer wanted to listen to "the experts" on the matter of arrests and interrogations. If the leading Eurocommunist's position might seem to contradict his party's public stance on rights and freedoms, perhaps that is one reason why the meeting was held in secret.

The resonant voice of Berlinguer added to Zaccagnini's rumble contained the politically delegated voice of nearly 75 per cent of the people, but the remaining three party secretaries had volume, too, in spite of their weakness at the polls. The dynamics of Italian history had often assigned them critical roles in times of trouble, which was almost always, and any one of them might emerge as the agency of this or that solution.

By far the strongest of the three was forty-four-year-old Bettino

Craxi. He was the head of the Socialists, which had slightly less than 10 per cent of the popular vote. Craxi and a whole new leadership of men and women in their thirties and forties had taken over from the old guard, which had been responsible for severe setbacks in the elections two years ago. The party under Craxi was at the start of a comeback phase. He was preparing to offer the electorate still another way to socialism, the modern, individualistic, Marlboro man's way, one might call it. He had already added a new-looking red rose to the hammer and sickle on the Socialist flag, but the rest was still on the storyboards, and the truth was that vigor and freshness alone were not much for a match with the Big Two. Attempting to shake loose from the hegemony of the Communist colossus, Craxi and all his young blood at the top had made of the Socialists a party in search of a cause.

They had not yet found it on the first day after the Moro kidnapping, but at the meeting in the Palazzo Chigi, Craxi seemed less interested in the brawny proposals of the others than in coming up with an angle all his own. He favored a cerebral approach, "a psychological counteroffensive." According to the minutes, he noted, "Superior minds are behind these subversive operations. The state, too, has to mobilize superior minds." The man and the cause were converging.

After Craxi, the meeting went back to the hardware measures. The secretaries of the two smallest parties, Oddo Biasini of the Social Democrats and Pierluigi Romita of the Republicans, concurred on the wiretappings, the preventive arrests, and everything else that might extend the long arm of the law, which is precisely what Andreotti said he would do when his turn came to sum up.

The record shows no disagreement, and when the meeting adjourned a communiqué was issued to the press. Although the provisions to be adopted would remain secret, the media were informed that everything would be done "in support of the constitutional and democratic system."[2]

In the same afternoon, more than thirty hours after the raid in Via Fani, an editor in the newsroom of the Rome daily *Il Messaggero* was telephoned by a man claiming to speak for the Red Brigades. The newsman was directed to a large square called Largo Argentina, which lies just north of the old Jewish ghetto. There was a message, said the caller, in a coin-operated photo machine located in the pedestrian underpass beneath the intersection.

A reporter and a photographer were dispatched at once. They searched in vain in and around the machine. Later another journalist returned with the jack of his car and he moved the machine away from the wall. He found nothing but a roll of old photographs and crumpled paper.

What had happened became somewhat clearer only after twenty hours more had gone by. Another editor received a call at about noon on Saturday. He later recorded the following conversation:

"Who is this?"

"This is the Red Brigades."

"And this is Buffalo Bill. . . . Who are you?"

"And you think I'm going to tell you my name. . . . How come you wrote that there aren't any messages?"

"Because there were none."

"That's not true. We told you yesterday where it was. Obviously your phones are tapped and the police got there first."

"All right, let's have another."

"It's still there. They didn't find it. . . . On the roof of the photo machine. Under a pile of scrap paper, there's a manila envelope. There's a photograph of Moro with it. Is there a [news] blackout on this thing?"

"No, honestly, why?"

"Because we're afraid that Cossiga and the others want everything made known only after it's all over."

He hung up. The Friday episode had been a trial run—a test to learn if the *Messaggero*'s lines were in fact clean and to see if this method of disseminating messages was secure. In spite of what the caller said, the *brigatisti* knew now that the phones were not tapped, at least not yet. Otherwise they would not have called for another wild-goose chase. This time the message was there, with a Polaroid shot of Aldo Moro.[3]

He was in the people's prison, awaiting trial, they said, for being Italy's "political godfather"; "the most faithful executor of all the directives imparted by the centers of imperialism"; "the undisputed theoretician and strategist" of thirty years of Christian Democratic oppression. He was their Hitler in Jerusalem, Stalin in the hands of a Gulag rebellion, and he seemed already in the dock.

In photographing him with their banner as a backdrop, they had copied the German way of the Red Army Fraction, who in turn had copied the press agents of presidents and kings, but only the Red Brigades—the *Brigate Rosse*—could seat their captive off-center so that he was directly beneath the SS in their logo, which of course, help it or not, they did. This was the man whom the poet Pasolini, who could loathe the bourgeoisie as soulfully as any *brigatista*, had called "the least implicated of them all,"[4] but now he wore a Nazi crown upon his head. It was a bad beginning.

Nevertheless, he was alive. "Praise God!" cried Honest Zac. "It looks as if they haven't harmed him," was what Mrs. Moro said when the picture was flashed on television. She alone noticed that he was not wearing the same shirt he had had on that morning, but he looked out at the rest of the world from under the stylized five-pointed star of the Red Brigades with enough enigma in the mien of his head and shoulders to haunt the generations.

Nature and circumstance had long ago pressed a Mona Lisan mystery on his face. Many had tried to describe it, but no one better than Sicilian writer Leonardo Sciascia, whose novel and later the film *Todo Modo* had seemed the last word on all that was unhallowed in Christian Democracy.

"Watching him on television," Sciascia said recently, "Moro seemed prey to an ancient weariness, to the deepest kind of boredom. Only in fleeting moments could you perceive in his eyes or on his lips a lightning bolt of irony or disdain, and immediately that weariness and boredom would again set in. But you had a sense that he knew 'something else,' the Italian, Catholic secret: the squandering of the new in the old, the use of every new technique in the service of time-worn ways; and, above all, a wholly negative awareness, the negativeness of human nature, which at the same time was his affliction and his weapon."[5]

A weapon used with visible pain, says Sciascia. But used. Now Aldo Moro, who had a passion, perhaps his only passion, for neckties, sat with an open collar, and across the image of his face, caught in the salts of flash photography, lay one of those momentary ironies. He did not look disarmed.

Only two other men had ever been in the people's prison, one in 1973 for a period of eight days and the other for thirty-five days in the spring of 1974. Their ordeals had been forgotten by nearly everyone except themselves, but now the family, the clue seekers, and all who tried to imagine what Moro's imprisonment might be like undusted the chronicles of those days.

The first man—the one who "enjoyed" the experience—was the then fifty-eight-year-old director of personnel of the Fiat automobile factory, Ettore Amerio, who was literally yanked out of his shoes on a street in Turin one cold December morning. He was wanted for questioning, said the Red Brigades, regarding Fiat's "Fascist policies" against leftist activists inside the factory, 250 of whom had recently been expelled. When the company agreed to withdraw an impending threat of mass layoffs, Amerio, given a brand-new pair of shoes, was released.

He had been led into the people's prison blindfolded and under a threat that can only be translated as "One false move and we'll kill you." When the tape was removed from his eyes, he found himself in a rectangular, windowless room, whose walls had been insulated with sheets of polystyrene for soundproofing. Hung like tapestry on one of the walls was the silk red banner and the circled yellow star with the computerlike printout letters that spelled *Brigate Rosse*. He saw a table, a chair, a lamp, a cot, and two men. They were in dark blue worker's coveralls. They wore matching hangman's hoods. They addressed him in the polite form of speech and identified themselves as "revolutionaries of the left." They told him that he would eventually be released unharmed, which, he said, did much to relieve his fear. "They were almost courteous." They removed his watch.

Four months later, it was the turn of Mario Sossi, dubbed at the time as "the most hated man in Italy." His kidnapping—codenamed Operation Sunflower—was qualitatively different from Amerio's and in retrospect it appears as a long rehearsal for the Moro affair, but that of course was as yet unknown.*

The capture and trial of Mario Sossi marks the departure of the Red Brigades from what they called "bite and run" operations to a new strategy "to strike at the heart of the state." Sossi, an assistant

---

* The similarities between these two episodes are striking, and as the earlier kidnapping was the handiwork of the founding fathers, they all but make the case for continuity in the organization as opposed to the more fashionable hypothesis of the "new Red Brigades," directed, perhaps, by foreign powers.

attorney general in Genoa, was more a hangnail than the heart, but as a pistol-packing, Red-hunting prosecutor, he had become a national figure and a public enemy of the extraparliamentary left, and was as good a beginning as any.

He was accosted one evening returning home from his office, lifted from the street like a sack of onions, and tossed into the back of a truck. The first words he heard were, "You've been looking for the Red Brigades; now you've found them." As in that last live image of Aldo Moro, Sossi was held firmly by the back of his head, which was continually being pressed downward, apparently to prevent him from looking at the faces of his assailants.

He was bound, blindfolded, and, he believed, given a substance to make him drowsy. When he came to his senses, he was on his feet inside the people's prison. "Be good," he heard someone say, "now we're going to untie you."

He was in a room about eight feet square. It had a small, low door with four locks. The walls and the ceiling were soundproofed. There were no windows, only a grated exhaust fan in a hole in the ceiling. The floor was covered with mats. A small table, a folding chair, a cot, weak light from a bare red bulb. The red-and-yellow standard was unfurled, and there was a slogan written on a wall: "Carry the attack to the heart of the state."†

In the dim light, Sossi later recounted, he saw two hooded men in blue coveralls. One was stocky; the other was tall and thin, and Sossi could see through the man's eyeslits that he was wearing glasses. They would be the only two persons he would come in contact with during his imprisonment, and they would conduct the people's trial.

"One of them," Sossi said, "seemed to me at once to be well prepared and quite cultured. It was he who would later take the part of the *dominus* in that sort of hearing, while the other man would act as the public prosecutor. He was uncouth, and he often used the word 'prick,' even when he was not in bad humor; he said 'prick' to show that he was sincere."

The two men left him alone briefly, then returned. They took his

† Almost a year later the police found the people's prison, and Sossi identified it as his own. It was nothing but an enormous wooden box erected inside a farmhouse about forty miles north of Genoa.

wallet, his watch, and two appointment books he had had in his pockets. They removed his shoes, his jacket, and his tie.

The shorter man, while he was searching him, said, "Don't think I'm a fag, now. We have to see what you've got."[6]

5.

The president was in a box. Masked men had taken away his navy-blue jacket and the matching vest he had been wearing beneath it and his silk tie and goodness knows why his striped shirt. They had taken his billfold and his cufflinks and his watch and a gold bracelet he carried around and probably his black moccasins, too. They had sat him on a backless chair and they had flashed hot light in his eyes from off center, this man who hated to be seen in shirtsleeves, who always wore his jacket buttoned. There was much he had to recover, and if they told him it would all be returned in the end, they had not lied. The people's prison, though its wardens pretended elsewise, was not very different from the state's.

No one remembered him in the place where he was born. Italians in general knew him as a *pezzo grosso*, a big shot, who if he were running true to form protected the Mafia, never paid his taxes, and had his hands in the national till. Probably he did none of these things, but he was not a man of the people. Not that anyone since Mussolini had wished to touch the people; the *duce* was not the first Italian populist to end hanging upside down. They knew Moro, too, as the fall guy under the political cartoonist's pen, the comic's TV routine ("that streak of white on his head is the only thing clear he's got up there"), the impersonator's *tour de force*, and the columnist's source of discontent.

"It's all a question of his face," one of the most widely read political commentators had written. "Moro's is anything but unpleasant. But it makes you yawn. He communicates with the people, but the only thing he communicates is lethargy. And if he does exercise a certain kind of magic, it's like that of an anesthetist, who has the power to procure the sweetest of sleeps for the patient but without any certainty that once the operation is over he will wake up."[1]*

In the very newspapers Moro had been reading going down Via Fani, his name was being linked—more by the word of a political hit man than reliable evidence—to the "Antilope Cobbler," the unidentified central demon in a bribery scandal involving the Lockheed Corporation. But that was on the sixteenth; on the seventeenth, in the name of the national interest, he was being beatified by the media, and on the nineteenth with the Polaroid shot in print, the icon of his sainthood was readily at hand.

"Stronger than a diamond, more tender than a mother," the headline of one newspaper read, and another daily, studying the photograph, said, "The image of Aldo Moro, of his serene and conscious dignity, reinforces our faith in reason and gives us a sign of hope."[2] No one asked why.

His was a sainthood that ought to be observed. It would soon be revoked, then rebestowed, then rewithdrawn, and so on, according to the shifting interpretations of the national interest. Now, however, they sang his virtues hoarsely; people looked the other way from the latest writing on the walls of the cities calling for "10–100–1,000 Moros," and few really knew who he was, what he had inside him, and no one, not even he, it seems, had any inkling of what he was yet to give.

He was born on September 23, 1916, in the dusty heel of the Italian boot, where people ate snakes and the hearts of swallows and puppy dogs cooked in a skillet to ward off rickets and TB.[3]

He was baptized Aldo Romeo Luigi. His father, Renato, was a provincial superintendent of schools, though schools were few in number in those days, and his father's father was a tailor and a merchant. His mother, Fida, was an elementary-school teacher

---

* There was an ominous remark in the same unfriendly article, written in 1974 when Moro resolved a government crisis, becoming Prime Minister for his fourth term. Every time Moro returned to power, the columnists said, he hears "the low roll of a drum, the kind that accompanies the march of the condemned in a scene in a melodrama."

when she was not producing and nurturing five children. She was from a family called Stinchi, and Aldo had the good fortune of being spared by the differentiations of language any childhood trauma from the hard "ch" pronunciation of his mother's maiden name.

In a country bled ashen by the First World War, then ravaged by conquering fascism, he was sheltered by geography and the monthly stipends of his parents, and so all his traumas were small— lessons driven home as neatly as cobbler's nails instead of the usual grapeshot. Through his stolid, bureaucratic father he seems to have received the age-old message that power is a function of order, and from taciturn Fida Stinchi came, no doubt, his faith in the ineffable.

His credo, Faith and Reason, would be buttressed and elaborated at an early age by Kant and the Gospels in a social hatchery where there were but two overt competitors for children's hearts and minds: the Catholic Church and the Fascist state. In Aldo Moro's case, the former, which did not shy from showing Charlie Chaplin and Tom Mix in the oratories, was the unassailable winner.

But not everyone who grew up warm and sang *Noi Vogliam Dio—We Want God*—instead of the *Giovinezza,* the Fascist hymn to youth, became an Aldo Moro. His character in formation was marked by a procession of commonplace experiences, of clichés about the clumsy boy taking refuge in books and overachieving by sheer hard work and study. If his most assiduous biographers have failed to turn up hardly more than a handful of banal anecdotes in a whole distinguished lifetime, probably that was due less to his predilection for privacy than to the simpler fact that there weren't any others, and even those known are best left unrepeated. It is a gratuitous exercise in armchair psychology to pretend to fathom why human beings with more or less the same milky beginnings go one way and another. Modern Italy has been governed by only three or four men of vision since Count Cavour showed the Pied-montese nobility how the immortal principles of the French Revo-lution, as he called them, could be used to gain and rule a greater kingdom. Moro, who came from a part of Italy Cavour never gave one thought to, was the last of this minuscule breed.

His call would come later, but Italy at the close of World War II was a country that had become undone, torn apart by foreign powers and betrayed and abandoned by its own. Politically, the

Italians had been hurled back into time, and many of the problems that had been faced one hundred years before, when Garibaldi chose to ride tall with his King, had to be faced once more. This time, the King who had let Mussolini march on Rome was banished, Italy was proclaimed a republic, and seventy-five men were picked to write its Constitution. Moro, who at the age of twenty-nine had been elected to the Constituent Assembly, was one of them. He had married Eleonora Chiaverelli, she, too, a book-worm, the daughter of a landed doctor in another town, his sweet-heart since they were twenty, and he had gone to Rome as a fresh-man representative from the southern city of Bari. They were Christians and democrats through and through and had been blessed by the then and a future Pope. In the capital, Aldo looked after the nation's Constitution and Noretta looked through sky-blue eyes after Aldo.

At a certain moment, when he had served all the mundane ap-prenticeships of mind, body, and soul, and had bounced four chil-dren on his knee, he emerged as a constant, a star in the political firmament. His constancy might fairly be described as an ingenu-ous, eighteenth-century, Jeffersonian belief in democracy and a Solomonic awareness of the low ways and means of a great part of human nature.

We see all this in action on one winter's day in 1969. An attempt had been made by factions in his party to isolate him and arrogate his power. After a long period of reflection, he came before the Na-tional Council of the Christian Democrats and in a memorable speech, told them why he refused to be crushed.

The sterile, closed circuit of power for the sake of power, he said, produces a detachment from society and dries up a party's vitality, weakening it electorally in the long run. He then gave his own con-cept of power:

The distribution and redistribution of power does not depend on the internal policies of a party. . . . In the end, there has to be a reason, a fundamental ideal, a human aim, for which power is constituted and exercised. Without this . . . a party sooner or later ceases to be a credible instrument in a free and progressive society. It is only by the unconditional acceptance of a moral reason that it develops coherently the heritage of our social ideals and the overall commitments of our time.[4]

In this haunted house of Kantian morality was lodged the kin of Bismarck too: old-fashioned *Realpolitik.*

In 1964, when an ambitious general and a mentally declining Chief of State had conspired with others to overthrow by a military *coup* the center-left government, Moro, prime target and Prime Minister, imposed a state secret on the affair as soon as he got wind of it. Documents were made to disappear, the general was offered the embassy in Brazil, and the President of the republic, who had grown increasingly terrified after the Kennedy assassination, broke down completely and was of necessity declared incapable of carrying out the functions of his office. The coverup lasted for years and remains a mysterious *omissis* in Italian history. There were so many people in high places who were compromised, Moro later confided, "it would have blown the whole system apart."[5]

He never dared like kings to claim *l'état c'est moi,* but at times he *was* Christian Democracy. In his last speech in the Chamber of Deputies, after a parliamentary commission of inquiry had accused numerous members of his party of involvement in the Lockheed bribery scandal, Moro, admitting their "political errors," made an impassioned plea for perspective. He warned against assigning guilt before due process, or creating distractions from national problems that had to be approached in harmony. Most of all, he warned against making a pariah of his party.

> Honorable colleagues [he said], if you have a shred of wisdom, and sometimes one is given to doubt that, do not underestimate, and we say this to you firmly, the great force of that part of public opinion which for more than three decades has found its expression and defense in Christian Democracy. . . . We represent not only votes, but ideas, hopes, values, rich human resources [and] democratic stability. . . . However this matter is ended, whatever be the fate of men for whom we have fought full of passion and hope, we Christian Democrats, faithful to tradition but capable of creativity, will continue to do our duty.[6]

He was perhaps more Christian than democrat in tolerating the imperfectness of men who would be tried and eventually convicted of corruption, but tolerance was the essence of his style.

He was a slow, reasoning star. He practiced the rare art of gentle persuasion, of trying first to understand the motives of dissent from his own view and then seeking the common ground where all kinds of opposites might stand, at least for a time. The question to ask, he had said on one recent occasion, is, "What can we do not to break, not to destroy, not to do anything catastrophic, but also not to damage the things that are essential to us . . . ?"[7]

He had often been described as, when not accused of having mastered the old Italian trick of *trasformismo,* of transforming opposition to support by the carrot and the stick, but all the great practitioners of *trasformismo* owed their greatness to the singular depth of their cynicism. Aldo Moro, unique in his party, which for thirty years had been run like a Tammany Society, profoundly *believed* in Christian Democracy. His sometimes oracular voice rose from the singular depth of this conviction, which may be defined as an idea of a democratic state where a political party inspired by the Church becomes the institution that exercises the power of Christ on history. Not that he was blind to the side of this party where the sun never shone, the side of influence peddling, neo-Fascist intrigue, Mafia connections, and all manner of organized evil. But men of faith, who are convinced of a Great Big Teleological Purpose to It All, or at least have made a favorable settlement with doubt, normally proceed on a different time scale than the rest of us, and Aldo Moro wore his tranquil, unself-righteous, Catholic conscience on the outside.

He cast the image of oriental suppleness, of some higher stage in the quest for *satori;* he had the color "of a slow autumn rain," as one of his colleagues put it in a happy phrase. His presence was an invitation to calm, discretion, prudence, slow-going, good manners, and that grand lost Italian trait always invoked but ever in vain: *pazienza.*

"We must fight," he once said, "but not necessarily to win,"[8] and of this stuff were openings to the left, larger majorities, and even parallel convergences made possible.

If he seemed forbidding, that was only true for those who had made no effort to understand him. He was only civilized. Beneath the heavy coats and suits and tightly knotted ties was a man who had to wash his hands a dozen times a day, who cringed when he was touched, who worried about his pregnant daughter Anna, who liked mystery novels and Westerns and Beethoven and Brecht and modern art and cigarette lighters; a man who shied from strangers and dirty words and all things uncouth; who could be coaxed into doing fair impersonations of celebrities, who knew how to win the affections of his students, and who, wherever he went with his traveling hypochondriacal medicines, carried among them a woman's golden bracelet, the tangible memory of one special sentimental moment in his life.

Such was the Gentle Builder who had fallen into the hands of the Revolutionary Razers. Now, before the people's tribunal, they told him that he would have to answer to the charge of his direct and maximum responsibility "for the basic political choices in actuating the counterrevolutionary programs of the imperialist bourgeoisie."[9]

Of himself, Aldo Moro once said, "I have always tried to avoid the worst,"[10] and in the people's prison, we know now, he began at once to search in the minds of his captors for a patch of common ground.

6.

The photograph of Aldo Moro and the news that at some unspecified time he was going to be tried were published in all the morning dailies of Sunday, March 19. What did not appear in the newspapers was an editorial that had been written the day before for publication in *Il Popolo,* Christian Democracy's daily. The editorial was to have been a trial balloon, broaching the idea that at some future date it might become necessary to negotiate for the life of the president. The copy had been taken personally by the editor-in-chief to Zaccagnini at party headquarters in the Square of Jesus, and on Saturday afternoon, Honest Zac read it carefully and approved it without changes. Somehow, however, Prime Minister Andreotti learned of its imminent publication, and he spent the rest of that afternoon mobilizing his strengths inside the party not only to suppress the editorial but to give Zaccagnini a lecture as well. The new majority had passed the first test of the hard line.[1]

At noon that Palm Sunday, Pope Paul addressed the faithful from his window high over St. Peter's Square. He asked them to pray for Aldo Moro, who was dear to him personally, he said. That was about all one could do if one was inclined to do something. The communiqué from the Red Brigades was a declaration that the capture and trial of their prisoner was but the beginning of a new phase in the "class war for communism," and it asked nothing of the enemy. It had already been widely reported that the Red Brigades were demanding the release of their fifteen comrades on trial in Turin, but this news was based on false information, of which there was suddenly an oversupply. The only reference to the Turin trial in the communiqué was a warning to the authorities not to take any retaliation against the defendants or any other "fighting communist" in their hands. Memories of the multiple deaths of leaders of the Baader-Meinhof gang at Stammheim Prison in Stuttgart were fresh, and the suicide theory had not yet gained much support (particularly among the imprisoned Red Brigade leaders, who in the weeks to come would continually protest their all-around good health). The only other point of interest in the communiqué—for those who cared little about the reasons it gave why the proletariat ought to unite—was an attempt to block disinformation: "All the communiqués," it concluded, "will be typed on the same machine. This one."[2]

Palm Sunday or not, the temporal authorities were actively trying to mend their state of unpreparedness. To their mortification, a third car used in the Via Fani raid had turned up in the predawn hours in Via Calvo in the spot where the first two abandoned cars had been parked. As Rome was surrounded by the Army and Via Calvo was in a zone of particularly dense police concentration, it was clear that the Red Brigades were mocking these operations, vaunting a capacity to swim like Maoist fish among the people, though it was more bravura than anything like that.*

On the credit side, Interior Minister Francesco Cossiga, yet another Christian Democrat who owed his career to Moro, began to put together an ad hoc think tank that included two behaviorists. The group was given the task of erecting a psychological model of the collective mind of the Red Brigades to forecast the probabilities of what its next moves might be. Cossiga also asked for assistance from the British Special Air Service, which had gained a great deal of sophistication from its long experience fighting the Provisional IRA. More important, Cossiga believed, was aid from the West Germans. Apart from their highly computerized antiterrorist tech-

---

* In a postoperation analysis for internal use only, the Red Brigades criticized this sort of brazenness, which was a running feature of the entire affair. "Many comrades," they said, "showed a low level of discipline due essentially to the pressure of time. Certain risks must not be taken . . . they can provoke a situation in which the strategic command may be forced to reconsider pre-established plans. And since improvements can be made, it is necessary that they are made."[3]

nology, their elite corps, the *Grenzschutzgruppe*-9, had conducted the spectacular raid at Mogadishu some months before, freeing all eighty-six passengers and a Yorkshire puppy from a hijacked plane.

Bonn and London responded with alacrity, as did the United States when requested to furnish all the intelligence it had on the Red Brigades. It was quickly discovered, however, that no one in Washington knew anything more than the Italians, and what was known was obsolete.

Cossiga himself vaguely recalled that an American psychiatrist had played a behind-the-scenes role in a recent major terrorist incident in the United States. He asked the American embassy to look into the matter, and though no one in Rome remembered who the psychiatrist was, he was readily identified in Washington as a full-time employee of the State Department, thirty-four-year-old Dr. Steve R. Pieczenik, a Deputy Assistant Secretary of State.

Under a request by the Italians for absolute secrecy, the softspoken U. S. Government expert in "crisis management" was sent to Rome to act as a consultant to Cossiga. His presence in the capital was kept hidden not only from the press and almost everyone outside the confines of Cossiga's office but from high officials in the U.S. embassy as well.

Pieczenik's job, he later revealed, was to advise on the formulation of "a number of very sophisticated strategies and tactics." They were in fact adopted, he said, though of exactly what they consisted remains secret and can only be inferred from how the government performed.

The young, Harvard-trained psychiatrist (and MIT political scientist) had dealt successfully with terrorist attacks involving the taking of hostages by Hanafi Muslims in Washington and a hijacking by Croatian émigrés in New York. But he viewed the raid of the Red Brigades as unprecedented in the history of modern terrorism, since, as he put it, "this was the first time a senior statesman was kidnapped for clear political purposes without any specific demands. . . ." These purposes, he said after speaking with Cossiga, were to create the conditions for civil war by provoking repressive measures. "It is also the strongest attempt we in the Western world have seen by terrorists to destabilize a democracy," Pieczenik said at the time. It was therefore essential to demonstrate, he said, "that no man is indispensable to the viability of the nation-state."[4]

Unfortunately, there is only one way to attempt such a demonstration, but all this remained to be seen. The government would insist on the nonrepressiveness of the new measures about to be decreed, and only the flealike opposition would disagree, but it was far too early for informed calculations. The absence of demands was no proof that they were not on the way, and if they were, everything would turn on what exactly the Red Brigades might want in exchange for Aldo Moro. The empty file in Washington and the puzzlement in Rome attested that no one had a clear idea of what the Red Brigades might or might not ask for—not even, the fact of the matter was, the Red Brigades.

For a long time—a year, perhaps—they had been tracking Aldo Moro. There were all too many other men of stature on their wanted list, but this was a particular moment in their little history, and no one more than Moro embodied in one frail, portable human objective the triumphs they hoped to bring home from their war.

In November 1975, the antiterrorist squad in Turin had arrested a known *brigatista* and found notes for a plan to kidnap the president of Fiat, Giovanni Agnelli. One would have to imagine a Ford, a Rockefeller, and a Kennedy all in one to find an American equivalent to the position in Italian society enjoyed by Agnelli, which may be why the rudimentary plan contained the annotation, "There are difficulties."

Difficulties, to put it mildly, had been wasting the Red Brigades since the bloodless conclusion of the Sossi affair in May 1974. In that instance they had demanded the release of eight members of another armed revolutionary organization who were on trial in Genoa. After twenty days of agonizing, their "provisional liberty" was ordered by the courts, but at the last moment the regional attorney general refused to actually release the men. The Red Brigades, believing that they had shown that the state does not respect its own laws, freed Sossi anyway with an admonition to "wise up."

They were universally damned by the makers of instant opinion, but Sossi said that they had cooked him *risotto*, had bought him medicine, and had otherwise treated him thoughtfully, enough so to prompt him to remark, "I respect them as enemies." This may have been their finest hour in terms of their impact on people's heart of hearts. They had never yet fired a shot, and the Red-baiting Sossi had given convincing evidence to the people's tribunal of political and criminal corruption in the Genoese magistrature and police department.[5] The image of a band of Italian Lone Rangers lay just behind the screen of public condemnation.

They *almost* got a good press. The influential newsweekly *L'Espresso* said that the Red Brigades had succeeded in showing that the state used methods as reprehensible as theirs, and *Panorama*, its larger competitor, found ordering the release of the captured revolutionaries in exchange for Sossi less offensive than the habitual release of captured Mafiosi in exchange for nothing.[6]

Italy had always loved its rough-riding bandits, even some Mafiosi. Terrorism, by whatever name is in fashion,† is as Italian as pasta. Half-baked notions about CIA and/or KGB Manchurian candidates as the real power in the Red Brigades persist in Rome, and the traditional love affair seems to be over, but the organization's most secret archives have been captured and revealed so many times that their fundamentally Italian past, at least their past, is as open as the Colosseum. They date back to childish dreams in the 1960s, but even childish dreams play from the bad script of history. Anyone grown tired of looking for which foreign devil's hand has got the Red Brigades by the short hairs ought to keep one eye on the sixties and the other on half of a whole millennium, for Italy,

† This may be the right place to try to defuse, at least for this reading, the political hand grenade that has been made of the word *terrorism*. One man's terrorism is another's liberation movement, and neither expression satisfies the truth. The only pure act of terrorism I can think of is the branding of every form of violence against established power as terrorism. George Washington was more than a terrorist, and the violent overthrow of the moneychangers in the Temple was much more than an act of terrorism. Political terror, whether used by the communist mercenary Carlos or a nation-state rattling nuclear warheads, is always a tactic and never a strategy. It is more instructive to examine what this or that terrorist is really up to, which usually induces one to seek out less emotional and thus more precise terminology. Oddly, words such as *radical, revolutionary,* and *guerrilla* have lately cooled down enough to be manageable, apparently in some proportion to the starry rise of the obscurant, catch-all word under discussion, and as one need not be terrorized by *terrorism,* I propose to use the word that seems best to fit.

gentle in so many ways, is a place where political banditry is a hoary institution.‡

The guns, from the first harquebus blast, have never been silent, and since the last war, Italy, refounded on the mystical aspects and not the firepower of the Resistance, had had to abide the anger of an old-fashioned Revolution Betrayed. All this, and the periodic visitations of the gods, Mao and Che and Ho, among others, pressed hard, but perhaps most indelible of all on the hearts and minds of those for whom the Resistance was a parent lost in childbirth, was 1968.

The origins of the Red Brigades are to be found in the story of two such orphans, and as the history of all things good or evil always leads back to a tender moment, theirs is a short Zhivagoan story of love. Margherita Cagol, the only person whom the Red Brigades have publicly recognized as their founder, was twenty when she met Renato Curcio, and he was twenty-four. They were sociology majors at the new University of Trent. She was a commuter student, and Curcio, the future chief and ideologue of the Red Brigades, was a shy mamma's boy—"Big Mamma," he called his mother and on one summer's day years ago simply left a note and Big Mamma behind ("I am grateful to you without end."). Cagol played the classical guitar. Curcio read. They were practicing Catholics, and after graduation, they would marry in a church, "without any bourgeois frills," she would say by then, but in a church all the same. They had grown up with frills; books and skis for both, a career in chemistry imagined by him, accounting for young Margherita. Instead, they became the Bonnie and Clyde of the permanently postponed revolution, and when her bullet-riddled body lay

‡ When Stendhal was in Rome in 1828 someone told him that banditry began in 1550, which seems a good enough beginning, though the bloody antics of the *condottieri* were already ancient political history in those days. "The malcontents," Stendhal wrote in *Promenades dans Rome,* ". . . glorified in fighting the despised government that oppressed the citizens. They regarded their calling as the most honorable of all, and what is singular and quite characteristic is that the people, full of shrewdness and spirit, whom they were fleecing, applauded their valor.[7] After the legendary Fra Diavolo and warrior Cardinal Ruffo, a historical rundown of Italian terrorism would have to give prominence to the trigger-happy exploits of Garibaldi and his Thousand, D'Annunzio and his Legionnaires, and Mussolini and his *squadristi.*

on a slab in a morgue, only a ring on her finger remained of what she had been before.[8]

They started small, of course; no one goes underground until every other road has been walked for a while and thought barred. The sixties in Europe and the Americas was a time the bewildered old man of history handed over to the student as if to see whether youth could make any sense of this world. Youth failed in the only way it can, sublimely, and by the end of '68, Curcio was writing and Cagol was reading that this was not a revolutionary moment, after all, but a prerevolutionary phase; what had to be done required not two years of struggle in a tight little island like Cuba, but "forty years of resistance."[9]

They married and moved to Milan to make contact with the proletariat, writing all along, both of them, now, to Big Mamma:

Curcio: "Margherita is magnificent. Every day I discover more and more how important and how beautiful it is to have her by my side."

Cagol: "With Renato life will be unpredictable, but this excites me. . . . I feel taken by the forces of life, of joy, of love."[10]

The proletariat, as usual, was not as enthusiastic as its would-be liberators, and even less was it full of love. Its sluggish affections had to be courted, and they tried everything to win its calloused hand. They refurbished and decked out all the old slogans about power growing out of the barrel of a gun, but this was Italy, not China, and the envisioned Long March wanted for men. The proletariat, as ever, was coy. It did not show displeasure when the Red Brigade—as Curcio, Cagol, and like-minded began in the singular to call themselves—burned the cars of well-known factory spies, or otherwise exposed, punished, or ridiculed the bosses and the goons, but it kept a respectable distance. In other words, the experience of the fledgling Red Brigades was one in which rewards were obtained only when they would do what no one else would dare, and that was almost always highly illegal. Thus was a process initiated. The logic of the underground, as one writer has observed, is a dynamic once begun that cannot halt halfway.[11]

Margherita had to abort a pregnancy following a clash with the police at a workers' demonstration, and they stopped writing to Big Mamma. Their apartment was searched. They moved to another and kept the address secret. Margherita cut her long black hair, curled what was left, and dyed it red. She was renamed "Mara." They went looking for guns and money and the sort of action that would ignite the forty-year fuse of the always-coming Revolution.

The action was a spiral of exemplary destruction, minikidnappings, people's trials, fund-raising "expropriations" of other people's wealth—that first round of bloodless derring-do ending in the spectacular Sossi affair.

By now, Curcio and Cagol, members of the "strategic command," were at the top of a clandestine military organization with "columns" in formation in the principal cities of the industrial North, and Mara was the head of one such column. Rome had begun to take notice, and three months after Sossi's release, Curcio was arrested. The Red Brigades had been infiltrated. Blood had started to flow. Arrests and shootouts followed in rapid succession, and for a while it seemed the *brigatisti* would all end in the dragnet. Curcio began to write the kind of history-will-absolve-me letters from prison *de rigueur* for the captured revolutionary chief, but few paid him any mind. In February 1975, however, Mara, with a submachine gun at the ready and five commandos behind her, raided Curcio's prison and freed him, stunning the nation once again with the armed one-upmanship of the attack against the state.

"I heard a voice that was dear to me," Curcio said later, recalling that wintry day of his rescue, and suddenly their pictures were on the covers of every magazine, the uncrowned but undisputed anti-idols of the day.[12]

It was a short season. Together in hiding, they helped draft the new directives of the strategic command, which named the ruling Christian Democrats as the primary target "to be liquidated,"[13] and in mid-May the first deliberate shot from the guns of the Red Brigades was fired: one round into the left leg of a municipal Christian Democratic leader. The "new" Red Brigades had arrived.

Three weeks later, Mara was dead, slain in an exchange of gunfire with the Carabinieri. "Fallen in combat" was how the Red Brigades described it in a Pauline-like message to their comrades, and they prophesied "a thousand hands" reaching to pick up her rifle.* But the following January 1976, Curcio and four other

---

* Mara became a martyr not only to the Red Brigades but to elements of the women's movement, too, and the mysterious circumstances of her death were contributing factors. Curcio later made a statement to the Carabinieri, which

brigatisti were tracked down by the Carabinieri. They found him in an apartment in a working-class neighborhood in Milan. "I know you've come to kill me," he said when they warned him that he was surrounded. He opened fire and after a twenty-two-minute gun battle, he surrendered, wounded. Still fearful they would kill him, he walked out backward, which would make the slaying somewhat more difficult to explain.[15] Instead he was merely arrested, and before long the entire group of founders was either dead or in prison. Their trial was scheduled for May 1976, and the peril seemed fading once more.

The thousand hands that had recovered Mara's gun were not nearly a thousand at all, but they began to use it fiercely, as never before. The official who had prevented the release of the communist prisoners in the Sossi episode was assassinated along with his bodyguards. More and more efficient assassinations, mutilations, and the threat of one or the other delayed the trial of Curcio and comrades interminably. For their part, the imprisoned founders claimed responsibility "past, present, and future" for every act of the Red Brigades, and the link between the old and the new was clamorously re-established in person when one of the main defendants escaped to return to the underground.

All this violent disruption, however, was little more than a holding operation against the massive police crackdown. It was that moment in the cruel dynamic when pure vengeance, spite, and personal hatreds begin to burn up the time once allocated to visions of the better world. Militarily, the Red Brigades were becoming an elite, a crack task force, undoubtedly attracting the mirror-image personnel of the best antiterrorist squads of, say, Israel or West

---

has since received some documentary support: "You Carabinieri killed Mara," he said speaking to an officer, "executing her with a *coup de grâce* . . . she was sitting on the ground, hit by a bullet in her torso during the shootout; it had passed through her chest from under her arm perforating both lungs. She would have died anyway of internal hemorrhage and asphyxiation. But you didn't wait for her to die that way. You finished her off with a bullet in the heart. Why? So that she shouldn't suffer more than she had to? Were you sure that by now she was done for?"[14] It is a commonplace belief among terrorists that the authorities have no wish to take prisoners, whose release may become the object and thus the cause of future terrorist actions. Moreover, they often go on to organize and politicize common criminals inside the penitentiaries and generally upset the penal system.

Germany. Politically, however, they were losing their grip. Even those autonomous groups of students and workers in the radical left who did not renounce the "armed struggle" were conspicuous in going their own way, and the strategic command of the Red Brigades began to feel the slight.

In February and March 1977, a series of violent events independent of the Red Brigades was interpreted by them as the arrival of a time to be seized like a pole for the "quality leap forward" that had become a shibboleth in their rhetoric. Protest riots in Rome and Bologna, ending in blood battles between the police and the *autonomi*, gave prominence to the "P.38s"—masked gunmen notorious for their use of .38-caliber specials who made phantasmagoric appearances at the end of every demonstration, turning them into shootouts. Hardly anyone could ever decide whether the P.38s were *autonomi* or plainclothes provocateurs, and probably they were a little of both, but the day of Revolution, viewed through a lingering fog of tear gas, certainly seemed nearer.

In June, the Red Brigades published a clandestine pamphlet critical of the armed *autonomi*, but only insofar as their rebellion was spontaneous and undisciplined. On the other hand, writing under the visual impact of barricades and fire in the streets, the strategic command saw the possibility of "formidable growth in the revolutionary process." It called for the unification of all this firepower, the first step being "the construction of the organization we call the Fighting [Communist] Party,"[16] and it decided on the most effective trick in the book, if and when it can be turned. They had in those months proved to their own satisfaction their capability to sustain an operation logistically more complex than the month-long Sossi affair. In a purely financial matter, they had kidnapped a Genoese armaments manufacturer, had moved him hundreds of miles down the peninsula, and had held him with impunity for eighty days. They had "taxed" their victim nearly two million dollars, slightly more than the amount for which he had been insured by Lloyds of London, and when Lloyds paid, they released him in Rome. Thus to their capability had they added the very funds that would be spent, almost in its entirety, for the kind of show they now had in mind.

What kind of show it would be was overtly advertised with startling clarity when in February 1978 the Red Brigades issued a thirty-thousand-word "Resolution of the Strategic Command." It was an underground document not easily obtained, but ten thousand copies had been printed, and while most of them were being passed around in the Movement, not a few had reached the desks, if not the eyes, of the police and the Carabinieri. In it, the *brigatisti* had resolved not only to raise their sights, they said, but also to engage the enemy by surprise attack in "prolonged actions that expose and exasperate all its internal contradictions." Enemy No. 1, they declared, developing the Curcio-Cagol line, was the "personnel" of the Christian Democrats.[17] Left to the guessing powers of their readers was exactly who No. 1 among the personnel might be, though only the most limited wit could guess wrongly, and quite soon many were the mornings that a car with counterfeit diplomatic-number plates passed slowly down Via Forte Trionfale to observe the early movements of Aldo Moro.

The plan to capture Italy's leading statesman went operational at the end of January 1978. On the twenty-sixth of that month, the departing agricultural attaché of the Venezuelan embassy in Rome returned the set of diplomatic plates issued to him by the Italian Foreign Office. They were stored in a safe to await reassignment, and would be off the streets for an indefinite but usually extended period. Somehow, the Red Brigades knew all this and knew it quickly.

Operating from a base—a rented apartment—within sight of the roofs of Via Fani, they promptly forged copies of the plates as well as the tax stamps, insurance certificates, and the whole gamut of documents they would need for all the automobiles used in the raid and beyond. The machinery and materials are more easily acquired than is generally believed.

The cars were stolen, vanishing one by one from the streets of Rome, between February 23 and March 13, three days before the attack. The getaway vehicles were fitted with police sirens and some with flipover license-plate holders, hiding a fresh series of numbers on the other side. The 128 bearing the diplomatic plates, reported missing since March 8, was seen several times outside Moro's apartment building during the week before the kidnapping —as recalled afterward—but long before that had the Red Brigades plotted the president's course.[18]

The organization that bit and ran in the early days had grown into a sinuous creature of the perpetual underground night. The second-generation *brigatista,* unlike the swashbuckling first, had to work hard for his/her glory. All the old errors of the founding fathers could be seen now as the dross that had bared an iron discipline, and it either ruled every moment of the *brigatista*'s day or his days were numbered.

By 1978, the Red Brigades, spending several "expropriated" millions of dollars annually, had established full-fledged columns in Genoa, Turin, Milan, and, more recently, Rome, an "armed vanguard" of up to four hundred underground regulars, and an aboveground undercover force ("irregulars") of at least as many and probably more. But the aim had never been bigness. "A few dozen fighters who go into action without endless talk," Ulrike Meinhof had said, repeating Lenin, "can fundamentally change the political scene."[19] While attempting to prove that point and that point only, they had built up an organization with several unique features.

The columnar structure (see chart, p. xv) was a hybrid of guerrilla enterprises reaching back to the Resistance by way of the Latin American Tupamaros and the theories and practices of the Brazilian revolutionary Carlos Marighella. All of these systems had evolved under the pressure to maximize the security of the organization and its operatives. The principal advantage of verticality was that each level was "sealed." In other words, A knows only what he needs to about B and nothing of what lies beyond, so the capture of A cannot normally lead to C, and vice versa.

The contribution of the Red Brigades was the formation of brigades (A-A-A-B-C) based on noncommunicating paired cells (B-A-A-A$\times$2) with three to five operatives per cell. Thus the breakup of one of these small units (by arrest, etc.) not only thwarts the police at that level of organization but also leaves the other half of the pair to continue the operations of the column uninterruptedly, while regenerating the lost limb.[20]

What life in those aptly named cells was like, was made very clear by the *brigatista*'s handbooks. They regulated every aspect of an operative's existence, his personal habits ("each comrade must be clean-shaven, hair cut"), his apartment ("modest, clean, orderly, and completely furnished"), his meals ("unless strictly necessary, meals are consumed at home"), his contacts with the outside world ("act with a reassuring air and be kind to your neighbors"), with his loved ones ("the modality of these relations are to be discussed with the column superior"), and his gun ("each militant will always carry his own sidearm"). Bedtime was no later than midnight, and training included constant reminders to look over one's shoulder and keep an eye on the rear-view mirror. A land of many monastic orders had made yet another, a brotherhood of revolutionary violence.

The rules for one were the rules for all. "There are no sacred cows," they had written and appear to have practiced. "The risks and privations are equal for all. The leaders take part in the action."[21] This seems to have been the case in the Moro operation. An organization within the organization, a *force de frappe*, appears to have been set up. One passage from the chapter on kidnapping in another Red Brigades manual gives a precise idea of how it all began—of how Aldo Moro's negligent route through Via Fani was simply but painstakingly traced by stationary observation, which was considered the safest method:

After recognition of his car has been firmly established, wait for it to make its first turn, noting the direction it takes. The next day, wait at the first turn for the second, and so forth.[22]

Such were the tiny paving stones on the road to the people's prison.

III

TRIAL

The sincerity of my intentions and of my political intuitions . . . despite the inevitable risk of error that exists in every choice, could inspire a generous judgment in my behalf.[1]

7·

In the people's prison, Aldo Moro began to prepare his defense. He more than anyone else, more than even the Red Brigades, understood the precariousness of his situation. By his own admission, he knew nothing at this stage of what was happening in the outside world, but he could easily imagine how the men of power were lining up in Rome, and when he began to be heard from it was plain that he had imagined all that was actually true.

The larger unknown was the price of freedom. It was axiomatic that guerrillas, like governments and armies, seized hostages to obtain the release of their comrades in prison. Moro appears initially to have taken that for granted and to have overestimated its importance, but from what he was told by his captors, he discerned quite soon that the Red Brigades had several objectives, and the priorities were anything but fixed. He was in a hand-rubbing, mediator's bailiwick.

The self-appointed mission of the Red Brigades of fashioning the Fighting Communist Party out of the scattered debris and hard feelings left in the wake of the rightward retreat of the official Communist Party was to be proselytized in the Moro case along three main themes: an exchange of prisoners, some kind of concession that could be interpreted in the Movement *de facto* political recognition by the enemy, and the "debriefing" of the hostage to obtain information for future operations.

It is true that for the theoreticians of guerrilla warfare the classic measure of a revolutionary organization's real power is its capacity to liberate its captured militants. Freeing prisoners is an indispensable rule of the game, since it bears directly on the organization's ability to recruit new adherents and on its own range of action. In the past, the Red Brigades made no secret of their steadfast subscription to this rule, but the only prisoner they had succeeded in liberating was when Mara freed Curcio, so by their own measurement they were not as strong as they tried so shrilly to make others believe. This was why the two other themes—recognition and information—were equally as important, if not more so, as they represented means to arrive at some later date at the desired capacity. In the forty-year resistance, as envisaged by Curcio, this was still the long January of year one.

Moro was not an *aficionado* of the theoretical works of Regis DeBray or Marighella, but he had, as will be seen, negotiated successfully with terrorists before, and now in an eye-to-eye dialogue with the Red Brigades he saw some room for maneuver. This might have been almost reassuring were it not for the political monolith that he knew lay wide on the outside.

All through Holy Week, the outside soliloquized like Hamlet on what ought to be done should the voice of Aldo Moro rise from the underworld of the Red Brigades. The government and the majority parties were besieging the media with appeals to exercise extreme "caution" should the dreaded message arrive, and on Wednesday, March 22, the Rome daily *La Repubblica*, considered one of the more enlightened publications in Italy, ran a survey in which eleven editors-in-chief of the nation's leading newspapers were asked whether they would publish what was termed a "confession" by Moro to the Red Brigades. A minority said no or were unsure and the rest said yes, but with disclaimers that included that Moro had either been drugged or had undergone physical or psychic torture. The source that would justify such disclaimers, it was agreed, was one's conscience. *La Repubblica* itself, in an editorial about the media's conscience, worried that the prevailing unanimity on self-censorship might transcend the present circumstances and also be used to cover up the past and the future.[1] Soon, however, *La Repubblica*, too, would stop worrying.

The Italian press even went as far as Toronto to interview media expert Marshall McLuhan, and he came up with the novel idea of a *total* blackout, of closing down the media entirely, as long as it might take "to restore people's sense of reality." He called it "beneficial shock," but that was the last time he was heard from.[2]

The truth was that the Red Brigades had imposed a blackout on the press. Day after day went by without one further word from the people's prison. Public interest in the case was dipping, and the nonnews on all fronts, particularly the police investigations, began to back into the low corners of the front pages.

The Easter tourist season was as much in bloom as the azaleas, which were being gathered by the tens of thousands for the traditional spring dressing of the Spanish Steps in Rome. The latest antiterrorist laws were decreed, to no one's satisfaction,* and Italy, with troops in combat fatigues on the streets, seemed a nation under siege. But it all looked innocuously surreal under the Mediterranean sun, and thanks to the supercop on every corner, the crime rate plunged. The house-to-house searches and the proliferation of checkpoints were hurting traffickers in contraband, and the word from the Mafia was out: "Free Moro or we'll kill a *brigatista* in prison."

Not for that reason, but attention focused briefly and hotly on the Turin trial, where on Monday, the twenty-first, Renato Curcio and comrades made their first appearance since the Moro kidnapping. Many had been expecting the imminent demand for their release in exchange for Moro's life, and the question under the klieg lights was whether the moment had come.

The fifteen "historic chiefs," as they were called, arrived in chains and were herded into an enormous security cage that could have held as many lions. They asked to read a statement. When reviewed by the judge, it was declared immaterial and the request was denied. This provoked visceral roars from the lions' den, followed by a verbal gang rumble against the public prosecutor, who had lost his nerve and ripped off his robes in the heat of battle. Curcio managed to get in the last word, vaunting in his flat, unmodulated voice, "We . . . have Moro in our hands." This was the

---

* They were precisely those Andreotti had proposed (preventive arrests, etc.), but one party leader of the new majority, the president of the Republicans, Ugo La Malfa, called them insufficient. He demanded a series of "unconstitutional methods to bring about the kind of democracy the Constitution aims at."[3]

headline the press corps had to settle for, since the *brigatisti* then exercised their right not to appear in court and were withdrawn, clanging off in single file.

The unread statement, however, which was sequestered by the court and made secret—not that it would have otherwise passed the self-censors—was much more edifying than the zoolike atmosphere in the courtroom. It revealed the full concordance of the old group and sought to develop the ideas of the new. It showed a complete grasp of what the operation was intended to promote in the overall—"UNIFICATION of the Movement" (emphasis in the original). Moreover, in pointing out that Moro, in spite of his preeminence, "bears no higher political responsibility" than any of the other Christian Democratic leaders, it went beyond the first communiqué from the people's prison, stressing the political nature of the problem and hence its openness to a political solution. The disappearance of Moro from the national scene meant nothing to the Red Brigades; it was the capture of his person that was all, and whoever wanted him back would have to give something in return. The statement gave no hint of what that might be, trying to create the impression that the organization, in or out of prison, was all of one piece.[4] That was untrue.

In that same week, Aldo Moro plotted his course—an attempt to circumvent the political reef in Rome. He needed pen and paper, and of course the co-operation of the strategic command. He was given the writing materials; co-operation would depend on what he proposed.

A system of communications had to be worked out. Wherever the people's prison might have been, it was not in the same place as the strategic command. Moro's guards were few, and his only contact with other human beings was limited to the two, perhaps in his case three or four, masked men or women who were conducting his interrogation-trial. They may or may not have been members of the strategic command, but evidence captured months later showed that all the decisions concerning the carrying out of Moro's mediation efforts were taken outside the people's prison on the basis of notes made by Moro himself or dictated by him to his interrogators.[5]

Once a working relationship had been agreed upon between captive and captor, at least six to eight *brigatisti* were pressed into service as couriers, not only between Moro and the strategic command but also between Moro and the various persons he would indicate as reliable "drops" for messages that would in turn have to be transmitted to men otherwise virtually inaccessible.

By the end of the week, the system was operational and ready for testing. On Sunday, Aldo Moro drafted a sixty-eight-word letter. The first message from the people's prison, written in a clear, upright hand on graph-ruled notepad paper, was for the president's wife. It would not be delivered until three days later and would remain secret throughout his ordeal; nevertheless, the voice so feared in Rome had begun to speak:

Easter, 1978

My dearest Noretta,

I want to send you on Easter day, you and everyone, my warmest and most affectionate good wishes, with all my tenderness for the family and especially the little one. Remember me to Anna whom I was supposed to have seen today. I ask Agnese to keep you company at night. I am fairly well, well-fed, and treated with kindness.

I bless you all; I send my dearest regards to all and a strong embrace.

Aldo[6]

On Easter Sunday and on *Pasquetta*, or "Little Easter," as the Monday of the Angel holiday is called, the men of power were unaware of the hot line between Moro and the outside world. The latest development being scrutinized was a second communiqué released by the Red Brigades in four cities on Saturday afternoon.

It was a document much longer than the first, but for anyone who was not in, or an observer of, the Movement, whose favor it clearly courted, Communiqué II was more interesting for what it did not say. It was a long indictment not as much of Moro as of the past quarter-century of Christian Democratic rule, charging it with all the unhappiest Italian political events of the times. Spanning the years Moro had some form of governmental power in Rome, it included the violent police repressions of strikes in July 1960, the 1964 plot for a military takeover, the "strategy of tension"—the name given to a wave of Fascist terrorism launched in 1969, for which there was evidence of collusion with the government Secret Service—and finally, the newest *bête noire* of the Red Brigades, an unsubstantiated long-range program to restructure and co-ordinate the nation's institutions to the needs of "multinational imperialism."

It would have been hard enough to answer to the smallest fraction of these charges, but the Red Brigades, picking up where the Curcio group had left off in Turin, said that they aimed "to ascertain the direct responsibility" of the prisoner, which was something slightly less grave than in Communiqué I, where it had been affirmed that Moro's responsibility was already demonstrated by his political godfatherhood. There was a hot line to Turin, too; it lay deep underground.

Few people could bear to study the language of the Red Brigades, which reads like Frankenstein's monster walks. That would turn to everyone's misfortune in the end, but now the only thing written that appeared new in Communiqué II was the phrase "the interrogation of Aldo Moro is under way."[7] This was disturbing enough for men who were hoping for a name-rank-and-serial-number response from the prisoner—and some came out and said so—but what was even more nerve-rattling was that ten days had passed and the Red Brigades still had asked nothing of the political class.

Just what they might be up to was the first subject being explored in the think tank Interior Minister Cossiga had set up with the counsel of U.S. adviser Steve Pieczenik. It had issued its first assessment, and before the Easter Sunday traditional baby-lamb dinner, Cossiga and his chief of police met with Andreotti in the deserted Palazzo Chigi to present the committee's report.

The behavior pattern of the Red Brigades had been analyzed, and until now, one member of the committee revealed the following day, "they have killed only in self-defense or as punishment, but never after a kidnapping." If murder was their intention, they could have done it in Via Fani, he said.

Somehow, the experts had arrived at the arithmetical conclusion that there was a 20 per cent probability or less that Moro would be killed. As for how to proceed, they said, the game had only begun; nothing remained but to wait.[8]

Twenty per cent or less was the best government rating Aldo Moro would ever receive.

The interrogation, or that part of it later to be transcribed from tapes and notes on forty-nine typewritten pages for the information of the organization, had not yet in fact begun. Under discussion in the people's prison and at the strategic command was Moro's plan to undramatize and above all depoliticize the situation he was in.

He had been caught in the trap of his own making. The alignment of unopposed political power was stacked in a manner that favored the predictable hard-line stance of the Communists. His strategy was to neutralize the situation. He proposed to ask for the intervention of the Vatican or some other extranational body, opening the way for a kind of moratorium during which none of the parties could either gain or lose at his expense.[9] It was the quickest and least painful solution to Moro's and the government's plight. It was one thing for the Vatican to ask Rome to give an inch or two, and quite another to contemplate ceding the same measure on demand of the Red Brigades.

The strategic command approved. That it did not agree entirely, however, would become apparent on the day Moro made his long-anticipated move.

8.

Since the kidnapping, Nicola Rana, a fleshy, middle-aged professor, had been coming each morning to Aldo Moro's office in Via Savoia. Rana for years had been Moro's *segretario particolare*, a job, usually reserved for males, that was somewhere between a private secretary and a right-hand man; after the raid in Via Fani, when all of the president's closest aides and assistants in both his public and university careers had been at a loss as to what to do, Mrs. Moro had instructed everyone to go on as if business were usual so that upon his return Papà would find everything in order.[1]

On Wednesday morning, March 29, Rana arrived at the office with a new mission. One of the Rome dailies, for want of harder news, had come out with a front-page headline questioning whether the Polaroid photo that had been made in the people's prison many rather newsless days ago was genuine. The implication was that if the photo, which was being analyzed by technicians at the Rome film studio Cinecittà, proved to be a montage, perhaps the whole affair was all an illusion, too. A plot within a plot and then one. Rana knew better. That morning he had spoken to the Red Brigades.

He had been telephoned at 8:00 A.M. and advised that a "packet" from the president would be delivered to the *concierge* of the Via Savoia building, and when it dutifully arrived before noon, Rana found three letters from Aldo Moro, one of which was for him:

My dear Rana,

I send you my most affectionate thoughts and many thanks for what you have done and are doing in support of my family and myself. And so it is that I still have need of you in this crucial moment. I enclose a letter for delivery to my wife and my loved ones about whom I've not heard a thing.

And then, on the political side, yet another letter to be handed personally to Minister Cossiga and with understandable immediacy. My idea and my hope is that this line of communication that I am trying to hook up will remain as secret as possible, to avoid dangerous polemics. This means that the reply, or a first reply, when it comes, should not be given to the newspapers, but should come as a letter or a message to you from the Minister. Later, we will figure out a way to forward it.

Presupposed over everything is that there be no surveillance of the building from the very first. The Minister should commit himself verbally to prevent all surveillance in the course of this operation. I tell you that an incident would ruin everything and cause incalculable damage. [Emphasis in original.]

Thank you very much and affectionate regards.

Aldo Moro[2]

The hot line was to be made two-way.

Immediately recognizing the president's handwriting, Rana began to move with the secrecy that had been asked for. He made several photocopies of the letter and went first to Mrs. Moro.

Although the street below the penthouse in Via Forte Trionfale was manned day and night by newsmen, they had thus far stood watch in vain. The family had announced at the very beginning that it would speak publicly, when it wished to, only by the written word. The intention was to frustrate the rewrite men of others' thoughts and speech, who were legion. Thus when one of them, to aid the majority cause, tried to peddle the notion that Eleonora Moro had said, "No one trades my husband for anybody," it was dear at any price and showed that there was more than Aldo Moro's wisdom at home. Now more than ever they maintained their reserve, withholding the happy news that at last they had had word from Papà.

Rana's appointment with Cossiga was not until the early afternoon. In the meantime, he had been asked by the minister to put together various specimens of Moro's handwriting. Cossiga himself was familiar with Moro's penmanship, but there was a graphologist in his think tank, and these matters were what experts were for.

The Ministry of Interior, the Viminal Palace, rises near the Opera on one of the Seven Hills. It was more an impenetrable fortress than a palace in these times, and the office of Francesco Cossiga could only be reached with a set of codex, electronic keys.

If there were one point of concord among the noncombinable elements of the ultraleft, it would have been that Cossiga, Italy's chief of all its chiefs of police, was a hangman. He had the misfortune of having those contiguous two s's in his surname, which helped promote this candidacy in all the graffiti allusions to the worst of nazism. It is doubtful that seeing his name sprayed wide along the embankments of the Tiber and elsewhere hurt him very deeply, but in fact he was an unusually sensitive man among his political peers, one of the few who had publicly recognized that the Red Brigades represented a social problem more amenable to political than police solutions.

What really hurt was the attack in Via Fani, which had caught him more than unprepared; it had thrown him into a tortured mood of self-reproach. As the person most responsible for internal security, he felt an anguish for not having foreseen that the demiurge of the great encounter between Christian Democracy and the Communists needed to be protected by all the potent means at his command.[3] He was a silver-haired man more than a decade younger than Aldo Moro, and Cossiga considered the president of his party his spiritual and political mentor. Moro years back had pulled him from the political chorus line and had moved him upstage.

Now the mentor was coming to him. To be sure, Moro had not, in his strategy to regain his own freedom, chosen Cossiga from all the power in Rome on the basis of close ties alone; the Interior Minister was the person placed best to guarantee the viability of the hot line, but the diplomatic task he had assigned him in the letter was not one he would have cared to entrust to anyone less than a friend.

We have it from one good source that Francesco Cossiga wept as he read Aldo Moro's long letter.[4] Said the mentor:

Dear Francesco,

> While sending you my dear regards, I am induced by these difficult circumstances to call your attention to a few clear and realistic considerations, having in mind your responsibilities (which obviously I respect). I willingly put aside every emotional aspect, and I shall stick to the facts.

The facts were, he said, that although he knew nothing of what had happened since his "withdrawal" to wherever he might be, he had been told in no uncertain terms that he was considered a political prisoner and that the entire affair was a political matter. He sought to make it perfectly clear that the Red Brigades would accept no ransom that did not represent a political concession, and that things more serious than his own present predicament could occur. The idea was to pay the smallest price, get out quickly, and "avoid worse troubles." This was why he was writing confidentially, he said, so that Cossiga might urge the other powers in their party, particularly the Prime Minister and the President of the republic, to reflect.

"Think profoundly," Moro said, "before you create an emotional and irrational situation." He then went on to suggest why the matter overshadowed his physical well-being. Humanitarian considerations should not be ignored, he said, but beyond that there were reasons of state involved. The man who had five times been the chief executive of a scandal-ridden country, the seventh major industrial power of the world, and a strategic member of NATO, found it necessary to remind his Christian Democratic friends in Rome precisely what he meant:

> Above all, to pick up where I left off about my present situation, the reason of State is that I am in a position of complete and uncontrollable domination, forced to undergo a people's trial that could go on at length; that I am in this state knowing all that I know as a result of a long experience, with the risk that I may be called upon or induced to speak in a way that could prove unpleasant and dangerous in certain situations.*

---

* This was of course read in Rome and abroad, notably in Washington and NATO, as a threat that had to be counteracted. For this reason, it was a serious error on Moro's part, but definitely intended only as a simple statement of

Having expounded the motivation as to why it might be advisable to get him out of the people's prison as precipitously as possible, he took up the problem of how. To begin with, law and legal custom were on his side. The doctrine that crime must not pay became debatable when human lives were at stake, he argued, and was insupportable in political circumstances where the damages were not only to the person but to the state as well. Nearly all countries had ascribed to this, he said, the big exception being Israel, and he gave examples, such as the release of left-wing extremists in West Germany in exchange for a kidnapped political figure, prisoner exchanges between states, and the continuous traffic in spy trades.

Finally, he repeated his appeal to cool reason as opposed to the facile passions he feared would prevail, and came at last to the way out:

I think a preventive step by the Holy See (Or some other [outside body]? Who?) could be useful. It would be a good idea for the Prime Minister and you to maintain very confidential contacts with a limited number of qualified political chiefs to convince those who may be reluctant. An attitude of hostility would be an abstraction and an error.

May God illuminate you all to the good, sparing you from getting bogged down in a painful episode, on which many things could depend. Most affectionate regards.

                                        Aldo Moro[5]

He hoped to resolve it all *in familias,* among "the friends," as he called them, a neat, swift, surgical operation, in which a friend-and-surgeon Pope would cut him loose from the people's prison. It could have worked if history had not already passed him by. Who would tell Aldo Moro by hot line that among his "friends" in Rome

---

reality. In the first place, he believed, and said so to Cossiga, that he was writing in strict confidence (*"in modo molto riservato"*), and second, when the twenty-five-thousand-word transcript of his interrogation was recovered, those who worried hardest were able to agree, breathing easily, that Moro had revealed nothing "new." True, he had kept the state and private secrets of men of power in many Western capitals, but in fact he revealed riches about the men themselves.

some were already saying that if he were to return there would be one man of power too many?

The only persons Moro had persuaded that a painless solution existed were the members of the strategic command. How genuinely convinced they were can be seen in what they did when second thoughts set in. Even before Moro's letter to Cossiga reached the ministry, someone, it seems, realized that quiet, behind-the-scenes negotiations were rather self-defeating for an operation designed as a "prolonged action" to expose and erode the government's internal weaknesses. In the theater of "armed propaganda," as the Red Brigades billed this kind of assault on the establishment, nothing that happens backstage is of any value to the guerrillas. It can always be denied, modified, or turned on its head by the enemy, whose higher credibility is built into the nature of the conflict.

By oversight or slow thinking, the Red Brigades had lost the initiative. They had given Rome relief from, and control over, the very thing that until now had been most fearsome: the voice of Aldo Moro. But within six hours after the confidential original was in Cossiga's hands, they had recovered, releasing photocopies of the letter to the press, along with a clarifying Communiqué III.

Taking some of the sting out of Moro's apparent threat to talk, the communiqué said that the prisoner had only "begun" to furnish enlightening replies, though the interrogation was proceeding with his "full co-operation." Moro, it said in its Gothic fashion, was perfectly prepared to own up to his responsibilities, but as he did not see why the other leaders of his party should not assume their responsibilities, he had asked to write a "secret letter." Such "occult maneuvers," it added in a parenthetical aside, "are the norm for the Demo-Christian Mafia." His request had been granted, explained the Red Brigades, "but as nothing must be hidden from the people, and this is our custom, we hereby make it public."[6]

Rome, that Rome behind closed doors, cringed. Aldo Moro had been given a fortune-sent opportunity to die a martyr's death, the Thomas More, Joan of Arc, Giordano Bruno, of that combination plate of earthly power called Statehood. He had already lived threescore and one, and for a damnable nine years he had refused an immortal crown, a mystical resurrection, or as in the ancient Greek rite of *pharmakos*, his complicity in sacrifice so that his blood might become the cleansing agent of his creation, and God knew how the fragile new majority still wanted. Instead, in spite of forcing many reappraisals and adjustments, of all the heartache and rancor he would cause, the president wanted to live.

The Red Brigades had dropped their mimeographed communiqué and the photocopies of the Moro letter to Cossiga in Rome, Milan, Turin, and Genoa, and at 7:40 P.M., they began telephoning newspapers in each of these cities as to where the material could be picked up. The newsmen, retrieving and copying the copies, informed the police, and by this train, it was still early evening when the Interior Ministry had all the essential elements in hand. The newspapers would not go to press until the predawn hours of the following day. There was, then, time enough for the government, the political parties, and the media to heed Aldo Moro's admonition to reflect, and even some left over to come into morning print with an answer.

Cossiga himself met with his closest associates—his political *consigliere*, Undersecretary Nicola Lettiere, and police, intelligence, and investigative officials—following which the matter was dumped into the think tank for rapid analysis both of the content and authenticity of Moro's letter and a deep reading of the new communiqué.

Apart from the family, only the government knew and possessed copies of the other two Moro letters. Communiqué III had by design not mentioned them, and furthermore it had continued to make no demands. Cossiga decided, in consultation with his staff, that the secrecy of these letters be maintained, and to keep options open, it seems, he would respect his mentor's desire that the two-way hot line not be placed under either physical or electronic surveillance. Thus, the government, informing Moro's aide Nicola Rana that the Via Savoia connection would be left intact, now had a secure channel of communications with the Red Brigades. Whether or not it would use it was a matter left pending.

As for the president's soon-to-be-public letter, Cossiga had already resolved that issue in a meeting at Palazzo Chigi with Prime Minister Andreotti. They had agreed on their official position, should the handwriting experts confirm its authorship. This and every future message of its kind should be presented as, to use Andreotti's laconic phrase, "not morally imputable to the subject."[7]

The family, as might be expected, believed otherwise. When Aldo and Eleonora were young, he had written and she had always held especially dear a short essay on one of life's meanings. In a schoolish, Thomist tone, he had commented that the day-to-day struggle for the truth of one's own life was the bearer of a harrowing grief through which the supreme joy of life was affirmed, and in some metaphysical way, one could grow to love that pain. "For this," the final words of his essay read, "to live is beautiful."[8] No one in Aldo Moro's home questioned the moral imputability of the letters from Papà; the family recognized his intellectual and literary constancy, and if he had never before used expressions such as a "people's trial" or had referred to the slaughter in Via Fani as his "withdrawal," these were seen as the signs of his perspicacity of how narrow must be the exit door of the people's prison.

The family had spent all that day pursuing the paths Moro had suggested. Most important, they had been in touch with the Vatican and had received assurances that the Holy Father was ready to act in whatever way he could to carry out the office Moro proposed in his letter. Indeed, the Vatican newspaper, *L'Osservatore Romano*, would come out publicly in this regard. It had been recalled that in the Sossi case Pope Paul had declared himself completely available, and only months back, in the Mogadishu hijack incident, he had offered himself as a hostage in exchange for the release of the passengers. It was a noble, if symbolic, gesture, and it was unlikely that he would do less for Aldo and Noretta:

The Christian Democratic Party, too, had extended its hand. In contacts with headquarters, it was arranged that one of the family spokesmen, Moro's press secretary, Corrado Guerzoni, would write an article for publication in the party paper, *Il Popolo,* the following morning. Guerzoni would contend that the Christian Democrats must prepare themselves for the possibility that a compromise with the Red Brigades may be unavoidable. True, ten days earlier, the party had killed a similar editorial, but the idea emanating from the family source would carry no official weight and would test the reactions of others. Furthermore, no one in the Square of Jesus could take lightly the risk of offending so mighty a clan as the Moros.

By nightfall, however, Guerzoni, Nicola Rana, and a third Moro aide, Sergio Freato, described as the hard-as-nails member of the group, found the party leaders unwilling once more to publish, and toughness and anger got nowhere. A meeting in the presence of the by now tormented Honest Zac went on for hours. Somehow, the glacier of intransigence was creeping everywhere, and to Zaccagnini's reported lament that it would never again be an easy thing to face the family, a reply from another member of the party directorate was said to have been, "My dear Benigno, the family has every right to gouge our eyes out, but they cannot force us to do anything less than our duty." Honest Zac saw logic in that one.[9] There were no more giants in the land where Vichian giants once sang before they learned to talk.

9.

The editorials and articles, the headlines and captions that were being cast in hot lead at that moment were a long way from the cause of Aldo Moro. He had cautioned against creating an emotional and irrational atmosphere, but he had not foreseen the Etna of intemperance running off the presses now. There had been a nasty frenzy hanging in the air since the first day. More, the interlock of friendly conversations among common-interest parties and the vigil kept on what the competition might be doing had a laser-like effect in concentrating power. But it would be difficult without some recourse to the rather shallow concept of mass psychosis to account for the rampant unanimity bundled and trucked to the nation's news kiosks the morning after the arrival of Moro's letter.

On the other hand, Andreotti after his meeting with Cossiga was immediately in touch with the leaders of the five majority parties—and most important with his own Christian Democrats and the Communists—and taken together these parties directly controlled or exercised an overwhelming influence on *all* of the mass-circulation newspapers in Italy. So it was with a touch of method to a madness, or as the case may be, vice versa, that "Operation Moro Isn't Moro" was launched.*

* The phrase belongs to Alessandro Silj, used in his critical study of the Italian press during the Moro affair. He writes that with the first letter "so much was said and written to negate its credibility that 'Operation Moro Isn't Moro' needed only two days, March 30 and 31, to more or less burn itself out and condition every future comment on the subsequent messages"[1] from Moro. On how this phenomenon fueled and was refueled by the foreign press, especially in the United States, see p. 137.

The *Corriere della Sera* is Italy's most prestigious daily and the one most widely read abroad. Though it is linked through the Rizzoli publishing empire to a wing of the Christian Democrats, it can be favorably compared in reliability, competence, and level-headedness to many of the best sometimes-conservative, sometimes-liberal newspapers in the West. By now, however, even the best level heads were swimming, and the front page, Thursday, the thirtieth, said the following about the advisory from the people's prison:

> Who wrote this letter? Was it written by Aldo Moro, president of the Christian Democrats, cautious strategist, supreme mediator and inspirer of Italian politics? Or was it written by a man who has the same name and the same face, who is still Aldo Moro, but reduced to impotence by a cruel imprisonment, isolated, perhaps in a drugged stupor or under some other control of the psyche?[2]

Lest anyone lack for a front-page answer, *La Repubblica,* to begin with, had this headline:

THOSE WORDS ARE NOT HIS[3]

The Communist-controlled *Paese Sera:*

RED BRIGADES EXTORT LETTER FROM MORO[4]

The progressive *Il Messaggero:*

A LETTER FROM MORO[5]
Real? Fake? How Was It Extorted?

During the day Moro's handwriting was definitively verified, and the two superparties in the Square of Jesus and the Street of the Dark Shops released to the state-owned Italian wire service, ANSA, the text of their position to appear in their official party papers the next day.

The Christian Democrats' *Il Popolo* would write: "The Honorable Moro is undergoing the gravest and most inhuman coercion."[6]

The Communist *L'Unità:* "The letter from Moro (if it can be called a letter from Moro) was written in a state of moral and physical constriction."[7]

The Communists, kept abreast by Cossiga, were as much aware

as the Christian Democrats of the other two Moro letters, which in being held secret did not entirely cut off the possibility of negotiation. Apparently this is why they felt obligated to go farther than their partners, saying that the known letter was deprived of "any significance or value." This was true, or was going to be true, "also for other documents compiled in the same handwriting, which, unfortunately, we must still expect from the kidnappers."[8]

Despite these *ex cathedra* pronunciamentos, some people still felt uncomfortable enough to explain how the new majority could be so sure that Moro wasn't Moro. One newsman consulted the think tank in the Ministry of Interior, and he was told that the five-page letter was actually a "collage." Some pages were written by Moro spontaneously, some under dictation, and without his knowledge, the pages were rearranged to alter the context.[9]

The Vatican's *L'Osservatore Romano* had not yet delivered its support of the family's position, but it had an interesting theory of its own: that the letter, however it might have been written, contained a secret message.[10] This notion was picked up on the following day by some of the coercion-constriction newspapers, and even on the same pages in which they were saying that the *words* were valueless, they were discovering hidden meanings between the lines.

A university professor, described in an interview with the *Corriere della Sera* as a psychographologist, found that Moro was actually saying the precise opposite of what he had written. The true reading, said the scholar, was that Moro "intends to sacrifice himself and that interiorially he is refusing the exchange" of prisoners. A key to understanding this was that at one point in the missive he had begun to write the letter T instead of the letter D, and this Freudian slip was "a sign of rebellion."[11]

One cryptologist succeeded in making some sense even of the fiendish words, or at least a few of them. He detected a decipherable repetition of the word "under," used either alone or as a prefix or a suffix. This and some other words associated with movement forward, up, and down, permitted him to break the code and led him to the conclusion that Moro was trying to signal that the people's prison was a submarine.[12]

The favored explanation, however, was the drug-and-torture theory. Moro's "state of constriction," said an authoritative Communist voice, who had seen the "language of the Mafia" in Moro's letter, was deepened by a presumed "prolonged deprivation of sleep, physical violence, the forced ingestion of drugs and other chemical preparations capable of disturbing the psycho-physical equilibrium."[13]

Suddenly every pharmacologist who cared to see his name in public print was ushered forward for a dissertation on mind-altering drugs. Not all of them, to their credit, entirely backed the idea that Moro had in fact been drugged, but that was in the fine print; it was the headlines that were mighty. The FIAT Agnelli's family-owned *La Stampa* found someone with satisfactory credentials who spoke of substances that "eliminate the powers of criticism and self-control . . . and render the subject susceptible to obey and follow imposed concepts." The drug Pentothal, among others, was mentioned and the headline became:

THE DRUGS THE RED BRIGADES
CAN USE ON MORO[14]

Finally, the *Corriere della Sera* came full circle and answered all its own questions twenty-four hours after they had been raised in a story under this banner headline:

ISOLATION, DRUGS, PROLONGED WAKEFULNESS
How a Personality Is Annihilated[15]

It meant nothing that there was a living witness, the survivor of the people's prison Mario Sossi, who had testified when freed and continued to relate to his interviewers how he had neither been drugged nor forced to write any words but his own in the three or four notes he had sent to his wife and the press during his imprisonment. Again it meant nothing, to the bearers of secrets in the inner circle of power, that Moro had written of his fair treatment to his family. Worst of all, it seems no one paused to wonder what fools Moro might make of men were he to be released and give a truer version of life in the people's prison.† This lapse was lethal

---

† This Moro succeeded in doing only in death. The autopsy proved that his body was free of any form of drug or maltreatment; on the contrary, although there had been a significant weight loss, tissue and organ studies confirmed that he had been soundly nourished, and the body showed a degree of cleanliness and self-care that indicated he had had easy access to toiletries and modern bathroom facilities. See pp. 245–46.

since it could not but warm the virus of the mind running around in those days, an insidious malaise that the president best not return.

The men and women of the 90 per cent slice of the political pie opposed to a Vatican solution had forgotten to tell the Vatican. No one yet had dared to recognize that Moro, sober, stoned, or Svengalied, had made a real proposal, and if it had gotten past his cell door it was clearly approved by his censors.

On Friday, March 31, the Vatican fulfilled the Holy Father's promise to the family and declared itself available. Repeating some of Moro's own language-of-the-Mafia words, *L'Osservatore Romano* wrote:

> The request for a preventive step intended to facilitate a solution to the very painful case of the Hon. Moro certainly cannot leave the Holy See indifferent.[16]

The situation, however, awaited clarification; concrete elements were needed before an intervention could be made. Obviously, the Vatican could not go to the negotiating table without something to give, and this was read correctly on the Italian side of the Tiber as an invitation to the government to ante.

It was also read with fury.

The men in the Street of the Dark Shops were nursing a suspicion that the men in the Square of Jesus would crumble under the pressure to negotiate, and the pressure would become excruciating, they knew, as the far-flung resources of the Catholic Church were drawn on. Rumor already circulated that two high prelates were seeking contact with the Red Brigades, and one name mentioned was that of the archbishop of Turin, formerly of Bari, Moro's political stronghold. Turin, of course, was the venue of the Curcio trial, and it seemed a sign of action that the archbishop announced a Monday-morning trip to Rome. The nuns at the Vatican switchboard were receiving dunning calls from reporters trying to learn if the Red Brigades had phoned.

The Communists, however, were not the only ones to take umbrage at the Pope's initiative. It had all happened without the advance knowledge of Andreotti's government and party. They had been taken by surprise, and worse, caught in an embarrassing contradiction. The party, on the day the Vatican announced its openness, was answering doubts raised by the Communists impugning the fiber of its resoluteness to defend the "national" interest once the Red Brigades began to turn the screw. Finding such a suggestion "offensive," the Christian Democrats responded indignantly, reiterating its holier-than-thou "line of suffering intransigence."[17]

Someone, either in the Prime Minister's palace or the Square of Jesus, heard a dripping inconsistency in the pipeline between Christian Democracy and the Mother Church, which was when the party plumbers were summoned.

On Saturday, April 1, Monsignor Giovanni Caprio, who held the equivalent rank of an Under Secretary of State in the Vatican Government—the Curia—was visited by two members of Parliament, Christian Democrats Guido Bodrato and Franco Salvi. Bodrato had often been described in the jargon of political infighters as a "lieutenant" of the party wing favoring the alliance with the Communists. Salvi was a well-known *moroteo,* a small group of the president's friends who formed an antithesis to the vertically and rigidly structured factions of the Christian Democrats. In his interrogation, Moro would speak of Salvi with fondness, commending him to his captors as a man with a "clear conscience."[18]

According to one source of Salvi's and Bodrato's informal encounter with Monsignor Caprio, "After listening to the reasons of his guests, the prelate gave them precise assurances: It was not the intention of the Vatican to create difficulties for the Christian Democrats. There will be no more initiatives taken by the Holy See in contrast with the firm line adopted by the party and the Italian Government."[19]

The Moro strategy seemed dead, but the monsignor and the Curia had underestimated the power of a last commitment in the heart of a dying Pope.

The eighth day of Easter in the liturgy of Catholicism is the time of the Marian Prayer to the Blessed Virgin, and on Sunday, the second, the Holy Father went before the faithful in St. Peter's Square to recite it with them for the last time.

His voice was a labored wheeze when he began to speak, saying that although this day was meant as a day of rejoicing, he felt him-

self a participant "in the painful episode that holds this beloved
City of Rome, our own diocese, and all of Italy in suspense."

He then read a brief appeal to the "unknown men" who had kidnapped Aldo Moro, imploring them to release him, and in a few
telling words of a single paragraph, he answered all the questions
of those who wished to know where he stood. With the phrase "We
have had no particular sign . . . ," he denied that there was anyone
in the Vatican in touch with the Red Brigades. This was true. With
the words that the Moro family was in "silent anguish" he meant
to convey that neither had there been any contact between the
Church and the Via Forte Trionfale. This was diplomatic. Finally,
he did not repeat the Vatican's offer to mediate; nor did he withdraw it. This was less than the monsignor had assured.[20]

In all, however, it was a step backward and showed that the
Curia had passed word of the government's discomfiture to the
Chair of St. Peter, but it was not submission. The Holy Father,
when he was Monsignor Montini in the pontificate of Pius XII, had
held a position not unlike Monsignor Caprio's. He had seen the
wartime Pope's policy of silence before the sacrifice of hostages
come under all but universal condemnation. Even after the short
reign of John, it became and was still a burning and in many ways
enfeebling issue in the Catholic Church, and Paul, though he had
always defended Pius, had by his deeds begun to give reason to
close the chapter of silence. Now, in the orchestration of the response to Aldo Moro, there was a feeling in the Vatican that the
Holy Father was a slightly unknown factor.

The next day, like a bolt of fire from a sullen sky, there was a
sudden crack in the political bloc. The Socialists, that searching
Pirandellian party, had gone to Turin on Thursday for an annual
convention and had come home on Monday with a cause. Not everyone in the party would agree with it—the Socialists were almost
as gutted with factions as the Christian Democrats—but now hardly
anyone knew of certain decisions that had been taken in Turin.

On Monday morning, it was still a secret, high-stakes gamble
being planned by party head Bettino Craxi and his Young Turks.
The idea of stepping into the vacant and forsaken role of the doves
had emerged when Craxi and his Valentino-look vice secretary,
Claudio Signorile took note of the Attilan sack of the president's

letter. Craxi had ordered his party newspaper, *Avanti!*, to tread lightly, and though many Socialist leaders gathered in Turin added redundant voices to the horde, Craxi held the party apparatus in rein.

In Turin, the city in which modern Italian politics was born, a very private meeting had been arranged between Craxi and one of the attorneys in the Curcio trial, Giannino Guiso, himself a Socialist but far to the left of his party. Guiso, a forty-five-year-old Sardinian who had defended the legendary bandit Grazianeddu, was in fact Curcio's own lawyer, though the Red Brigades were in the process of fighting for the right to defend themselves, and Guiso on Curcio's request had withdrawn from the trial. Nevertheless, he had the authority and exercised it daily to see his client in privacy, which made him the man for Craxi.

"In Turin," Guiso said later, "I had a way to check out the existence of possible openings" for negotiations.

The primary question for the lions' cage was whether there was berth for dealing at all, and Guiso's answer was that if there were no negotiable solutions there would have been no letters from the people's prison.

This was what Craxi needed, and as both men agreed on a flexible line in opposition to the "suffering intransigence," a working connection was made.[21]

Craxi, in his address to the forty-first congress of the Socialist Party, called the Red Brigades "the worst of all evils," which had the ring of what everyone else was saying on that day, but he managed, almost subliminally, to ease in the heresy that "if a reasonable margin for negotiations were to crop up, it should not be destroyed prejudicially."[22] And he got by.

The space was scant for this kind of talk in the newspapers, and the Socialist-watchers were too busy looking for the sticky stuff with which Craxi might bind the subgroups in his party; the stuff had been buried in Craxi's message.

10.

The balding, bespectacled secretary general of the Socialist Party was above suspicion when on Monday afternoon, April 3, Andreotti and Cossiga stood before the second meeting of the five chiefs of the new majority.

The dike had gone high against the peril of talking to the Red Brigades since last they had met in Palazzo Chigi, but there were many holes yet unplugged. Parliament would be in session the following day, and there was already a long list of speakers even among the majority parties with questions about the government's position. The tiny opposition was getting some attention, complaining that the new decree laws and the hundreds of arrests that had ensued had succeeded only in creating a climate of witch-hunt.

The Prime Minister had hoped to avoid a public debate in Parliament. He had argued that any open discussion of the matter would inevitably show different shades of opinion, which might appear to the terrorists as weaknesses in the hard line. He would prefer, he had let it be known, a more "elastic" mandate in handling the Moro affair,[1] but democracies die hard in any country, and Andreotti, with his brilliantined, trimmed-once-a-day hair style and his solemn bank-manager demeanor, was not a cut of Mussolini.

Giulio Andreotti had his own exceptional qualities, and what he lacked in flair was filled in with eighteen-hour workdays. He had been aptly characterized by one qualified observer as the "perfect product" of Italian politics.[2] By this was meant that the man who had long been a leader of the right wing of the Christian Democrats, in and out of power for thirty years, but mostly in, a friend of criminals of high finance, and bribers and the bribed; the man who had built a political fiefdom in Rome's Latium region, with long tentacles that had been traced to the Mafia and the Fascist-Secret Service "strategy of tension,"[3] who was highly regarded in the Vatican and seen as Washington's favored man in Rome, was the man for all political seasons chosen in the Square of Jesus to minister the Coming of Age of the party with "the clean hands" in the Street of the Dark Shops.

The fifty-nine-year-old Roman-born Prime Minister opened the meeting with the same-as-last-time heavy air of secrecy prevailing beyond the palace doors. The same, too, was the cast of characters, with the addition of Cossiga: Zaccagnini for the Christian Democrats, Berlinguer for the Communists, Craxi the Socialists, the Social Democrat Biasini, and the Republican Romita. Now, however, the positions that emerged were extremely clear, and the minutes of the meeting, taken down sometimes in direct quotation and sometimes in paraphrase, read like a Hollywood scriptwriter's morning output on a sun-smacked Malibu beach.

The Prime Minister began, commenting on all three letters from Moro, offering a quote within the quote:

ANDREOTTI: "Not morally imputable to the subject": This is the reply to give to the public, because it corresponds to the truth. A reply, a political reply, also has to be given to the Red Brigades. It has to be a reply of great firmness. Some newspapers . . . are talking about our two-faced game: a façade of firmness and negotiations under the table. Our firmness has to come out looking like it is, that is, authentic. This is the way the government has been conducting itself. We've also notified the Vatican with clarity, and now the Vatican no longer has any room to maneuver. If the firm line slackens, the State may not be able to avoid reactions from the armed right. . . . *

* This justification of the hard line by reference to a fear of neo-Fascist terrorism is unique in the entire affair. It is difficult to imagine a higher act of submission to terrorism than for the state to have discarded all its options to appease a projected unenunciated threat from the extreme right.

COSSIGA: . . . Moro had no sense of danger about himself. Now we need to give more protection for the most important people of the State. We have to expect a new move by the Red Brigades.

BERLINGUER: The most pressing problem is tomorrow's [parliamentary] debate. Tomorrow the government must reaffirm with great clarity its own intransigent position. The same for the parties. Express it clearly. What would happen among the law-enforcement agencies if they were to feel we're giving in?

ZACCAGNINI: I'm in agreement with Andreotti. Tomorrow we have to reaffirm in Parliament that our position was taken "not without suffering and a profound awareness of the value of a life like Moro's." To this line of firmness we consent, without forgetting the human aspect. That is, to continue to try to recover Moro . . . . firmness but not excluding any legal way that might serve to recover Moro.

CRAXI: If you want to save Moro, you have got to move from words to deeds. [Craxi] thinks he has to be saved at any cost.

BIASINI: Not at any cost. The government already has an outline directive. We have decided on not entering into any bargaining. . . .

ZACCAGNINI: Says he was not speaking about bargaining.

BERLINGUER: But we don't want to give the impression that we're affirming one thing and we're ready to do another. We must avoid discussion of principles. Which is worth more: a human life or a reason of State? We are facing a mortal challenge.

CRAXI: Mortal above all for Moro. It's not a question of examining matters of principle. The only thing being asked is that the State do everything that is realistically possible. Negotiations do not mean giving in.

The Social Democrat said that the government ought to look decisive. The Republican wanted a "state of public danger" declared if necessary. Andreotti then summed up.

ANDREOTTI: We must agree on the need for clarity being asked of us by the people. We can do this best by pursuing the line already chosen. Hypotheses about other kinds of initiatives must not be talked about, for now. If we're confronted with new things, we'll examine them at that time.[4]

When it was over, three hours had gone by. The programmed substance of the parley was compressed into a one-line communiqué for the media, who were assured that what had taken place represented a "concordant evaluation of the situation and on the attitudes to adopt."[5] Although Honest Zac had appeared somewhat less hawkish than the majority, after the meeting broke Craxi seems to have had a moment's reconsideration about taking flight as a dove. When he passed the Palazzo Chigi pressroom, the reporters, who had not gotten a word from the others that was not in the communiqué, tagged after him and asked what was meant by "concordant."

"Unanimous," said the Socialist, getting into his blue armored car.

There would be no going back, however. Craxi on his way to the meeting had given a brief radio interview in which he said that the problem of Moro's release was political and that "We must explore every possibility to free the president."[6] This time his words would not be entirely overlooked.

Soon Craxi would hear from the family and receive an offer hard to ignore.

If ever there was torture in the people's prison, it was when Aldo Moro's captors brought him a sampling of the public massacre of his letter to Cossiga. Investigators later found some evidence indicating that the very first "independent" news the president received from the outside were copies of the March 30th *Corriere della Sera*, *La Repubblica*, and the Communist *L'Unità*, in all three of which he was portrayed as a man in the terminal stages of brainwashing.

Whatever effect this had on the prisoner, who was accustomed to reading a hundred newspapers a week and who it seems hungered more for news than any physical nutrient, within forty-eight hours he had sprung back and had once again taken the offensive. If beyond the three in hand he had had all the newspapers in the world, they would have been superfluous. Indeed, given Moro's, or any seasoned politician's knowledge of the process of unnatural selection that determines which political thought gets into print, any one of the three would have sufficed on that day. In any case, receiving the confirmation of the fears expressed in his letter to Cossiga, he tried to develop a new strategy. Craxi was still under cover, and all that Moro could go on was his perception of the strengths and weaknesses of the men into whose power his earthly future had fallen.

His captors, being foremost among them, had less faith than Moro in his ability to obtain a prisoner exchange. In the Sossi case not only had the state reneged, but also the country in which the released prisoners were to be exiled, Cuba, had declared its refusal to accept them. It was after this episode that the Red Brigades, regarding Castro's position as representative of what they called the "socialimperialists," or Communist countries in general, began to rethink the hostage method of freeing their comrades. Nevertheless, they were clearly not giving Moro any reason to believe that he was on the wrong track. Nor were they preventing him from trying. Moreover, judging by the focus of their attention at this moment, they were more concerned with the impression they were making on the Movement—which was all too little thus far—than with the "secondary" status of the prisoner.

Of all the other human impediments to his freedom, Moro again putting pen to paper now singled out suffering, honest Zaccagnini, trying in a new letter to grab him by the moral lapels and shake him to his senses. Moro was going for the weakest link, and in Zaccagnini he found it.

"Hard days are coming,"[7] Zaccagnini had said on his election as party secretary two years earlier. Awkward, unable to fill his own clothing no matter how it was tailored, Zaccagnini had always been depicted as emotional, naïve, and a pathetic sort of man, though this was untrue, and Moro knew him otherwise. They were contemporaries, but Moro was the mover and Zaccagnini was moved. He had been moved like a Steinway into the party secretaryship against the favorites in the running; he had won only because Moro had presented him as a provisional but necessary captain in the Columbian voyage with the Communists, who could be dazzled by reputations of honesty. Zaccagnini's celebrated sensitivity and ingenuousness were composed more of style than of substance. Moro knew him better as crafty, ambitious, impressionable, sentimental, and, as he told his captors, a man of "good heart."[8] His heart was what Moro took aim at.

From the internal evidence the first letter to Zaccagnini appears to have been written on Saturday, April 1, but it did not arrive until Tuesday afternoon, the fourth, when the mightiest battalion of the political class was seated in Parliament listening to Andreotti expound the hard line. The Red Brigades had a star performer's sense of timing.

The Prime Minister had spoken briefly and had taken his green baize place in the Chamber, when Cossiga, seated beside him, was handed a message. Communiqué IV had just been released in the now-customary four cities, and with it a letter for Zaccagnini. Cossiga went out quietly and returned shortly afterward with the texts, which he handed to Andreotti.

No announcement was made and the session continued with debate from the floor. But suddenly there was a rush of distracting movement and whisper in the great amphitheater. Someone had begun to circulate copies of the letter down the walnut benches. Heads shook forlornly, eyes widened, and in the meantime, by a more direct route, the arrow shot from the people's prison reached the seventh row right of center, where at a black-top little desk sat Benigno Zaccagnini. Zaccagnini left the chamber, withdrawing to the adjacent Hall of Ministers to read the letter.

Moro thundered at him with immense authority, in an attempt unlike the understated message to Cossiga to blister his heart and soul, and it promised tacitly that this was but the mild beginning.

It had been Zaccagnini who had pleaded with Moro when he had wanted to devote more time to his family to accept the presidency, and reminding him of this and of the vulnerability of his bodyguard, which for dubious "administrative reasons" had not been reinforced, he said, "Morally it is you who are in the place where I am materially." The party must act, he demanded, whatever anyone else might say, and he meant above all the Communists. Lashing out at them, Moro wrote that while they now found it politically convenient to adopt the hard line, they "cannot forget that my dramatic withdrawal happened on my way to the chamber for the consecration of the government I had worked at length to construct."

He was not the first man to suffer ingratitude, however, and he placed all this in the past. As for the present, he said:

> I am a political prisoner, and your brusque decision to cut off all discourse relative to others similarly detained puts me in an untenable situation. Time is passing quickly, and unfortunately it's short. Any moment could be the last.

The only positive solution was to propose the liberation of prisoners on both sides. He recalled that this had always been his position, including in the Sossi case, and he mentioned the names of two of his Interior Ministers who could corroborate him. Negotiation along these lines was the reality that had to be faced in one way or another.

"If the others don't have the courage, let it be done by the Christian Democrats, who have always had the virtue of divining how to move in the most difficult situations."

Pointing a long finger from the darkness that obscured him, he said, "If this is not meant to be, you will have wanted, and I say this without animosity, the inevitable consequences, which will recur upon the Party and yourselves."

Finally, he had some closing lines on the great national distress about his mental health:

> I want to state precisely that I say these things in complete lucidness and without having suffered any coercion of my person, as much lucidness, at least, as a man can have after fifteen days in exceptional circumstances with no one to console him and knowing what awaits him. And to tell the truth, I also feel a little bit abandoned by all of you. . . . Having done my duty to inform and remind, I entrust myself to God, my loved ones, and myself. If I didn't have a family so needful of me it would be a little different. But the way things are, one really needs courage to pay for the whole of Christian Democracy. . . . Most affectionate regards.

Aldo Moro[9]

As the copy of the letter moved from hand to hand, Parliament lost its taste for speeches. The men of power began to slip away from their places and gather in the corridors outside. In the Hall of Ministers, a stand-up meeting of the Christian Democratic leadership, including Andreotti and Cossiga, huddled around Zaccagnini. Asked to comment as the group left the parliamentary palace, Cossiga said, "Our impression is that the letter from Moro was completely extorted."[10]

Zaccagnini, according to those who saw him, seemed less certain. One eyewitness said that the party secretary came out "looking ashen, curved, stepping slowly." Someone was holding his arm. It was night. They all went by bulletproof car to the Square of Jesus.

Andreotti and Cossiga and at least eight other leaders of the highest councils of Christian Democracy regrouped in Zaccagnini's office on the third floor of party headquarters. They had, of course, interpreted Moro's first frontal attack against the party correctly, and if ever Honest Zac needed the support of his colleagues, it was now.

After what was later described as a "calm" rereading of the letter, everyone was in agreement that the most hurting phrase was the reference to Zaccagnini being morally where Moro was physically. This was the psychological hardware designed to crush poor Zaccagnini, and for this reason, one reconstruction of what happened at the meeting disclosed, "all the Christian Democratic leaders gathered closely around Zaccagnini assuring him that in this moment his role as the guiding force of Christian Democracy is indispensable."[11]

Once the secretary had been comforted, there were practical matters to be considered. The party daily *Il Popolo* would soon go to press, and present in the room was its editor-in-chief, Corrado Belci, who had always been a Moroite, but now could do no better than to stand in wait for instructions. If in the first instance the instructions had been that the president was under coercion, now Belci was to write that he was under "absolute coercion," and the already hackneyed phrase about the letters not being morally imputable to Moro was now rewritten as not being morally "ascribable." For some reason, perhaps because it contained an association to *scribe,* "ascribable" rang truer in their ears.[12]

They also worked up a spot analysis for public consumption as to why Moro would write such things, though if people really believed he were under absolute coercion, who needed an analysis? In any event it was imagined that the captors were telling the prisoner that the negotiations for his release were already under way, and all that was required for their successful conclusion was a good word from the Christian Democrats. Therefore, to signal the Red Brigades that cynicism will get them nowhere, whatever Moro might say—and they were expecting him to get tougher—would be regarded as nil. What possible form of negotiations there could be without the consent of the party that controlled every institution of state in the land was left unanalyzed.

Spurious analyses, breast-beating, and crocodile tears, as might be surmised, were felt to be insufficient. Moro had after all laid claim to a consistency of views on the matter of negotiations that predated his capture. If true, it would become more and more difficult to sustain the absolute-coercion thesis; it simply does not take much coercion to force someone to say what he has often said freely. Furthermore, if Moro was as supreme a statesman as he had been made out to be, why was his position on negotiations, which he said was on record, any less valid than the stance adopted by men of inferior credentials? To be sure, these were the very sort of internal contradictions the Red Brigades had set out to "expose and exasperate," and that seemed a good reason now to attempt to recrate them before the shoddy box of their safekeeping burst open.

A search among Moro's voluminous publications and papers had already been made following his letter to Cossiga in hopes of finding a more comfortable version of Moro's thinking, but nothing "useful" had been uncovered.[13] This was because Moro's conception of the state, dating back to an important series of lectures he gave on the philosophy of law and the state in the mid-1940s, had always been founded on the principle of flexibility. Laws, he had taught, were made for men and not the other way around, and when the needs of law became incompatible with the needs of men, there was only one of the two that was alterable, and that of course was the law.[14] Cicero had gone around Rome saying more or less the same thing in the first century, and Italy owed a thousand years of greatness to its adaptability, and nothing but tears and ruin to rigidity; Moro was no pioneer.

Nevertheless, at the meeting in Zaccagnini's office, Cossiga proceeded by telephone to check out Moro's assertion about the two men—both Christian Democratic senators now—who he said could testify in his favor. His actual words were that his ideas on negotiations and flexibility had been "already expressed to Taviani on the Sossi case and to Gui regarding a contested law on kidnappings." Luigi Gui had been Minister of Interior in Moro's fourth government, formed in 1974, some months after the Sossi case. Gui confirmed Moro to the letter, adding that he had been opposed to taking the hard line in kidnap cases of any kind.[15] The second man, Paolo Taviani, had held the Interior portfolio in Moro's first three governments, between 1964 and 1968, and had had the same post throughout the Sossi episode, when Moro was Foreign Minister. Taviani in 1974 was the hard-liner *par excellence* who had supported the state's turnabout after the release of the communist prisoners had been ordered by the courts. It seemed odd that Moro would summon Taviani, since they were known as traditional political enemies, though the situation called for standing a little taller than the tide. As it turned out, Taviani let it be known that, if need be, he could be relied on to dispute the president's claim.

"I told the Minister of Interior and the secretary of my party," Taviani said thirty-six hours later, "that the Hon. Moro did not—I repeat, did not—ever express either any judgment or any opinion to me in connection with the Sossi kidnapping."[16]†

Senator Taviani's denial would be front-page headline news; Senator Gui's confirmation would be no news at all.

The night's work done, everyone went home.

Zaccagnini, however, had really only been partially salvaged. Haunted, he was now among the slightly unpredictables. More important, one man who had been present in Zaccagnini's room no longer believed that the hard line was the best line, though he had said nothing as yet. He was the president of the Senate, one of the most powerful Italians and one of the very few with a prestigious international reputation. Moro had often been called a political

---

† Against this, Moro replied indignantly some days later with an attack on Taviani's forgetfulness. He gave the approximate time, place, and nature of the conversation, and went on at length about Taviani's "excess of zeal" in having always been a timeserver to wherever the power shifted. Asked for his response, Taviani said, "I don't argue with the Red Brigades."[17]

"thoroughbred," of which, the saying went, there were only two. This man was the other. His name was Amintore Fanfani.

The media's Operation Moro Isn't Moro resumed like planetary motion the following morning. As has been suggested, it was more of the same. New was the idea of Moro having been turned into a "puppet," and the *Corriere della Sera* cited a generic RAND Corporation study to show that he had by psychological reversion been turned into a "baby."[18]‡ That he had protested his clarity of thought was seen by the Communists as the proof of his coercion, since by prior definition he had been forced to write exactly that. The depth of his confusion was revealed by the indisputable fact that although the letter had been received on the nineteenth day of his imprisonment, he had written that he had been in "exceptional circumstances" for *fifteen* days. Worse, he had forgotten to begin the letter with the date. And so on.[19]

By sheer overkill, the "news" of Aldo Moro's psychological ills began now to assume the aspect of revealed truth not only in Italy but also throughout Europe and the United States. In a "news analysis," the Rome correspondent of New York *Times*, Henry Tanner, spoke without qualification or attribution of "the brutality of the act of slowly destroying the hostage, and giving the public periodic glimpses of his deterioration." Tanner indicated that his sources for such judgments were Italian "politicians and newspapers."[20] By week's end the *Times*'s news summary was telling of Moro's "deteriorating state of mind," his "begging" and his "pleading."[21] The source for this, it seems, was the *Times* correspondent. As for the readers, the text for the Moro letters themselves were left to their imagination.

Lost in all the concern for Moro's mental well-being was the precious time for a careful reading of Communiqué IV. It had been dispatched with a long enclosure, the sixty-page resolution of the strategic command issued clandestinely in February. Taken to-

‡ The theory of the hostage developing a parent-child relationship with his captor as a result of his total dependency—also known as the Stockholm Syndrome after a documented case of this kind—would become the mascot of the political class. Given enough time, it may even be impeccable, but it cannot have any other relevance than to explain an observed *change* in the behavior of the victim. If, as in the Moro case, the overall *continuity* of personality is demonstrated, there is simply no evidence of the syndrome.

gether it was possible to conclude that not only Moro, but the Red Brigades, too, were feeling a little abandoned. Moreover, the new document showed different emphases and contrasting lines of thought inside the strategic command. Read along with a declaration made by the Curcio group in Turin on the same day as the arrival of Communiqué IV, these tendencies seemed eminently exploitable in favor of Aldo Moro even in the context of the hard line, provided it had been taken in good faith. At this moment, the price of Moro's freedom was plunging; it was much lower than many people imagined, including the prisoner.

In the first place, two thirds of the communiqué, the largest proportion thus far, had nothing to do with Aldo Moro. It was a plaintive, antihistoric scream at the rather surprisingly inert ultraleft to show some sign of life after all the risk and bother the Red Brigades had gone to for the Good Cause. The revolution was "necessary and possible!" There was, comrades, "no need to be afraid" of the enemy, and "ONE CAN AND MUST LIVE CLANDESTINELY"; unite, extend, intensify, "CONSTRUCTING THE FIGHTING COMMUNIST PARTY," etc. What had been proposed as the primary purpose of the capture of Aldo Moro was evidently being evaluated inside the strategic command as foundering, failing dismally. Furthermore, the release to the establishment press of the long resolution—which received, predictably, only the barest and nonsensical references—was an admission that the underground lines of communication were short.

Second, those in the strategic command with much more modest aims, as expressed in their one third of the communiqué, had a reasonable chance of succeeding. Indeed, they already had succeeded in dramatizing the faults and foibles of the system. The police investigation was becoming a national embarrassment, and the think tank in the Interior Ministry in spite of the hard line was giving a 30 per cent probability rating to negotiations, which were not even needed from the less ambitious group's standpoint. This placed the macroliners, who were undoubtedly the same persons who would later take the role of the Red Brigades' very own hardliners, on the defensive. The dovish-micros were near to the Curcio group in outlook and probably formed the older, definitely the more "conservative" component of the strategic command, though it is certain there was much overlapping.

Their segment of the communiqué was directed at backing up the prisoner's strategic letter to Zaccagnini, and in disassociating itself from Moro's approach, it implied that other solutions existed. It commented on the "treacherous and vulgar" behavior of the press with regard to Moro's message to Cossiga, and seemed almost to sympathize with his expressions of being left behind by his own kind. The interrogation was continuing and Moro was "clarifying" his responsibilities, which was phrasing designed not to press the threat of a secret-spilling confession.

While Moro's references to prisoner exchanges showed no lack of political realism, the communiqué went on, "This is his position [and], it is useful to make clear, not ours." Restating a commitment to free imprisoned comrades, it cited, however, examples of jailbreak and escape rather than negotiated releases, of which there were none that had succeeded. It continued to refrain from making any demands and stated that the Red Brigades had no interest in "secret negotiations" and "mysterious intermediaries," which it charged was the government's game, not its own game. "The trial of Aldo Moro will go on to its conclusion," it said in what would almost have been serene language had not the macros come next to bat, and nothing on the outside could intervene to modify the judgment that would in due course be handed down from the people's tribunal.[22]

When placed in conjunction with the simultaneous statement of the Curcio group, the insistence of the Red Brigades on the trial, the shying from demands, and the possibilities that might be pried open became clear. Moro's trial, said the Turin Fifteen, was of *itself* an act of war against the class enemy, and was not against the individual. It was therefore in the interests of the Red Brigades to recognize the prisoner's political identity, and, mocking the charges of torture, they said it would be self-defeating "to repress the individual either physically or psychologically." In contrast to Operation Moro Isn't Moro, Moro *as* Moro was both the medium and the message. It was all.

This was compared with the conditions of political prisoners in the hands of the state. They were incarcerated in newly instituted maximum-security antiterrorist centers in various degrees of isolation from one another and from contacts with their families, friends, and the outside world in general. The severity of the "special prisons," as they were euphemistically called, was already under heavy criticism by Italian civil-rights groups, and the Curcio statement used Moro as an example of the sort of treatment the Turin defendants wanted for themselves and their fellows: "the maintenance of their political identity." This meant, as a "minimum program," more social intercourse both in prison and with the outside.[23]

Was the life of the president redeemable by a mere loosening of an already controversial penal routine? The question would lie buried for weeks.

I I .

The doves nested in one of a block of buildings built to the ponderous taste of Mussolini. It stood between the tomb of Augustus
and the Via del Corso, the great central spear of the Piazza del
Popolo trident. Here, at the home of some forgotten Fascist bureaus,
the red flag of socialism flew.

Party headquarters had been emitting a religious lip service to its
intransigent partners in the new majority, but Bettino Craxi by now
was in another league: a concealed triple alliance to break the hard
line. After his radio interview, Craxi had been contacted by Sereno
Freato, the tough, unsubtle Venetian of the Moro family clan, and
when the power and prestige of Amintore Fanfani was added to
the equation, a three-way deal was projected.

Craxi met with the family and some members of the faction in
the Christian Democrats led by Fanfani. The *fanfaniani* said that if
the path were properly beaten, their leader would come forward to
champion the soft line. It would be up to Craxi to formulate and
advance this position, which really meant that Craxi was being
asked to take all of the considerable political risks and manhandling
and less than the lion's share of the credit, if credit would ever
accrue. Craxi, though he knew he would have backbiting in his
own party, agreed. As for the credit, lions do not always get their
share. To the family fell the first task of sounding out by hot line
the minimum terms of the president's release.[1] The arrangement
was struck.

It was, then, the family's move, but there was trouble in the hot line. Since the government had chosen not to use it, no system had been established to transmit messages back to the Red Brigades. They in turn did not fully trust the no-surveillance pact and had begun to use other drops as indicated by the prisoner. On Tuesday, April 4, however, along with the original of the letter to Zaccagnini, Moro had enclosed a second message to his wife, asking her to send, along with news of the family, her evaluation of the political mood in Rome.[2] By now it was all too clear in the people's prison that of his two offensives—the Vatican solution and the Zaccagnini weak link—the former was blocked in the absence of progress in the latter and Moro needed a firsthand assessment. Eleonora Moro was instructed by her husband to cast her reply in the most cryptic way possible and send it as a letter to the editor of the Milan daily *Il Giorno*, a newspaper with a national circulation. The confidentiality of this missive was respected by the Red Brigades, who were undoubtedly as eager as Moro to have an inside view.

On Wednesday, Mrs. Moro met with Zaccagnini, who came to the Via Forte Trionfale looking as grim as old paint and left looking thoroughly excavated. She had given neither solace nor pause to suffering Zac, and after he had been tongue-lashed and sent off, she wrote her letter to the editor. It was published with front-page prominence on Friday, and read:

Rome, April 6

Dear Editor,

In this situation that allows us no contact, I avail myself of the courtesy of your newspaper, for which my husband has often written* . . . to reassure him that all the members of the family are united and in good health.

This was the first "coded" news, a highly personal reference to their daughter Anna, about whose fragile well-being and lack of physical closeness to the family Moro never ceased to grieve.

Mrs. Moro turned next to her opinion of the effect her husband's strategy was having on the men of power:

* Moro had frequently contributed political analyses to *Il Giorno*, usually at the start of an academic semester when extra money was needed for the children's education.

Unfortunately we have not had any sign that might comfort our hope of his return.

All was not lost, however:

We would like him to know nevertheless . . . that in spite of everything we have faith in men and believe it is still possible, after so much pain, to embrace him once again.

With much gratitude,

Eleonora Moro[3]

The letter was answered immediately with new and very sensitive instructions intended by both Moro and the strategic command to remain secret. But the troubled hot line broke down completely by a police action that precipitated a weekend of high tension. It propelled the strategic command into a risk endangering the entire operation, prisoner and captors alike.

What happened was that the police had begun to make note and investigate virtually everyone seen visiting the Moro household, and at least three such callers had already been used by the Red Brigades as postmen between the people's prison and the family. On Saturday morning, the day after Eleonora Moro's letter to the editor, a courier from the strategic command slipped the president's long reply under a sidewalk control booth of the city bus company, and telephoned one of these go betweens. His name was Franco Tritto, the youngest of Moro's teaching assistants at the University of Rome.

Tritto, who lived in the same general area as the Moros, had already carried a message to the family. Since then his phone had gone under police surveillance.

"Listen," said the *brigatista* without identifying himself in any way, "the president has decided to abuse your courtesy once again." He then informed Tritto precisely where to find a white envelope containing a message for delivery only to Mrs. Moro.

Tritto replied that he might encounter some difficulty in seeing the *signora* because of the "confusion" in Via Forte Trionfale and he asked if he could give it to anyone in the family group.

If it were really impossible to do otherwise, the courier said, revealing the importance attached to this message, that would be all right, as long as it did not fall into the hands of "either the police or executives of the party."[4]

The letter was in the hands of both before Tritto arrived at the appointed place. It was immediately classified as top secret by Cossiga, but an unusual rush of Saturday-afternoon consultations at the Square of Jesus and meetings in the Interior Ministry ignited a conflagration of rumor that swept the entire peninsula. By evening, Andreotti, who had been away from Rome, had flown in and had met with Zaccagnini, and Cossiga had flown out on what appeared as a mysterious mission to Switzerland. That anything at all had occured received repeated denials, from which the media distilled its own brew. The president's moral resistance had given out entirely, they said. It was all on video-cassette, and an apocalyptic conclusion was thought to be nigh.[5]

While the men of power were contemplating their next counteractions, the Red Brigades tried again to get a copy of the letter to Mrs. Moro. Checking back with Tritto, they had a confirmation of the interception and consequently that his wire was tapped. They had then to assume that the no-surveillance pact was off and that any messenger they would call on might not only be bugged but be under police observance as well. This raised the risk sharply of transmitting communications of this kind. It had to be expected that the police would always arrive first at the drop point unless it were dangerously close to the messenger himself, and in fact there would be no further messages meant to be kept from the eyes of the authorities. Moreover, it placed a strict time limit on any future phone contact with the family, since the origin of their calls could be traced. Nevertheless, they went ahead in their attempt to get a copy of the sequestered letter to Mrs. Moro.

The *brigatista* who had earlier spoken to Franco Tritto now telephoned another contact suggested by Moro, a young parish priest by the name of Antonello Mennini. The Red Brigades' operative had already been in touch with Father Mennini before his line, too, had been tapped, saying that whenever he would call he would use the name Professor Nikolai. Now, after he had lost about forty seconds trying to get this across to the person at the other end and then waiting for Don Antonello to come to the phone, he told him that he had to hang up but would call back. The Red Brigades had calculated that they had a telephone security margin of at least three minutes, but apparently Professor Nikolai felt uncomfortable from wherever he was calling and he moved to a new phone.

"Listen," he said a few minutes later, "you should get this letter right away. You'll do it easily, and you should tell the *signora* that we're very sorry. This letter was supposed to have been delivered much earlier, but the intermediary we picked was unable to collect it. So we had to call on you again. Tell her all these things."

The letter, he went on, was inside a crumpled newspaper in a sidewalk litter basket and he described the corner it was on.

"Why, that's just outside," said the priest.

"Yes, right next to you. Go immediately or they'll get it first."[6]

If there had been a police watch on Don Antonello, they had wittingly or not let a *brigatista* and all the places he might have led them slip by.

Before the weekend was over, Mrs. Moro possessed and had read her letter. She had also met with envoys of both the government and the Vatican. Everyone now knew what Moro was planning and that he understood with as much lucidness as he claimed to have what was going on in Rome. Thus it was agreed on all sides not to break each other's secrets.

If Aldo Moro's public letters were the divisions he fielded in his battle, this private letter to his wife was his Pentagon. In it were the outlines and suggestions of all the several plans he had drawn and was drawing to outflank, if not defeat, the obdurate foe. Beside an underlying perplexity at why there had to be a fight at all was a full acceptance of the reality of power and the terms in which it had to be affirmed. In a declaration of love for his family and friends, the president called them all to arms.

He wrote:

My dearest Noretta,

Even if the content of your letter to Il Giorno brought me no reason to hope (not that I expected it would), it did me an immense good, giving me in my sorrow a confirmation of a love that remains firm in all of you and accompanies me and will accompany me in my calvary. To all, then, my warmest thanks, my most heartfelt kiss, my greatest love.

I'm sorry, my dearest, to have to give you additional commitments and grief, but I believe that even you, however disheartened you may be, would never forgive me if I were not to ask you to do something which may be a useless act of love, but is an act of love.

And now, within these limits, I should give you some indications regarding your delicate task. . . .

Mentioning the names of the family intimates to call on for help, he said it seemed to him that Parliament, and his best friends among the members, had held silent, perhaps because of intimidation, of a fear of being the cause of undermining a united front. "And instead," he said, "one must have the courage to break this fictitious unity."

What really is astounding [Moro wrote] is that within a few minutes the government believed it had evaluated the significance and the implications of an event of such importance, and that in such great haste and superficiality it elaborated a hard line that has yet to be scratched. . . . And then all this rigor in the very country of disarray which is Italy.

To bring down this façade, which he saw as an unprincipled expedient, the first thing to do was to organize what he felt most lacking thus far: "the voice of my friends." He asked his wife to convoke a working group of those men and women of power he believed were his closest followers, men and women he had known for decades and who had built their political fortunes in the Moroite movement within Christian Democracy. They were to be asked to initiate a dissent.

"Incite them to a disassociation," Moro instructed, "to rupture the unity. It's the only thing our leaders fear. They don't care a thing about the rest." The leadership was ignoring the troubles that would arise "after," he added, adopting what it thought was the lesser evil.

The organized dissent from the hard line, he said, "should be firm and unemotional." The meetings Mrs. Moro would have with the dissidents ("if you get to have any") were to be publicized. Private pressures were to be backed up with public declarations. And it all had to be done swiftly "because time is closing in."

The objective to work for was a negotiated exchange of prisoners and the expulsion from the national territory of those freed on the Red Brigades' side. The idea of the expatriation of undesirable citizens, as practiced by the Soviet Union and other states, was new to Moro's position. It added technical problems, such as finding a host country, but introduced the possibility of seeking a solution by already established international laws—one in particular being the Geneva Convention on internal armed conflict.

Moro turned next to the Vatican. He said that on the reverse side of the clipping he had seen of Mrs. Moro's letter, he had read a report of an article in *L'Osservatore Romano*, which in substance was a "no to blackmail."† Thus the Vatican, Moro wrote with particular horror, "denies its whole humanitarian tradition, and today condemns me, and tomorrow it will be children who will fall victim so as not to consent to blackmail." This thesis was in contradiction to prior positions taken by the Church in cases like his own, and with it, he said, the Holy See had placed itself in the service of the Communists.

"It is incredible how far we have gone in the confusion of the tongues," said Moro, alluding to the biblical destruction of Babel. Despairing on what appeared to him as an about-face of the institution that was dearest of all to his being, he suggested an encounter with Cardinal Poletti "to rectify this enormity."

From this thousandth blow, he fell now into the throes of bitterness, and speaking of his son, who had become active in a progressive Catholic movement, he said, "You must tell Giovanni what it means to be in politics." Was there no one in his party who regretted having placed him in a position he had not sought? "And what of Zaccagnini? How can he remain tranquil in his post? And Cossiga, who was incapable of imagining any way to defend me?"

Finally:

But it's not this I wish to speak of; it is of all of you whom I love and will always love; it is of the gratitude I owe you, of the indescribable joy you have given me in life. . . . If at least

† The article, entitled "The Hour of Truth" and written by Father Virgilio Levi, sanctioned a hard line that transcended politics and ideology and a moral crusade against the "dark forces" that had coerced Moro into giving "ignominious and false confessions."[7]

I were to have your hands in mine, your kisses, your photographs. The Christian Democrats (and Levi of *L'Osservatore*) take even this away from me. What evil can come from all this evil?

I embrace you, I hold you my dearest Noretta and you must do the same with everyone else and with the same feeling. Is it true that Anna has come back? May God bless her. I embrace you all.

Aldo[8]

Eleonora Moro and the family had thus been entrusted with no lesser task than the formation of a new political movement—an outcast party of dissidents to counterpose to the Catholic-Communist axis. It was to be a motley bunch of every persuasion from the threshold of the neo-Fascists to the core of the Red Brigades.

The family had few illusions about the malleability of the Andreotti government, and it knew more or less what leverage it retained among the Christian Democrats, not only in the party but also in other institutions, reaching as high as the President of the republic. The Chief of State had powers independent of the government, and thus far President Leone had spoken nothing but kindness to the Moros.

True, the article by Father Levi was the hard-line voice of the Roman Curia, but the Curia was not the Church in its entirety. Eleonora Moro had received Cardinal Poletti on the very day her husband's letter had urged such a meeting upon her, and the cardinal had gone to Pope Paul the next day bearing the president's misgivings. Then, if stock were taken, there were the Socialists, being primed internally by Craxi for their promised offensive, and there were, thanks to the letter from Papà and fresh ideas emanating at home, many avenues yet to be explored. Moro, of course, had stressed the element of time, but the people's trial had only begun, and, in the worst instance, matters would necessarily become a great deal more harried before the end was visibly at hand. There was a magnificent sense of realism in the family's motion, except for one unknown into which some wishful thinking had seeped.

There were those in the family circle, particularly around young Giovanni Moro, who believed with Giovanni that if Moro, and

Moro alone, had brought the Communist and Catholic parties together, it was to the advantage of the former, more so than anyone
else, to bring the statesman home.[9] Images of a famous handshake
between Moro and Berlinguer were hard in fading, and they
suggested the very man the Moros ought privately to see.

Until rather recently, Giovanni Moro considered himself a
member of the "disappointed generation." They were children, by
his own description, who had been nourished by the belief that the
all-new and good society was theirs for the making, only to discover
at twenty that everything had long ago been decided and it seemed
ever would be "in the comfortable cage of moderation that was
Christian Democracy." The president's son, who was the facial
reflection of the president's wife, felt himself to be a "disenchanted
Catholic" and had gone in search of new ideas.[10]

His father had publicly proposed the "strategy of attention"—
keeping an unjaundiced eye on the Communists—and Giovanni
watched, too, looking from another angle. He, his sister Agnese,
and many of their friends began to see in Italian Marxism, or that
large portion of it led by the Communist Party, the missing vitality
in political Catholicism. They were inspired and guided by a forty-
year-old lawyer named Giancarlo Quaranta, who had been Giovanni's scoutmaster in the Catholic Boy Scouts of Italy. Quaranta, a
man with an enthusiasm that was catching, had founded a national
group provisionally called the February '74 Movement. He believed
less in the political engineering of joining the two mass parties—according to the blueprints of Aldo Moro—than in an atomic fusion
of the best of both possible worlds in a "cultural revolution."

Quaranta had written a book titled *The Politics of Culture*, and
Giovanni had contributed the Introduction, in which he praised the
work of his old Scout leader as "a great sign of hope." The little
green paperback had come out a few days before Moro's capture,
and had been designed as the ideological handbook for "democratic
Catholics and Communists" to foment the cultural revolution and
usher in the "new humanism."[11] Its intended impact, however, was
totally pre-empted by the guns in Via Fani.

All this by way of explaining how it was that a nationwide movement of frustrated cultural revolutionaries, boys and girls up from

Scouting, attached itself from the beginning to the Moro family cause.

The dissident party was waxing, and the first mission invested by Giovanni Moro in February '74, given its Marxist connection, was to search for light in the Street of the Dark Shops.

By coincidental circumstance, history had provided for the Communists, as it had for the Socialists, a Fascist edifice for its headquarters—the old studios of the long-silent radio voice of fascism, EIAR. Once, in wartime, the building had had to be protected from ill-wishers by an around-the-clock guard of German troops, but that was eggshell compared with the recently installed security system to assure the tranquillity of its present occupants. In the past few terror-struck years all the seats of power in Rome had been fortified, but the job had been done most efficiently, as usual, by the party with the clean hands.

Nighttime or not, the outer walls of the building were in the constant wash of natural or artificial light, by which a battery of television cameras kept an unblinking watch on all the surrounding streets, the windows and roofs, and the alertness of a deployed police contingent. This was monitored from a booth on the ground floor inside, which looked out on the tall arched entranceways lately sealed by bulletproof, electronically operated glass doors. When on the infrequent occasions each day these doors were opened to permit the comings and goings of the highest party officials, they would slide wide, swallowing or disgorging the caller, his car, armed escort, and all.

In this way, party secretary Enrico Berlinguer had arrived in his silver-blue Alfa Romeo on the day he met with Giancarlo Quaranta, top Scout again, on behalf of the family clan. Berlinguer, the red aristocrat who had found Karl Marx in his uncle's library and had thus received his call, was, according to Quaranta, an easy man to talk with in the confines of his office. They spoke quite freely for an hour or so. Quaranta tried to persuade the Communist leader not only to unbend the intransigent line but also to try to make contact with the Red Brigades and open the negotiations. Of the party that had propounded the "scorched earth" policy against every living thing on its left, this was like asking Stalin to invite

Trotsky to tea, but Berlinguer was of a milder temper than either of those men.

"Not to negotiate," he replied when he had heard out Quaranta with charm, "is the best way to save the life of Aldo Moro."

"He told me not to worry," Quaranta would report to the family. "He said, 'It's not in the Red Brigades' interest to kill him.' He said, 'They will release him.' "[12]

Coming directly and confidentially from Berlinguer, so sanguine a prognosis of Moro's health might almost have been reassuring. Of all the men of power in Rome, he had more ways than any other of knowing what the Red Brigades were up to. It meant nothing that on television that very evening, Berlinguer, the head of the proletarian party, made an uncompromising defense of the working class as being free of any trace of terrorist activity. The only "proof" he offered was an unworried appeal to all citizens to report to the authorities any "sensation or suspicion" that a crime against another person or the state might be committed.[13] This was an incitement to witch-hunt, and clearly he felt that *his* Communists had nothing to fear, but with 1.8 million card-carrying members, the party received a continuous flow of firsthand information from the nation's industrial centers. These were the same working-class centers where the Red Brigades, the *autonomi,* and the entire ultraleft had taken root and had the bulk of their supporters. On the other hand, it was becoming more and more problematical for the nonviolent Communists to gather news about the fighting Communists since the party had begun turning over what one of its officials has called "useful elements of information" to the police.[14]

In the end, Quaranta had discovered that the only light scouted for in the Street of the Dark Shops was on the outside, and the family decided not to trust their fortune in the counsel of Enrico Berlinguer.

I 2.

Aldo Moro on trial was in the same place as a man and his cigarette at the battered wall of a firing squad. After the last drag, in
the absence of reprieve, there is little more than to be done with it.
The president smoked slowly.

In their Monday-morning quarterbacking of the Sossi case, the
Red Brigades had attached greater importance to the trial than to
any other phase of Operation Sunflower, including the question of
prisoner exchanges. Sossi's interrogation, which had taken place
two hours daily, had been the means to verify their political
analyses, they said, and "to identify who in the shadows of power
was really pulling the strings."[1]

"It was not a policelike interrogation," they revealed on another
occasion, "but an attempt to understand how men most exposed to
power reason."[2]

Rome was given a glimpse of what was going on before the people's tribunal when on April 10 the Red Brigades distributed Communiqué V with an excerpt from the interrogation. It contained
Moro's angry response to the repudiations of his ex-Interior Minister, Taviani. His denial, the president said, was "incomprehensible and anyway, considering my situation, in my judgment
disrespectful and provocatory." He also wondered aloud if behind
the hard line subtle pressure was being applied to maintain it by
the United States and West Germany, which was perfectly true.[3]*

* The communiqué itself added little to its predecessors. It aimed at making
the points that the trial was proceeding calmly, in absolute security, and that
the Red Brigades were uninterested in secret negotiations ("nothing must be
hidden from the people"). Its message to the Movement was "Organize!"[4]

The overall transcript of the interrogation, which the Red Brigades would keep secret throughout the affair, speaks eloquently of how well the prisoner perceived what his judges were after. In being true to himself at the same time, his testimony, given the circumstances, is a tour de force of his own style, with an internal momentum that might have carried it to a longer, more natural end were not time and the cops closing in.

The rather long period I have passed as a political prisoner of the Red Brigades has naturally been hard, and as is the nature of things, it has also been edifying. I must say that under the pressure of various stimuli, and most of all a reflection that recalls to each his own, the often turbulent events of my political and social life come back to me with a rhythm and an order that make them more intelligible.

With those two sentences, which could have opened a Victorian novel that had taken years from its author's life, Aldo Moro began his partly written, partly spoken deposition.

According to the indications of the communiqués, the trial lasted twenty-one days, from March 25 to April 15, but the transcript seems to cover only the last fifteen of those days, and it is unlikely that there was anything taken down before. It began, then, at about the time Moro received the news, following his letter to Cossiga, of his overnight transformation by his peers into a nonperson. Early in the document, however, he speaks of being a prisoner for twenty days, which was on April 5, so most of the material was accumulated in the ten-day period after his letter to Zaccagnini. This was when the positions of the government, his party, and the Communists were perfectly clear to him, and the icy front continued throughout to appear unscratched.

At no time during the trial did he, or for that matter, the Red Brigades, have any clue whether his instructions to the family were obtaining results. Although at one point in his testimony he expressed a faith that the Red Brigades, even turned back by Rome empty-handed, would spare him, the underlying tenor was of a man left alone on a barren island, knowing by the vacant horizon that he is soon to die.

Thus it is not surprising that if he testified for ten days, he reserved one day to vent an Olympian anger at the men he held responsible for the impasse in his predicament. What does evoke some wonder is the unique, deep descent that all ten days provide into the dark, unswept cellars of national and international *Realpolitik.*†

He had been called upon to give an accounting of what for three decades had gone on at the top, which is precisely what he did in twenty-five thousand words or more. If the Red Brigades still wished to know who pulled the strings of power, they learned now that there were no strings. Their disappointment is on record. The revolutionary organization that was sounding the alert for a Washington- and Bonn-based "project" to restructure Italy and other European countries as satellite States of Multinational Imperialism had to reconcile high conspiracy with Moro's exquisite description of a party everlastingly in power incapable of organizing community youth centers for political discussion. Not that he was being less than candid. He drew a picture of thirty years of Christian Democratic rule that recalled the last of Dorian Gray. There was nothing but an amorphous, man-eating ooze, into which only the most ambitious men dared to dip, and whatever happens "happens by the force of things." Indolence, inertia, and decadence were the reigning conditions, and the need to flake away the rot from time to time was the prime inspiration and mover. The rest was the rise and fall of petty alliances, the doggish search for the vulnerability of one's enemies, lure, deceit, duplicity, tergiversation, treachery, cynicism, cold-bloodedness, and the interiorization of it all in a brotherhood of *omertà*. He did not quite explain where he fit in, and said he was more often a victim than a victor, but he never pretended, nor could he, that all the while he had been elsewhere.

Moro produced a document that will or ought to be read for

† Moro was head of the Foreign Office in five different governments from 1969 to 1974. Accordingly, a large part of his testimony deals with international affairs. Most striking is his firsthand portrayal of the father-and-son relationship between the United States and Italy. This has long been a subject for scholars in both countries, but rarely has it been made so plain. Nothing, it seems, ever happens in Christian Democratic Italy without a glance across the Atlantic for approval, which is not always forthcoming. Moro's disclosures of Washington's attitudes toward his opening to the Eurocommunists are telling: At first Nixon's "blood boiled" and Kissinger reacted with animosity and a "dose of vulgarity," but later, President Carter looked at Moro, if not with favor, then with a "perplexed eye," though of things Italian "he doesn't know very much."

years by those who care to know how big power is wielded by small men. But our story is about how a somewhat bigger man wielded a personal power that was shrinking like soap in water, and, as such, the document as a fighting instrument, rather than as a textbook, is more to the point.

In telling his interrogators something about everything they wished to know, and not vice versa, he had not surrendered the hope that the people's tribunal would pardon or acquit him, but he also had gone farther. There was more than his life on the block. There was pride, dignity, the continuity of life into death, and the immortal afterlife every statesman believes in: his place in the crowded kingdom of History.

His adversaries could go on maintaining his psychic paraplegia only as long as the season of silence held out, but he could insist to eternity that the situation was otherwise. Which is why an early passage reads like the start of a will, with proverbial references to the soundness of his body and mind, despite "many disrespectful insinuations."

Certain that his testimony would sooner or later surface, he burned all the bridges behind him ("recognizing my complete incompatibility with the party . . . I resign from the Christian Democrats") and mined the foreseeable future with political time bombs meant to shatter the official "truth" of his ordeal bound to be handed down by the men of power. In a caveat not to believe his would-be political heirs, he declared of his own case:

> It cannot be said tomorrow that I found just and supported the positions taken by the political forces, beginning with the Christian Democrats; rather, one will have to say that I considered them inhuman, dangerous, and politically unproductive.

He was prerecording his voice from the grave, and in doing so he went after the heirs themselves, marking them one by one for haunting.

First, he took note of the dramatic irony of his own fate. In constructing the new majority, he had had a choice between Andreotti and Fanfani to head the government. The irony was even greater than he knew, since Fanfani was already at work against the Andreotti hard line. Nevertheless, Moro remarked that while he esteemed Fanfani, he harbored a "forty-year, innate, irreducible distrust" of Andreotti. "I have always rejected," he said, "and I reject to this day to try to understand the underlying reasons for this feeling, this psychological given." Yet he chose Andreotti, he said, because he believed at the time that it was in the best interests of the country that Fanfani remain president of the Senate.

His crystalline exposition of the trap he had unwittingly set and fallen into made a lasting impression on his judges. In the present situation, the Christian Democrats had to show, he told them, "how much efficiency and holding capacity it acquired from the pact it has just stipulated [with the Communists]. For the Communists, the rigorous refusal to be flexible and humane is the certificate of their unimpeachable conduct. For the Christian Democrats, this is the counterproof of a good deal."

Evidently, it was not an easy matter for Moro to come to terms with this quirk in his fortunes. Recalling how Andreotti had solicited his good offices to gain control of the new government and that once assured of power he had closed himself off in "a dark dream of glory," Moro went on to plant future accusations of deadly cunning. With Moro in the hands of the Red Brigades, all Andreotti needed to become *padrone* "was Berlinguer to play his game, which he did with incredible flippancy." This, in the "pale shadow of Zaccagnini, who suffers without pain, worries without worries, is impassioned without passion . . ."

At last, self-reproach and a moral:

In the future, inventors of [political] formulas should prefer prudence when thinking about such things.

If such were the men and institutions he had numbered among his own kind, he was grateful, he told the people's tribunal, "that I owe the salvation of my life and the restitution of my freedom to the Red Brigades."[5]

His testimony given, the prisoner awaited a verdict.

IV

SENTENCE

*What a price
for this spectacle
of apparent greatness!*[1]

13.

Elsa Mazzoni concentrated. She saw a white car entering the rear of a white truck. She saw the white truck begin to make for the sea by the old Aurelian Way. She saw Aldo Moro. He was covered with blood, but not his own. He was in the people's prison. He was near still water, a lake, or perhaps a slow-moving river like the Tiber.

Massimo Inardi received. He received Aldo Moro. The president was in a farmhouse by a stream, a water mill somewhere near to Rome.[1]

The ghost of Giorgio La Pira spoke through a make-do planchette, an ashtray. He pointed it at letters penciled on white paper. Aldo Moro, said he, was beside a lake; no, not *beside* a lake but in a nearby village, a tiny hamlet called Gradoli fifty miles north of Rome.

The men of power were trying everything not taboo to save the president's life. Elsa Mazzoni, a celebrated clairvoyant, had been hired by the Ministry of Defense. Massimo Inardi was a cherubic parapsychologist who had proved to the satisfaction of the nation to be endowed with some special mental talent. He had accumulated unprecedented winnings on a television quiz show. He was concentrating for Cossiga's ministry. Giorgio La Pira, a messianic founding father of Christian Democracy, was Zaccagnini's spiritual candidate for the solution to the whereabouts of Aldo Moro.

The mediums summoned hard, but the work of running down the extrasensory clues was left to Cossiga and his chief of police,

Giuseppe Parlato, a man with career trouble antedating the case at hand. They had put together an Italian version of the *Grenzschutz-gruppe-9*'s "leatherheads," a strike force equipped with the latest antiterrorist technology, such as the stun grenades used in the Mogadishu assault.*

The Italian leatherheads had everything they needed but the target, and the voices from beyond seemed to be homing in on just that. Moro, they all agreed, was in an isolated place near Rome and a body of water, and the ghost of La Pira (Don Sturzo, the great forebear of Christian Democracy, had refused to talk) had given the precise location.

So it was that on at least five occasions during the first fortnight of April hundreds of police, Carabinieri, and search dogs, backed up by helicopter reconnaissance, combed the banks of the Tiber, the Latium coastline, and the village of Gradoli (population, one hundred). None of this was done to pander the sizable superstitious vote, since it was carried out with no publicity, though the authorities might have had other reasons not to reveal their sources and informants. It was, in any event, part of the latest government and new majority policy, to be reiterated along with the old policy of no negotiations, of "leaving nothing untried." Moreover, it went far in proving one thing: Moro was not in an isolated place near Rome and a body of water. Indeed, according to later evidence, he was within a five-mile radius of the geographical center of the city.†

Of all the facts and fancies, by the thirtieth day, Saturday, April 15, only the ghost of Giorgio La Pira had offered some semblance of a clue to the disappearance of the president (Gradoli), and that had been wrongly interpreted. The rather inconclusive month was summed up by the think tank in its second report, which was issued that day. All the probability ratings gravitated around 50 per cent,

* This weapon is made of cardboard and is relatively harmless, but when exploded it causes instant temporary blindness and deafness.
† Strangely, the spirits would return to rattle at the beleaguered chief of police. On April 18, some ten days after the search at Gradoli, an apartment in Rome used as a base by the Red Brigades for the attack in Via Fani and occupied at least until April 17 would be discovered in a residential street called Via *Gradoli* (see p. 134).

meaning that Moro might survive but might not, negotiations either would or would not be forced open, and as for whether the prisoner had talked, maybe yes or maybe no.[2]

Crisis manager Steve Pieczenik went back to Washington. He was convinced, or said he was, that the Italians were managing their crisis in an exemplary fashion.

Cossiga, commenting that Saturday evening on the think tank's report, said that the "real troubles" were yet to arrive. In a matter of minutes, they arrived. Police chief Parlato, via the routine four-city channels, brought him the latest communiqué from the Red Brigades, the sixth in the series.

"The interrogation of prisoner Aldo Moro," it began, "has terminated. . . . As far as we are concerned, the trial of Aldo Moro ends here."

The people's tribunal pronounced its judgment:

Aldo Moro's responsibilities are the same as those for which this State is on trial. His guilt is the same as that for which the Christian Democrats and their regime will in the end be beaten, dissolved, and dispersed on the initiatives of the fighting communist forces. There are no doubts. ALDO MORO IS GUILTY AND IS THEREFORE SENTENCED TO DEATH [emphasis in original].[3]

Not a word from the man condemned. Not a word from the Red Brigades as to what might happen next. The question could not be repressed: When, if not done already, was the execution?

Cossiga was heard to say, "All right. Now we move."[4]

Cossiga moved. He telephoned Andreotti. The Prime Minister had just received a personal message from Jimmy Carter promising "my steadfast support" of the government's position,[5] so he knew he was traveling straight. Cossiga telephoned the Chief of State of Italy. President Leone had come under criticism in recent days for having held silent thus far, and there were suspicions that he might even be a dove under cover. This was true. But Leone, a Neapolitan lawyer who had climbed all the rungs of Christian Democracy, was so compromised in the Lockheed scandal and in other peccadillos yet unannounced that his freedom of independent action was seriously restricted.[6] His political future depended on the willingness of the other men of power to respect the code of *omertà*. Andreotti believed that the time had come for the Chief of State to speak, and an appointment was set for Leone to receive him and Cossiga the following morning immediately after Mass. Everything but Mass was cleared with the Communist Party.

The news of Aldo Moro's bad turn was long on the wires by now, and both Andreotti and Cossiga thought of fragile Zaccagnini. It being night and the weekend, Zaccagnini was very much alone in his office, brooding in the Square of Jesus. Cossiga dispatched his Under Secretary, Nicola Lettieri, to reanimate him, and a member of the Christian Democratic five-man directorate, Flaminio Piccoli, was summoned from a dinner party for the same purpose. According to one source, both Lettieri and Piccoli found Zaccagnini "prostrate across his desk, his eyes gaping, and almost incapable of speech."[7]

Piccoli took charge. A member of Parliament, he had been an editor of a local newspaper in Trent, his home ground, at the time Curcio and Cagol were at the university stirring the caldrons abrew with the Red Brigades. Moro had described Piccoli to his interrogators as a man basically without ill intentions, but "he has always made mistakes and always will because he is constitutionally attracted to error."[8]

Presumably something was done to nurse Zaccagnini back to a more erect posture, and Piccoli gave his reading of the new communiqué. He thought it hard to explain why the sentence had precipitated so abruptly. Many had forecast, including the men in the think tank, that the interrogation would produce the sporadic release of sensational disclosures about the misdeeds of this or that Christian Democrat, and there were reasons to believe that this would take a rather long time. But Communiqué VI, while declaring that the prisoner had confirmed the "despicable complicity" of the Christian Democrats in thirty years of wickedness, admitted frankly—and as it turned out, truthfully—that the trial elicited "no clamorous revelations." The communiqué had had to content itself with such phrases as "there are no secrets" and "what mysteries can there be" about so "putrid" a party as the Christian Democrats. The Red Brigades, despite all the mind-bending and arm-twisting tortures described by the media, had wrung nothing out of Aldo Moro that was not already known *ad nauseam* to the proletariat, they said, and not without an air of disappointment.

From all this, as well as the unexpected foreshortening of the affair and the absence of a message from Moro, Piccoli was led to speculate that perhaps the president had died of a sudden illness in the people's prison and the Red Brigades were playing on nothing but bluff. Or maybe they were planning to kill him on the thirtieth anniversary of Christian Democratic rule, which would fall on April 18, only three days away. Or was this a hammer blow to split the party the way Moro himself had counseled the family? Or might it be the signal for the doves to mobilize and march?

Zaccagnini knew less. Wracked, gutted, a visible ruin, he decided to raise the probability risk of negotiating with the Red Brigades.[9]

Flaminio Piccoli may or may not have been error-prone, but his suppositions were flawless. They were the same as those being posed everywhere in Rome.

In the penthouse in Via Forte Trionfale, however, no one could accept, much less discuss, the idea that Papà might already be dead. It was macabre to even imagine that the death sentence favored the family cause insofar as it might soften the talons of the hawks and spur the doves into motion. But the cliff-hanging verdict and the prisoner's mysterious silence seemed like mighty tactical support in Moro's overall design to return from the people's prison. In the grotesque logic of raw power under siege, it was the best news so far.

The family decided to press for an international solution. Giovanni Moro's February '74 group had been studying the prospects of an intervention by the International Red Cross, but this was found to be a complicated matter, and while it appeared promising because of a specific article in the Geneva Convention of 1949, it was entrusted to a consultant in international law, and was not yet ready for launching. A second possibility was the United Nations. Secretary General Kurt Waldheim was related by family ties to an Italian diplomat who had been Aldo Moro's *consigliere* in the Foreign Office. Contacted through this channel, Waldheim had agreed to co-operate, but the most effective way had yet to be determined. Third was the good offices of Amnesty International. This London-based human-rights organization had recently been awarded a

Nobel prize for peace. Unlike the Red Cross, the UN, and the Vatican, Amnesty had no authority sanctioned by international law. This could make it more palatable to the hard-liners, since any negotiations could be said to be "not official." This was a medicine the Christian Democrats might down.

It had rained on Saturday and it had rained on the days before, and it rained a wet fury on Sunday. In April, the Mediterranean climbs into the sky for a while; it falls on thousands of freshly pruned vineyards and olive groves, and when the soil has had a drink that may have to do until autumn, it swells the earth and then the rivers that carry it home to the sea.

Violently. A train derailed in a mudslide; forty-seven dead. Snow, wind, and rain invaded the North. The earth shook Sicily. An old woman died of fear. The Tiber rose higher than many of the graffiti scrawled on its embankments. Mercifully, it covered a claim that one side of the river was neo-Fascist territory complete with a Dantean warning to abandon hope all Communists who entered there. Another writing still bobbed on the water line: "As long as the violence of the state is called justice, the justice of the proletariat will be called violence." Only the violence of the gods offends no one but the victims.

It was a gloomy beginning, but it was a beginning. Everything that had happened before the death sentence seemed a prelude in the gray light of Sunday. Zaccagnini went to Mass in the Church of Jesus across the street from party headquarters. Here the devil was supposed to have entered when the Jesuits built their mother church four hundred years ago. Satan had been walking with the wind through the Square of Jesus, and when he, if "he" it is, came across the church, he wished to go inside to see if it were all the warrior Jesuits were vaunting. The wind agreed to wait outside, where it waits to this day, since the devil has yet to emerge. Which is why, Romans say, the Square of Jesus is the windiest square in town.

On this day, it all seemed true. The wind was beating the rain outside and the devil gnawed at the edges of Zaccagnini—caught in an intrusive photograph of him at prayer. He is wearing a dark, heavy overcoat, seated, doubled over, in an empty pew. His eyes are covered and he holds his head like a heavy stone in his hand.[10]

His party had come out that morning with a new resolve "to find a way at once" to save the president's life. But now those were words and words only, and Zaccagnini looked unrelieved. Privately, secretly, he had succumbed to the family's bidding. He had asked, or would ask sometime that day, Amnesty International to come to the president's aid.

The undeniable role of Prime Minister Andreotti as the Grand Spoiler of the family's labors in pursuit of a softer line became clear that Sunday.

Some days after the events in Via Fani, which had upset Andreotti to a degree that would only be revealed months later, he telephoned Mrs. Moro to extend his sympathy. He asked the president's wife if there were anything she needed. He asked her if she needed money. Mrs. Moro said no, the least of her reasons being that her husband had an income equivalent to about five thousand dollars a month, not to speak of his and her properties, and it did not appear likely that the Parliament, the party, or the university would cut off his salary while he was still alive. Nevertheless, it had gotten back to the family that a rumor was making the rounds in the places of power that she had asked the Prime Minister for a large sum of money, and the rumor within the rumor was that Andreotti himself had let the story be known. Lacking credibility, and completely unprovable, it was a rumor that did not travel well, but it did have the unfortunate effect of breaking direct communication between Mrs. Moro and Andreotti, since she did not reciprocate his first call, and he never phoned again.[11]

Andreotti's offer to Eleonora Moro was looked upon by the family as wanting in good taste, but they had no solid reason to believe that he would not respond positively if an all-around, face-saving solution could be found to ransom the kidnap victim. Certainly, a search for a middle ground was the present position of the party, or of Zaccagnini and many other Christian Democrats in high places, and this was what was meant by *Il Popolo*'s morning statement about finding a way. Later in the day and on Monday, however, the beginning signs appeared that the Prime Minister was executing a preventive policy of neutralizing what remained of Aldo Moro's and the family's powers.

On Sunday morning, as scheduled, Andreotti and Cossiga went to the Quirinal Palace, once the residence of popes and kings and now of Giovanni Leone. The Chief of State had already answered the attack on his silence in the Moro case, saying that he would only speak out to mediate dissent in the government or to call it to action should the need arise. This was a wise way of defending the presidential prerogatives, but that was yesterday. Now, in some undisclosed fashion, Leone was induced to issue a public message to Eleonora Moro, and within a couple of hours, she had it in hand. Leone, speaking for every Italian, said that the kidnappers were and would continue to be totally isolated from the entire nation. To tell this to a woman sharing precisely the same position as that of the Red Brigades on the matter of the release of her husband— that it was negotiable—was more revealing of Leone's meeting with Andreotti than of the true state of affairs.[12]

From the Quirinal, Andreotti and Cossiga went to a meeting in the Square of Jesus with Zaccagnini and the rest of the party directorate. Here it was decided to publish a special edition of *Il Popolo,* which normally did not appear on Monday. With the publication of the Sunday paper, word began to circulate that the party was softening, and that its appeal to find a way to rescue Moro was directed at the other parties, particularly the Communists, to join them. The correctives were released immediately. A Christian Democratic spokesman declared at a press conference that today's appeal was directed at no one,[13] though how this was possible was lost in the rush to print. What *Il Popolo* would say tomorrow went by teletype today. The weight of the party's solidarity was shifted noticeably from the presumably living president to all the dead victims of the Red Brigades. This emphasis was a theme that would characterize the presence, behind the scenes or on-camera, of Giulio Andreotti.

In the evening, another emergency repair job became necessary when it was somehow learned in Rome that Amnesty International would release an appeal on Monday, and that this was an appeal with an intended audience: the Red Brigades. For the first time, the word *discuss* was going to be unfrozen, and what Amnesty wanted to discuss were "the facts" that might lead to the prisoner's release. Furthermore, there were reports that the party itself had solicited the London organization.

This placed enormous pressure on the already decomposing links between the party and the family. On Sunday and Monday, prior to the issuance of Amnesty's appeal, there were multiple exchanges between the two, with Health Minister Tina Anselmi making five round trips from the Square of Jesus to Via Forte Trionfale. Anselmi, the only woman member of Andreotti's cabinet, was in the Moroite group in the party and she was considered a family friend. She was thought to be the contact person with Amnesty, which not only made the party look "bad" but also involved the government by virtue of her high office.

In London, Dick Oosting, Amnesty's vice secretary, suddenly found himself drawn into the vortex of Italian politics. The Christian Democrats and the government wanted disclaimers written into the appeal. From the Street of the Dark Shops, the Communists telephoned London to remind Amnesty of its own charter. They considered this development as "the antechamber to negotiations,"[14] and even with the disclaimers it would appear that the family was trying to leap over the hard line. Amnesty, London was told, could act nonofficially only and for nothing other than humanitarian purposes. Furthermore, the Communists warned, Amnesty had to be extremely careful not to confer any hint of political status on the Red Brigades, the consequences of which would be incalculable.

As a result, when Amnesty's statement came out on Monday it contained one or another kind of adulteration in three of its four paragraphs, appearing as though it had been written by an ecumenical committee that had included the Red Brigades. Within twenty-four hours the matter was completely forgotten.[15]

There were some things, however, that could not be "fixed," and the more the fixers bore down the more the untouchables felt called upon to act. On Sunday afternoon, Craxi visited Mrs. Moro to reassure her that the Socialist D-Day was coming. He had gained the tacit support of all but one of the factions in his party and would declare his position before this week was over. The following day, Fanfani raised his voice in the Senate. He expressed his "bitterness" about the poor reception accorded the "direct solicitations to take appropriate, timely, and democratic decisions to forestall feared events."[16] In Fanfanian language "direct solicitations" could be read, if one wished to, as the letters of Aldo Moro.

Neither could the Pope be fixed. The Holy Father in his Sunday-noon appearance in St. Peter's Square had said nothing about the

Moro death sentence. His silence left the Vatican-watchers bewildered. The Church-inspired but nonofficial relief organization Caritas Internationalis, which on that same busy Sunday presented itself as a willing mediator, was the Curia's latest substitute for a Vatican intervention, and this had been approved by the Christian Democrats. But Caritas would have even less impact than Amnesty, and Pope Paul favored another approach, of which the Curia was unaware. The Holy Father would authorize a highly secret mission seeking deep contact with the Red Brigades to learn just what within the powers of a Pope alone could he give them in exchange for a live Aldo Moro.

14.

Then, like a glove across the face of Rome, came Communiqué VII:

THE TRIAL OF ALDO MORO

Today, April 18, 1978, is the end of the dictatorial period of Christian Democracy, which for a full thirty years has ruled with wickedness and a heavy hand. Concomitant with this date, we announce the execution of the president of Christian Democracy, Aldo Moro, by means of "suicide." We consent to recovery of the corpse and give its exact location. Aldo Moro's corpse is immersed in the slimy bottom of Lake Duchessa (this is what he meant by getting bogged down) . . .

> In the name of Communism
> The Red Brigades[1]

This repulsive statement contained three additional sentences of scarce consequence as well as a hysterical "p.s." It was picked up midmorning by a reporter for *Il Messaggero* following telephoned instructions from a caller claiming to be speaking for the Red Brigades. Conforming to past procedure, the newsman turned over the material to an official of DIGOS (Division of General Investigations and Special Operations), which was the brand-new name for the political branch of the police. As with all the previous communiqués, the DIGOS personnel and the police laboratory began routinely to determine the authenticity, while the information it contained passed immediately to Cossiga's ministry—this time with an advisory that there were doubts at first sight about its authorship.[2]

In fact, Communiqué VII, it would be swiftly concluded, was a clumsy forgery of its predecessors. It had not been typed on the machine that the Red Brigades at the outset had said they would use throughout; it had been photocopied rather than mimeographed, and it had not been distributed in any of the other three cities. More transparent was the uninformed attempt to imitate the language and style of the *brigatisti*, as everyone familiar with these characteristics immediately recognized. All of the early news reports carried clear references to the communiqué's dubious origin.

Nevertheless, in the couple of morning hours while all this was being ascertained, there was some reason to suspect that the Red Brigades might be up to something devious and big.

At about the time the communiqué was revealed, the Rome fire department received an emergency call reporting a serious water loss in an unoccupied apartment on the north side of town. The leak had been discovered by the tenant below, whose bathroom was being flooded. When the firemen arrived, they entered the top-floor apartment by ladder, forcing a balcony door. The water was jetting full force from the shower, and the nozzle, propped in a horizontal position by a broomstick, was aimed at five wide cracks in the tiles. The leak was genuine, but someone had either purposely been trying to call attention to the apartment or was signaling something less obvious.

While the damage was being repaired, one of the firemen looked around the apartment. It was a modern, studio-type flat in an upper-middle-class district called Tomba di Nerone, or Nero's Tomb. The name of the winding street was Via Gradoli. On a divider that separated the tiny kitchen from the rest of the apartment, the fireman saw a bowl of fresh fruit and yesterday's newspaper, and on another shelf was a powerful radio, equipped to receive police bands, and several copies of a pamphlet with the stylized five-pointed star of the Red Brigades—a logo more common these days than the shape of a Coca-Cola bottle.

DIGOS was alerted, and within a half hour or so, the police had uncovered in closets, drawers, and from under the bed an enormous

cache of various types of hand weapons, ammunition, hand grenades and other explosives, bulletproof vests, police and military
uniforms, first-aid equipment and pharmaceuticals, counterfeit
identity documents, and a trunk full of automobile number plates,
one of which checked out as the original removed from the stolen
white Fiat 128 that had backed into Moro's car in Via Fani.

For a moment, it seemed they were in the people's prison, and
from a window in Via Gradoli they could look across an undeveloped tract of low hills and see the buildings in Via Forte
Trionfale. This notion was dispelled as quickly as it took to learn
from the neighbors that the apartment had been occupied by a
rather reserved young "engineer" and his female companion, who
rarely received visitors. Besides, there was no trace of anything that
might indicate that the prisoner had ever been present here.

The find in Via Gradoli was little more than a supply station for
the Rome column of the Red Brigades. The apartment had been
rented two years earlier, and the tenant, later identified as veteran
brigatista Mario Moretti, had fled when the water problem became
unmanageable. Cleaning the apartment of anything that might lead
the investigators elsewhere, Moretti, with the evanescent flair of
the older *brigatisti*, had staged the police "discovery" as a diver-
sionary maneuver.[3]

All this, except the identities of Moretti and friend, was known or
surmised in the Interior Ministry by midday, just as the falseness of
Communiqué VII was confirmed by a ground and helicopter
glance at Lake Duchessa, where Moro's body was said to be submerged.

The lake, fifty miles northeast of Rome, was tucked into a remote
snow-covered mountain at an altitude of six thousand feet. It would
have taken a band of Sherpas on snowshoes a whole day or a night
to have hauled Aldo Moro's body up the mountainside, longer if he
had been forced to climb with them alive. No one had been seen in
those parts since Easter. The inclement weather of recent days had
erased every old footprint and there were no fresh ones. Furthermore, Lake Duchessa, an uninviting glint to a bird's eye, was frozen
thick on the surface and had been for the past four months. To the
convoy on snowshoes, the Red Brigades would have had to have
added a team of frogmen equipped with explosives and heavy
weights to penetrate the ice and anchor the president's body to the

boggy bottom. The state official picked to direct the investigation reported after an aerial inspection of the area, "The body of Hon. Moro absolutely cannot be up there."[4]

Why, then, today's game, as programmed in the Interior Ministry, was played in one-on-one opposition to reality remains an enigma best left to the shamans of wishful thinking to ponder and unravel. Months later, someone would recount how frightened the men of power looked when, on another occasion, a rumor of Moro's release had spread; now they would act piously relieved.

Against the visiting team of reality, Rome, managed by Cossiga and diverse coaches, decided to play down the "doubts" about the new communiqué and play up the "breakthrough" in Via Gradoli. The playing up came by the simple omission of the shower-and-broomstick detail, which of course withheld the design and thus the insignificance of the discovery. The playing down was accomplished when in the early afternoon both Cossiga's and Andreotti's political Under Secretaries declared, respectively, that the announcement of Aldo Moro's execution had to be considered reliable and "we feel this dramatic certainty in our heart."[5] Whereupon, Enrico Berlinguer added sting to the drama by theatrical gesture. The Communist chieftain and a small, heavily guarded entourage went by traffic-stopping foot to the Square of Jesus to pay their respects to Zaccagnini and Andreotti, who was already at his grieving party secretary's side.[*] Twenty minutes later, Berlinguer told reporters waiting for him at the elevator, "We have brought the solidarity of our party to the Christian Democrats, Zaccagnini, and the Moro family."[7]

They had promised to leave nothing untried, and so, while the men of power mourned tentatively, they sent two thousand lawmen to look for the president's body. Police ski squads and mountaineers on snowshoes climbed through subfreezing fog and twelve feet of snow to reach Lake Duchessa, while Chinook helicopters dropped frogmen from an ugly sky. Electronic underwater detection devices

---

[*] Berlinguer's shadow Minister of Interior, Senator Pecchioli, had received the news on his direct telephone line to Cossiga. Pecchioli was an experienced mountaineer and he ridiculed the idea, given the prevailing climatic conditions, that Moro's body could have been dumped in Lake Duchessa, but that was said on a calmer day.[6]

were lowered through holes blasted in the ice, and the frogmen, in their orange-trim rubber suits, went down the same holes to rake the muck below. As for the less hardy, the uninvited, and people with nothing more urgent in their day, they could follow it all on color TV.

The announcement of Moro's death refocused world attention on Rome and its nearby mountain lakes. Provisional regrets and solidarity arrived without hesitation from around the globe. The full-blown obituaries were in a holding pattern in newsrooms East and West on both sides of the equator, and in the meantime the mass and not-so-mass media sought to bring the public up to date.

Even in the best of circumstances, foreign press coverage of second-rate powers is rarely more than second-rate, based as it usually is on official and secondhand sources. Now, however, this shortcoming, innocuous most of the time, became yet another pollutant as it wafted back to the Roman air.

When, for example, *Time, Newsweek,* and the Washington *Post,* not to speak of the British and continental press, gave prominence to the notion of Aldo Moro being morally and spiritually destroyed, much of this was reported back to Rome in translation by Italian foreign correspondents. The casual reader in Italy might have seen it as "confirmation" of what was being said at home, but more important—since it invariably reappeared in the parliamentary press review—it was read by the men of power as uncritical support for the government's line. Rome had become a star enchanted by the studio's publicity.[8]

To make matters worse, the lack of comprehension abroad reinforced the general worldwide indifference to the fate of Aldo Moro. James Reston, writing in the New York *Times* at the time of the Lake Duchessa body hunt, made headlines in Italy with his suggestion that Moro, cast in the past tense, was only a symbol of a problem. The problem was the Soviet Union, which was responsible for international terrorism, including the Red Brigades. He let it be known that the Carter administration "is trying to say to Moscow that what happened to Mr. Moro could happen to anybody" and to stop "financing the terrorists and getting into a serious confrontation in Africa, Europe, and the Middle East."[9]

In a dispatch from New York, veteran U.S. correspondent for

Rome's *Messaggero*, Lucio Manisco, called Reston's article "disconcerting . . . an analysis that seems inspired by a seven-martini
lunch." Manisco also expressed concern that "instant experts"—
foreign reporters on special assignment in Rome to cover the Moro
case—were disorientating American public opinion.[10] It was Reston's not Manisco's article that was reprinted in the parliamentary
press digest,[11] however, and with Moscow accusing Washington
and Peking for the violence of the Red Brigades, Rome looked and
felt off the hook.

Berlinguer extended his condolences to the family no farther than
Zaccagnini, but Zaccagnini felt he had to face Eleonora Moro in
person. This would not be easy. The scene at Christian Democratic
headquarters was material for students of eschatology or the Second Coming. Men and women were weeping in the hallways. The
media, cluttering the Renaissance courtyard, found many people
struck dumb. The traffic of high officials to and from Zaccagnini's
third-story office was almost as dense as the crowd in the piazza
outside. Transistor radios, tuned to Lake Duchessa and Via Gradoli, were stuck by many an ear.

Zaccagnini was described that day by a fellow Christian Democrat coming down from his office as having no illusions about the
president's fate. Zaccagnini was well composed, it was said, and
every now and then he opened up, remembering the old days with
Aldo Moro, only to grow tense again whenever his phone rang. He
went to the penthouse with his personal physician.[12]

Via Forte Trionfale was as jammed with police, newsmen, and
onlookers as the other theaters of operations, though a great deal
more funereal. The street was choked with vehicles that could do
no better than crawl, but no one dared sound a horn. A woman reporter keeping a day-long watch on the visitors to the family noted
the order of procession. Zaccagnini came and went within ten minutes, appearing as he left, she said, "terrified and still incredulous."
His call, or perhaps the look on his face, was interpreted by observers as a confirmation that he had brought official news of "the
worst."

After Maria Fida, Moro's oldest daughter, arrived with her baby,
Luca, "the little one," the reporter climbed to the top floor of an ad-

jacent building to try, she said, "to steal an image of the family's intimacy." She gave the following account:

> But the only thing we see is a normal apartment, a long terrace rounding the penthouse. All the windows are open, and through the curtains we see bookshelves reaching as high as the ceiling. The huge rectangular terrace is deserted. There's a swing without cushions, a hammock, some folded lounge chairs, and geraniums that haven't yet flowered. Beyond the living-room windows, we make out some shapes. Someone gets up, then sits down again. . . . We see a person with white hair, standing, pacing back and forth, but we're too far away to figure out who it is.[18]

From this and a hard day's legwork she felt she could say that the family was holding up well, and that holding up the family was a "memorably courageous" Eleonora Moro. Her fantasy was near enough to fact, but the anguish in the Moro household did not concern Communiqué VII.

No one but the willing believers could easily succumb to the gross cruelty of that senseless document. Later, the Red Brigades would accuse Andreotti and his "accomplices" as the perpetrators of Communiqué VII, and the men of power would return the blame to the accusers. But it is extremely doubtful that either version is true. If the Red Brigades had wished to draw some advantage by throwing the enemy off balance, as was charged, they would neither have mimicked themselves so poorly nor have chosen a site so ludicrously unreachable as Lake Duchessa. On the other hand, there is no conceivable gain that might have accrued to the hardliners. One could be driven momentarily to loathe the terrorists more than ever, but that would only shift one's sympathy nearer the victim, and when the terrorists would make themselves heard the pressure to negotiate could be expected to heighten.

That Communiqué VII was not taken for what it most assuredly was—an anonymous, contemptuous hoax—is a good measure of how much warp there was in those days in the collective state of mind.

The problem faced by the family on that day of premature bereavement was how to communicate the solid fact that the president in one breathing piece could still be brought home. If anyone were to know whether Aldo Moro was dead or alive, it would be Mrs. Moro. The existence of the telephone contacts between the Red Brigades and the family, and the transmission of private letters from Aldo Moro to his wife, had been publicly revealed. These exchanges, in fact, were generally thought to be far more extensive than they actually were. Yet almost no one listened when the family tried to report on the status of the president's situation.

For days, at least since the death sentence, they had been working in vain to interest the press in their news. To be sure, they wished to present it in the form of a broadly signed petition. They had gathered a large number of signatures, and among them were distinguished names at home and abroad, including a Nobel laureate, prominent Church figures, and even two prestigious members of the Communist Party. The appeal was addressed to the Red Brigades to spare their prisoner and to the state to slacken its intransigence. It was the latter clause that offended, and thus when every major newspaper refused to print it,[14] they were merely exercising their rights—though such exercise may not always be a virtue, and in this case it was lumpen journalism.

Only when the family began to feel at a loss did Giovanni Moro's cultural revolutionaries hazard the suggestion of going to the small dailies of the extreme left. One such newspaper, a Rome tabloid called Lotta Continua, or Continuous Struggle, had recently come out unequivocally for negotiations. It was more popular than the others, especially among university students, and had a national circulation. It also enjoyed a certain back-door respectability in establishment political circles. Known to report what the men of power preferred to leave unsaid, it was usually digested in the daily press review prepared by Parliament and scrupulously read by Andreotti and everyone else in charge.

Nothing but the Red Brigades themselves, however, could have been farther removed from the family of Aldo Moro than the likes of Lotta Continua. Lotta Continua was also the name of a political party in the ultraleft that had precisely the same origins as the Red Brigades, the great distinction being their mutual repudiation some years back. Lotta Continua was a revolutionary movement within the Movement that had abjured armed violence at this "stage" of the class struggle. It believed in organizing the proletariat against the bourgeoisie by democratic means. In effect, however, the only

thing continuous about Lotta Continua and its homonymic newspaper was its interminable and implacable critique of the revi-
sionist Communist Party, and the irascible party rarely resisted re-
sponding, as the elephant shoos the fly.

As a consequence of this lopsided feud and Lotta Continua's
equal abhorrence of the Red Brigades, the sharply edited tabloid
had made itself the staunchest supporter of Aldo Moro's cause.
With nothing to lose but its chains, it had been conducting a unique
and fearless campaign against the hard line.

On the morning of the eighteenth, it had come out prior to the
release of Communiqué VII with a somewhat prophetic editorial.
Entitled "In Search of a Martyr," it accused the Christian Democrats as being a party in need of an illustrious cadaver and the
Communists of bad faith in their "firmness." If the Red Brigades
were thinking of avenging thirty years of Christian Democracy on
this anniversary day, said *Lotta Continua*, "let them bear in mind
that the execution of Aldo Moro would only be a repetition of [the
party's triumph] of April 18, 1948."[15]

This was not very different from the family's thinking, not to
mention Aldo Moro's, and when hirsute editor-in-chief Enrico
Deaglio was contacted at his tousled offices in a Roman working-
class district, he agreed to do "as much as possible."[16]

On the following day, while the operations at Lake Duchessa
were running up a bill for the state of some $350,000, and the lead-
ing dailies were wearing out the letters that spell *anguish, Lotta
Continua* published what the family thought of the provisional
demise of Aldo Moro. "Notwithstanding Communiqué No. 7 . . ."
they said, "we in fact believe that there are legitimate reasons to
suspect . . . a different truth." Since the only different truth about
death is life, they apparently had not felt the necessity to elaborate;
nor did they give the motives for their suspicions, which in any
case were only circumstantial.

Their brief assessment had been inserted into the appeal. Although *Lotta Continua* had disclosed that the document had originated "in circles close to the Moro family," it was not signed by
anyone in the family camp but only by those who had subscribed,
the majority after having been solicited by Giovanni Moro's group.
Among the non-Italians was novelist Heinrich Böll and economist
Paulo Freyre, but the signatories were mainly Italians of national

renown. Of the state, they asked that it eschew its "fideistic and fet-ishist" defense of its institutions and rather allow these institutions to express the troubled reality of the times. It was a short plea for tolerance on all sides, for meeting halfway, for cooling down, for joining hands, for affirming the supremacy of one old and battered life over the latest, chrome-trimmed accessory for a throwaway po-litical class.[17]

The reaction of such an appeal by the persons it was directed at was about as predictable as nightfall. The newspapers that had rejected it in the first instance remained more or less consistent. The Communist *Paese Sera* published a "summary," which dropped all the references to the state. The official party paper, however, went a long way to overstate and magnify the expurgated part, but only to disown the thinking of the two Communist signers, saying that they had not cleared such thoughts with the Central Committee.[18]

Nevertheless, the reputations of the signatories and the diversity of the views they represented gave the appeal a thrust of moral au-thority that had a striking effect in the tug-of-war on the hard line. It added impetus to both sides and exhausted the weak all the more.

15.

On Thursday, April 20, after persistent reports about a body that had, or perhaps had not, been found at Lake Duchessa, a telephone rang in Rome.

"This is the Red Brigades," said the caller.

He paused, hearing the unmistakable sounds of a line routinely tapped.

"How many little games do you have to play?"

The person at the other end of the line, an editor at *Il Messaggero*, assured the *brigatista* that none of the "games" were his or his newspaper's.

"All right. Anyway, we're claiming the attack last night against the 11th Mechanized Brigade of the Carabinieri. We're claiming it officially. Understand?"*

"Okay."

"Now, we've got a message for you. Communiqué VII. The real

* Here the Red Brigades are taking responsibility for a grenade assault on a police barracks north of Rome, the residence of General Dalla Chiesa, ideator of the maximum-security antiterrorist holding centers—"concentration camps" to the *brigatisti*. Raids on persons and property, in accordance with the February "strategic resolution," were taking place throughout the Moro case. That morning, for example, the vice commander of the San Vittore prison guard was assassinated in Milan as a "torturer." Since the Via Fani attack, two other men—one the ex-Christian Democratic mayor of Turin—had been shot in the legs (the infamous "kneecapping"), and a third man, a "sadistic" prison guard where the Curcio group was being held, had been killed. In that incident, the victim managed to seriously wound a *brigatista*, who was later left at a hospital by his comrades.

one. It's in Via dei Maroniti, back entrance of the Upim [department store], just after it, against the wall, in a trash can. There's a photo, too. But run. Otherwise Cossiga's houseboys will get there before you."[1]

Someone ran. The material was in a manila envelope beside a *trattoria* less than a hundred yards from the *Il Messaggero* building at one of the busiest intersections of Rome. Cossiga's "houseboys" ran last. The communiqué, but not the photograph, had already been released in the northern cities, and the afternoon newspapers were coming out with front-page "buts" that Moro may be dead anyway.

He was alive. Ten days had passed since last he had been heard from, thirty-three since seen. As in the first photograph, he appears before the standard of the Red Brigades. He has been tried and convicted in the meantime, and in many ways not only in the people's prison. His hair has grown longer. He appears rounder, less drawn than before. The differences between the two photographs seem to end here, but to those who knew him well, particularly to whom he was dear, there was a world of subtle changes. In the first photograph, his face, his countenance, his bearing unite like atoms to raise a question; he asks the men of power what are their intentions, and sitting as someone quietly ailing might sit in the outer office of an overworked physician, he waits for a reply. Few people had ever seen Aldo Moro as he is in the second photograph. He leans forward now, taut, a step or two less than combative. His look is a look engraved in stone. His question has been answered and is gone. His eyes seek out the camera lens, as though he wills that no one may avoid his penetrating stare. He accuses. He threatens. He has spoken unburdening volumes at his trial. He seems released from an intricately woven past, a net. He seems renewed. Steeled. He holds a newspaper in his hands, and though his hands are not visible and would give a factlet to be barked at as a sign of a montage, he lays this as his claim to life against the death-wish mood on the outside. It is yesterday's *La Repubblica*, and we know this at once, not by the date, which is illegible, but by the inky headline. Stretched between two ads for J and B scotch whiskey are the words: MORO ASSASSINATED?

MORO IS ALIVE was the streamer *Il Messaggero* went to press with now, bringing out a special edition that afternoon. The photograph and Communiqué VII were reproduced on the front page, and the originals went to the police. All the men of power were notified immediately in the usual fashion. A wirephoto of the new Polaroid and the text of the communiqué were teletyped to the headquarters of all the political parties. The meetings began anew. The good but chilled Samaritans at Lake Duchessa were sent home. In the labor of it all no one thought of showing the photograph to the prisoner's wife, though at 7 P.M., hours after the picture had been retrieved, a policeman on duty at the Moro home brought her several copies of the *Il Messaggero* extra. "Signora Moro was very relieved," the officer said.[2]

Earlier in the day, the family had had word of the communiqué, and the text had been acquired and studied in the afternoon. Unknown to the others, they had also received two new letters from Papà, to be read and delivered to men he hoped to enlist to his cause. From their evaluation of all this material, the family knew now that they would have to haul out all their reserves over the next forty-eight hours. Forty-eight hours, beginning at 3 P.M. on Thursday—when the photographic proof that Moro was alive was in hand—was the amount of time the new communiqué had given the Christian Democrats to decide and reply whether or not they would pay more than tears and hortatory words for the life of their president.

> The time has come [said Communiqué VII] when Christian Democracy can no longer shirk its own political responsibilities. It can choose whoever it wants as accomplices, but on trial first of all is this foul party, this lurid organization of State power. As far as Aldo Moro is concerned, we repeat—the Christian Democrats can pretend not to understand but they will not succeed in changing the matter—that he is a political prisoner condemned to death. . . . The problem to which Christian Democracy must respond is political and not one of humanity, a humanity which it does not possess, which it cannot erect as a façade to hide behind, and which, when proclaimed by its bosses, sounds like an insult.

The word *humanity* on the mouths of the Red Brigades did not look like lipstick; nor did it sound much better, but at least they were ruling it out on both sides. In a lengthy exposition of the severe conditions in the antiguerrilla prison system, with charges of "political genocide" not only in Italy but also throughout Western Europe, the Red Brigades, following the Curcio group, compared this with how they had treated Aldo Moro ("scrupulously, as a political prisoner and with all the rights that qualification confers; nothing more but also nothing less"). This was the matter that had to be negotiated. They said:

An essential part of our political program is the freedom of all communist prisoners.

For the first time in the entire ungodly affair, they spoke now of Moro's freedom:

The release of Aldo Moro can be taken into consideration only in relation to the FREEDOM OF COMMUNIST PRISONERS.

Let the Christian Democrats give *a clear and definitive* reply whether they intend to pursue this path. Let it also be clear that there are no other possibilities. [Emphases in original.]

They had until 3 P.M. on Saturday, April 22, to do so, and if they did not, the Red Brigades would answer to no one but the Movement, "assuming the responsibility of carrying out the sentence handed down by the People's Tribunal."[3]

All the world turns when they hear an ultimatum, and when the clocks were consulted, from the digital blinks in Tokyo to the old sundial outside the Chamber of Deputies in Rome, they saw that the countdown was on.

The trouble with ultimatums is that they expose the weaknesses on both sides. The receiver is forced to take a position, which, because of the time limit, brings out *all* the dissent in his own ranks, and his position risks being overthrown. The giver, having already admitted in his one-last-chance-to-be-good offer that he fears he may lose, now has no more moves, cards, chips, or whatever. Given the tick of the clock, this is the sort of scenario, when the stakes are right, that packs the Super Bowls of this or that high drama. The grand finale, the denouement, the no-draw ending, catharsis, and even an Aesopian moral are all built in. This is also the reason why some ultimatums are less ultimate than others.

The think tank was finding the "faults" in the latest photograph (the missing hands, etc.), which could prove useful in a stalling, give-us-more-proof maneuver, but an educated reading of the ultimatum would have been a more profitable expenditure of thinking time.

The Red Brigades in finally announcing their long-awaited demands had asked a great deal less than was feared. In the first place, they had completely discharged the government or any other official entity of the state from the arena of the negotiations. Although Christian Democracy, by virtue of pervasiveness, influence, and good fortune at the polls, had become identified with the state, it was still nothing more than a political party, and thus a private, nongovernmental organization. A nationwide sounding of public opinion, taken about ten days earlier, showed that 60 per cent of Italians polled were in favor of negotiations with the Red Brigades, as long as the government was not involved.[4] This in spite of the 100 per cent rejection by the mass-circulation press and the state-owned radio and television networks. If there was a poll-watching wing in the Red Brigades, it had succeeded in imposing a still more cautious approach when the Christian Democratic Party was told that it could choose whatever "accomplices" it liked. The implication was that it could delegate the stigma of dealing with the *brigatisti* to a neutral, unsulliable third party, such as Amnesty or Caritas.

Moreover, Moro's party was being asked to merely reply whether it intended to pursue a path, and at the end of the path lay only the *freedom* (*liberazione*) of communist prisoners unspecified in name or number in exchange for the *release* (*rilascio*) of Aldo Moro. Considering the incessant references to "physical, psychological, and political annihilation" said to be going on in the special prisons, to speak of freedom for their comrades in relation to the actual release of their prisoner was a clear indication that the Red Brigades would accept something less than they were willing to give.† "Release" has only one possible meaning in this context; "Freedom" has many. It could mean the freedom to choose one's cellmate, to

† It was also a signal that at the moment the minimalist, soft line was holding sway in the strategic command. The larger objective of uniting the Movement had been recognized by now as failed. The Moro operation in the end would divide it more than ever (see pp. 267–68), and the evidence was accumulating rapidly. The communiqués had already dropped the entire affair, concentrating totally on cracking the power front in Rome.

speak with one's wife or family without the use of a sometimes bugged intercom between a plate-glass separation, or to spend a little more time in the sun—all of which were being fought for by the 175 *brigatisti* in the hands of the state.

Finally, the ultimatum, which would bring on the quickening of respiration as the hours dissolved into minutes, then seconds, had threatened foxily. The Red Brigades, in the absence of a reply of intent from the Christian Democrats, would respond by "assuming the responsibility" of carrying out the sentence, which was something less than actually carrying it out. This was also muscle-flexing. If they were willing first now to "pursue a path" of unspecified length, the Red Brigades apparently felt that the people's prison was secure and that time was on their side. It was in the Christian Democrats' own interest, they seemed to be saying, that a quick deal would save the party from further erosion and spare the police operations of further embarrassment.

All this, however, was only one interpretation of Communiqué VII. Others would see it very much like the head of the GR2 radio network news, Gustavo Selva. He was keeping a diary in those days, and in the predawn hours of April 21, he made the following entry in the editorial "we":

> We are watching the hands of the clock moving, and we're thinking of those forty-eight hours—a good ten of which are gone—and the expiry of the ultimatum set by the Red Brigades with icy dryness: Free the communist prisoners or else we execute the death sentence. . . . The anguish for the fate of Moro, somewhat eased in knowing that fortunately he's alive, has been immediately replaced by the terrible dilemma, to deal or not to deal. There are those whose reply is decided, and they have no doubts. No deals . . .[5]

At the same moment that Selva was going on to reaffirm his belief in the righteousness of the nondoubters, *La Repubblica* was preparing an even less complex interpretation for that morning's opinion consumers:

> It is a matter of the sacrifice of the life of a man or the loss of the republic. Unfortunately, for democrats the choice leaves no room for doubt.[6]

Of the many possible ways to read the ultimatum, however, the first, longer version, given above, was the only correct way; it was the interpretation being given openly and privately, to anyone who cared to listen, by sources in touch with the Red Brigades.

One of the very few who listened was a former chaplain of San Vittore Prison in Milan, an aging priest named Don Angelo Curione. Many *brigatisti* had passed through San Vittore on their way to the special prisons, and while Father Curione himself had never heard their confessions, he had come to know the man who had. His name was Eduardo Di Giovanni, a slim, forty-seven-year-old Sicilian attorney who had been carrying out a continuous legal defense of captured *brigatisti* since the first arrest, which was that of Renato Curcio. Di Giovanni, his taciturn associate Giovanna Lombardi, and two or three other lawyers in Italy were the repository of the deepest confidences of the Red Brigades, and the Sicilian had also been indicted as their accomplice—a charge, however, that was later dismissed by the courts.

Of this group of lawyers, Di Giovanni was part of a *de facto* triumvirate who were acting as unofficial interpreters of the often arcane thinking of the Red Brigades, and until now they had been interpreting with micrometric accuracy. The other two men were Giannino Guiso (Craxi's source) and a battle-scarred Milanese named Sergio Spazzali, both of whom were engaged in the Curcio trial in Turin. Di Giovanni, maintaining far less visibility than the others, was in Rome.

The son of a man who had dueled undefeatedly to defend his honor in the Sicilian dawn, and the grandson of a combative senator (still alive at 103), Di Giovanni may be described as one of those fighting communists the Red Brigades were trying at such bloody expense to unite, though he did his fighting exclusively in court. He later recalled his meeting with the ex-chaplain as beginning when at the time of the ultimatum he walked into his offices in a residential part of town and found Don Angelo sitting patiently in the waiting room.

"What can *we* do?" asked the priest when they had retired to the lawyer's study and he had explained the object but not the origin of his call.

"He didn't say who 'we' were, and I didn't ask," Di Giovanni would remember, "but from the way he spoke, I knew who had sent him."

With an equal measure of tact, Don Angelo would not question the authority of the Sicilian's reply, though, for his part, he claimed only to be speaking for himself.

So it was that in the confines of an office bombed by neo-Fascist terrorists in 1974 and watched now by great danes, the personal emissary of the Vicar of Christ met with a trustee of the Red Brigades, and neither would part the worse for it.

"I told him," said Di Giovanni, "that the Red Brigades were seeking above all some sort of recognition of their political identity." This could be accomplished by a prisoner exchange but it was not the only way. His colleagues in Turin were already suggesting that a change in the prison regimen or even a sign of the Red Brigades' existence as an armed political enemy might be sufficient. What hurt was the brand of a common criminal or of *indiscriminate* terrorism.

The pathetic yearning of the Red Brigades for certification by the state as though they were a group of lobbyists or a new kind of charity appears to have been lost on everyone. As for what the Pope would do, given this situation, neither Di Giovanni, Don Angelo, nor anyone could possibly foresee.[7]

16.

Since the ultimatum, according to the more picturesque press reports, Pope Paul had not missed a single television newscast and in between kept a radio going while remaining in constant communication with the Christian Democrats and the government. Most of the information about the Pope was emanating from Vatican spokesman Monsignor Romeo Panciroli, but by now, like all of Rome, the Holy See was sharply divided into many hawks and few doves, and what the Vatican, particularly *L'Osservatore Romano,* was saying about the Pope was much less reliable than usual.

On the other hand, the Holy Father had probably not told anyone on the Curia side about Don Angelo's mission or that the Pope's private secretary, Monsignor Pasquale Macchi, had met a messenger from the family in the early hours of the ultimatum to collect one of the two latest letters from Aldo Moro.

In the Apostolic Palace, Paul VI withdrew from the clattering instruments of telecommunications. He retired to the papal chambers to read the president's news:

Most Holy Father,

In my very difficult circumstances, and remembering the paternal benevolence Your Holiness has often bestowed upon me . . . I am emboldened to turn to Your Holiness in the hope that you may wish to encourage in the most suitable way at least the start of a process for an exchange of prisoners. . . .

I can imagine the anxieties of the government. But I must point out that this humanitarian practice is in use by very many governments, who give priority to the salvation of human lives, and to satisfy their sense of security, provide for the removal from the national territory of the prisoners from the other side. Besides, dealing as we are with acts of guerrilla warfare, I do not see how there can be any other effective form of reducing tension in a situation that promises terrible times.

Having come across a stern article in *L'Osservatore Romano* here in my prison, I am deeply concerned because whose voice, if not the Church's can fracture the crystallization of views that has been formed by now; what higher humanism is there than Christianity? Therefore, my prayers, my hopes, and those of my family, whom Your Holiness some years ago benevolently wished to receive, are addressed to Your Holiness, the only person who can turn the Italian Government toward a gesture of wisdom. . . .*

Aldo Moro[1]

The effect this letter had on Pope Paul is known: With all the elements he had now assembled and under the burdens that had been mounted on his old frame, he began to draft a message that would quake the power in Rome.

At the urging of the family, but also spontaneously, all of the forces in favor of a negotiated solution to the plight of Aldo Moro began in the early hours of the ultimatum to move to the front.

The first shot fired was the loudest. Bettino Craxi, in the second or third hour, taking even his own party by surprise, released a statement breaking off the Socialists from the hard line. He would have a difficult time tomorrow at a meeting of the party directorate, but his timing was devastating.[2]

Beyond the walls of the Vatican, ten Italian bishops and arch-

---

* In a closing paragraph, Moro referred to a precedent well known to the Pope, in which he himself as Monsignor Montini had an active role. In that case, Pope Pius XII, during the German occupation of Rome in 1944, personally intervened to obtain the release of an Italian being held by the Germans in the city as a political prisoner. His name was Giuliano Vassalli, and he had risen to prominence in Rome. He would shortly enter the picture on the Aldo Moro side (see pp. 179–80).

bishops added their names to the family-inspired appeal in the ultra-leftist *Lotta Continua*. The presidium of the Conference of Italian Bishops, a national organization, asked the intransigents to "desist." Adopting the same phrase as the ultimatum, it said that the search for accord was the just "path to pursue."[3]

Two former Italian Chiefs of State, now Senators Giovanni Gronchi and Giuseppe Saragat, declared themselves on the side of the soft line. Gronchi, a Christian Democrat, signed a document for which the names of other Christian Democratic parliamentarians were being collected by the family for presentation to the party before the ultimatum ran out. Ex-President Saragat, of the Social Democrats, said, "the thing to do is negotiate."[4]

The hawks were being driven over to the defensive, and the hardest blows were coming. It suddenly seemed insufficient to merely reiterate state intransigence for its own sake. There were too many doubters among the nondoubters, too many potential defectors. The old bulwarks were crumbling. Lights would burn late again.

For years, Benigno Zaccagnini had a craggy vertical crease on the right side of his face, a crevice in a jowl of tired flesh. But in recent days, it had sunk, and when on the night before the ultimatum he went on television to speak brokenly of his party's "terrible days," it had seemed a trembling abyss. He had been in the Resistance during World War II. He was a physician. He had a son not much older than Giovanni Moro, he too involved in counterculture politics. Benigno Zaccagnini's celebrated honesty was as real as party life allowed. He had been called the Pope John of Christian Democracy, and if Aldo Moro had rejected Isaacian passivity in the test of faith demanded by the fantasy of power, someone, it seemed, had to fill what was missing. Someone, as Moro himself had suggested, had to go spiritually to the place where the president was only physically present.

In the fourth hour of the ultimatum, Zaccagnini crossed the Square of Jesus to attend a *messa della speranza,* or a Hope Mass, in the church of the Jesuits, and when he returned, at about 7 P.M., there was a message on his desk from Eleonora Moro. She asked the party to save her husband's life, in whose hands she believed it lay exclusively now.[5] She had also sent along the second of the letters she had received that day, addressed as it was to Zaccagnini.

Now it would be Zaccagnini and his party to want a letter from Aldo Moro held secret.

The stony, unpitying, accusatory face in the photograph sprung to life, as Moro went after Zaccagnini with the stiletto of his ire. It was almost as if he was determined that Zaccagnini had to share his destiny. Only to him would he speak in this fashion, though he used him as a stepping-stone to address himself to the entire leadership in the Square of Jesus. He began on a note of mordant sarcasm ("I still allow myself to invoke my title as party president"), then he said: "Certainly the country is faced with problems, and I do not want to ignore them, but there are also fair solutions . . . and in fact against the problems of the country there are problems that regard my person and my family." He went on:

> I do not believe you can rid yourself of these problems, neither in the present nor before history, with the ease, with the indifference, with the cynicism you have shown until now. . . . Voices of dissent, inevitable in a democratic party like ours, have been artificially held back. My own unfortunate family has, in a certain sense, been suffocated, unable to cry out desperately their pain and their need of me. Is it possible that everyone is in agreement in wanting my death for some presumed reason of State which someone lividly suggests almost as a solution to all of the country's problems?†

The hard line, Moro said, would bring on anything but a solution. He made a prophecy:

> If this crime is perpetrated, a terrible spiral will emerge, which you will be unable to manage. You will be overwhelmed by it. You will be split off from the humanitarian forces that still exist in this country. You will cause, in spite of first appearances, a fracture in the party, which you will not be able to dominate.

In a passage that followed, he reminded the party of his constituency, of the voters who identified Christian Democracy with him personally, of his politically powerful friends—of all the people who, we know from other letters, he was at this moment wondering

---

† In this case, "someone" is an unmistakable allusion to the Communist Party, although in other letters Moro hints (correctly) at pressures on his party coming via Cossiga from West Germany, and the United States (see pp. 281–83).

to the core of his troubled soul whether they had ever existed and where on earth they had gone. With Zaccagnini, however, his pen was the vector of strength only.

I tell you clearly: for my part, I will absolve and I will justify no one. . . . Any opening, however problematic the position, any immediate sign of awareness of the magnitude of the problem, in these hours that are flying, would be extremely important. . . .

Declare at once that you do not accept the simple and immediate reply, the reply of death. Dissipate at once the impression of a party united in a decision of death. . . . Whether the sentence is executed depends on all of you. . . .

If you do not intervene, you will be writing a cold-blooded page in the history of Italy. My blood will fall on all of you, on the party, on the country.

Think it over, dear friends. Be independent. Don't watch tomorrow. Watch the days after tomorrow.

So much for the leaders as a group. The rest was for Zaccagnini alone:

Think it over, you too, Zaccagnini, chief executive. Remember in this moment—it must be stinging for you to remember it—your extraordinary insistence . . . on making me responsible for the new [political] phase being opened and known to be very difficult. Remember how strongly I resisted, above all for family reasons everyone was aware of. Then I gave in, as always, to the will of the party. And here I am, at death's door, for having said yes to you, and yes to Christian Democracy. You have, then, a very personal responsibility. Your yes or your no will be decisive. But you should also know that if you take me again from my family, you will have willed it twice. From this weight, you will never unburden yourself anymore.

May God enlighten you, dear Zaccagnini, and enlighten the friends to whom I address this despairing message. . . .

Thanks and cordially yours,

Aldo Moro[6]

Zaccagnini left party headquarters at two o'clock in the morning in the company of his fellow leaders. He was silent and he appeared unseeing. The others told long-waiting reporters that he had had a letter from Moro, but it was in the hands of the police investigators as a clue and would thus be kept secret. The party secretary went home in his Alfa. The newspaper *Lotta Continua*, then on the presses, had no more inkling of the contents of the letter than the other dailies, but it expressed in a headline what all the men of power either feared or relied on. It said: "Now the life of Aldo Moro is in the hands of Benigno Zaccagnini."[7]

17.

In the twenty-first hour of the ultimatum, which fell on the edge of a dreary Friday morning, Bettino Craxi went before the leadership of his party to explain his heresy. It was a day of heresies revisited, in which the nonconformist positions were being evaluated, when not abhorred, and one sorrowful man—a member of the Communist Party's Central Committee who had signed the appeal in *Lotta Continua*—was persuaded by his comrades to publicly recant ("no, we must not negotiate, to negotiate is impossible").[1] Important figures in the Socialist Party had known that Craxi was soft on the hard line, but now he had made himself an embarrassment. Craxi, however, faced his own peers, some of whom were second to none in indignation, with more resolve than the penitent Communist and a great deal more leverage.

A protégé of Pietro Nenni, the dean of Italian socialism, Craxi came to the meeting with a letter in his pocket from another grand old man in his party and a green light from yet a third. The letter, signed by ex-party secretary Francesco De Martino, called the publicized notion that it was either Aldo Moro or the republic that had to be sacrificed an "absurd dilemma" and gave Craxi carte blanche support for whatever he might propose to the party directorate. The other big-name backing was from Riccardo Lombardi, who had underscored an additional folly in the hard line by pointing out that if in Via Fani Moro had been killed and the Red Brigades had captured the five police officers no one would have dared question the need for negotiations.

Craxi also came prepared with a draft document that would give him a mandate to search for a "reasonable and legitimate" solution. The solution, or an outline of it, was already in mind. He was convinced, he told the heads of all the other factions in his party, that acting swiftly Moro could be saved with small concession. His source, his *gola profonda*—to use an expression going around at the time, meaning, literally, *deep throat*—was Red Brigades lawyer Giannino Guiso. Guiso had been advising that to forestall Moro's execution indefinitely, the negotiations need only *begin*. Indeed, they did not even have to take place, in any formal sense. The Christian Democrats had only to *say* that they would negotiate. Still less, without even uttering the cursed word, they had only to *ask* what the Red Brigades wanted, and at some point make a counteroffer. Or, since they had already proposed the "freedom of communist prisoners," the Christian Democrats had only to respond with an invitation to be more specific. The disputants did not have to come within a thousand miles of one another, which is about as far apart as human beings can get and still be in Italy.

"The natural intermediary," Guiso had said, "is Moro. It is he, the statesman, however you care to argue about his messages, who has always remained at the height of the situation."

This was why Craxi, fresh with these ideas when breaking with the hard line on Friday, had asked the Red Brigades to allow Moro to specify the terms of his release, as he had begun to do in his previous letters. At the time, Craxi and Guiso were unaware that just such a letter was on its way to Zaccagnini. In it, as we saw, the president confirmed Guiso's counsel indubitably. Any sign, he said, however problematical, "would be extremely important." This was also why Mrs. Moro, having read the letter first, sent it with her own appeal to Zaccagnini to simply declare the party's *willingness* to learn the precise terms of Moro's release.

Craxi had the idea of putting together an expert task force to study what, within the "reasonable and legitimate" framework, the counteroffer might consist of, and to be certain of the outcome, the ad hoc group would be advised by the *gola profondissima* of the entire triumvirate of the *brigatisti* lawyers. It was a fail-safe operation, or the closest humanly possible equivalent, requiring nothing but the consent of the men in the Square of Jesus.

In terms of political horse sense, which is the only sense under

the thick hide of power, Craxi's plan, if it worked, offered inesti-
mable advantages. It would alleviate the current pressure on the
Christian Democrats and give the Socialists a privileged relationship with the ruling party. It would isolate the Communists and
provide Craxi with the discrete identity on the left he had been empowered to establish. And finally, as Moro's rescue squad, the
Socialist Party, sending home to the grassroots the image of
daredevil youngbloods, could collect its reward at the polls. Not for
one instant during the entire affair did any of the political parties in
Rome forget that significant local elections were to be held on May
14—now exactly three weeks away.

None of the details of Craxi's strategy went beyond the meeting
room that day. The mandate he had asked for was approved
unanimously, a point emphasized when the text was released in the
early afternoon, but this was really only a pact of silence to allow
him to develop his line—and hang by it if he failed. It was also
noted everywhere in Rome that Craxi, coming out of his meeting,
went directly to Zaccagnini. It was a rescue plan still on paper
only.[2]

"Rough treatment."

Such was the directive that came down from the third floor in the
Street of the Dark Shops after Enrico Berlinguer had a ten-minute
talk with Craxi in the early hours of the ultimatum.[3] The order
was meant for the party paper, L'Unità, a morning daily, which
was food for the rest of the party apparatus to think and act upon
all day.

The Communists felt their position to be foundering. While Craxi
was meeting with his fellow leaders, Berlinguer's right-hand man,
Gerardo Chiaromonte, made a spot check at the Square of Jesus
and reported "serious wavering" among the Christian Democrats.
That day's L'Unità had appeared with an uncompromising reiteration of the party's "democratic firmness," but its preoccupations
about negotiations as the "end of everything" and its defense of the
hard line as not being a "caricature of a Prussian State" were indications that the supply of sound argument was shrinking.[4] The
auto-da-fé one comrade had undergone that morning was yet another sign of shortage, notably of magnanimity.

The scene at party headquarters as the Communists awaited

word of Craxi's confrontation with his fellow Socialists, as well as the mood, the visceral fear of isolation and a deal being made behind their backs, was aptly described by an eyewitness reporter in the next day's *La Repubblica:*

> High officials and other executives, present in an unusually large number; going in and out of their offices, standing around in the corridors, speaking almost in whispers. A day of waiting and suspicion, yesterday in the Dark Shops. Will the Socialist directorate correct the proposal advanced by Craxi to open negotiations with the Red Brigades? And what will the Christian Democrats do? Will they hold or will they fold under the weight of emotion? . . . Are they perhaps looking for a new political balance and a break between the Communists and the Socialists?

> "In the end, a human life has never been an absolute value to sacrifice everything for," says [Central Committee member] Paolo Bufalini, reasoning more with himself than with his listeners. "Just because it is of incalculable worth, a life, that's why it can't be bartered."[5]

When the news arrived that Craxi's position had been endorsed by his party, this was defined as "laxism" and a "false sense of humanity." The Communists made no secret of their feeling that the Red Brigades were a direct threat.

Someone among the beleaguered Christian Democrats had the artful idea that the best way to prevent a change in the official party line was to disconnect the mechanism by which such a change could occur. In other words, the five-man party directorate, which Zaccagnini had called into permanent session on the day of the Via Fani attack, was unplugged, and it was announced that for the duration of the ultimatum the wavering leadership would not meet. The fear of course was that the five might split, and with Zaccagnini nearer to toppling than wavering, the president's will could prevail.

The disadvantage of this ploy was also considered. It could be misunderstood as the "clear and definitive" answer being sought by the Red Brigades: an unequivocal *no,* which would be the pistol-

shot end of the game. Furthermore, the family had had the fore-
sight to make a public statement renewing Eleonora Moro's personal appeal to the party,[6] revealing that she had done so. This, at
least for the suffering intransigents, would be hard to ignore, and
Zaccagnini's rack was turned when the new letter he had hoped to
keep secret was released to the press, either by the family or the
Red Brigades.

So, while the party directorate was dismeeting, the party directors met. In the event, it was a maneuver of tiny consequence, but
it showed some of the discomfort of sitting on a fence. It was also
solace for Zaccagnini. He was not a man alone; there was a whole
wavering crowd.

In the Prime Minister's palace, the government was doing its
share to counteract the gains being registered hourly by the "negotiations party"—as the heterogeneous group of doves was now
being called—by the Cabinet's approval of three bills to be introduced into Parliament. In the past two or three days, the Communists and other intransigent forces were exercising their influence on
the trade unions to bring out the police unions in favor of the hard
line. All grades of police officials and heads of police organizations
were suddenly sending out press releases that fell short of being
threats, but not by a losing margin. Ordinary policemen were said
to be telephoning Christian Democratic leaders by the "tens" to
remind them to respect the law, and two unidentified officers on
duty in the Square of Jesus were reported to be stopping members
of Parliament at the entrance to party headquarters to tell them
angrily that if they negotiate it would mean the end of the state
and that they would resign from the force.

True or not, Andreotti, Cossiga, and the other Cabinet members,
by the bills they sent off to the Chamber of Deputies, sought to
provide for an expenditure of more than one billion dollars for law-
enforcement agencies; policemen, Carabinieri, prison guards, and
other lawmen would get a pay raise of fifteen dollars a week.[7]

The unmeetable Christian Democratic Party met without respite
between the twenty-eighth and the thirty-second hours. A search
among the twenty-odd participants for waverers was not very occupying timewise, and only one man had actually supported the presi-

dent's view until now. Senator Fanfani was present, too, but he was still saving himself for some bigger and better moment, should it come, and to offset the fainthearted was the attendance of Andreotti and Cossiga, who like Fanfani and several others were not members of the directorate.

At about 10 P.M., seventeen hours before the ultimatum ran down, the meeting ended and the party issued its reply to the Red Brigades. It could hardly be a *no* and there was no chance for an outright *si;* it was a mediocre mixture of both, what Italians call a *ni.*

It was one long sentence, half of which was a reaffirmation of the party's loyalty to the state and its institutions. The other half agreed with the family that there was a necessity to identify the "possible ways" to restore Moro's freedom. As for the family-requested willingness to do so, the party believed that the willingness shown by the Catholic relief organization Caritas Internationalis satisfied Eleonora Moro's appeal.[8]

The Red Brigades had only to telephone Rome area code 06, No. 698-7214, or others that would be flashed on television screens from here on, and enumerate the possible ways. This looked fine on television, but as it was a repetition of what the party had been saying for days *before* the ultimatum, it was understood by the men of power that the hard-liners were still in command.

To the extent that it might be interpreted the same way by the Red Brigades, it was a dangerous suspension of decision-taking. For the family, there remained nothing but to keep one eye on the clock and haul out its heaviest battering rams. No one had more than a fleeting hope that the *brigatisti* would call Caritas, though its phones in Rome and the head office in Fribourg, Switzerland, began at once to ring. Between reports from the usual bunch of mythomaniacs, oral diarrheics, nympholeptics, jackanapes, and the simply depraved, someone called to ask, "Any news?"

18.

In the morning, an old Franciscan nun passed below the penthouse in Via Forte Trionfale. She halted by the iron fence that closed in the pines and cypress around the building. She prayed, and when she continued on her way, she was heard to murmur, "It will rain again today." It poured.

In the apartment upstairs, Eleonora Moro was meeting with Health Minister Tina Anselmi, who was the last remaining link between the family and both the party and the government. Zaccagnini no longer had the wherewithal to face Mrs. Moro, and Andreotti never did. Anselmi, an oaklike, fair-haired woman from the North, had for days been taking the full force of Eleonora Moro's wrath, and when no one in Rome had thought of sending her a copy of the latest Polaroid, she had raged at Tina Anselmi, sending her off in tears. Now the minister had the unhappy mission of having to report on the party's decision of the night before. Her visits, too, were numbered.

The city slowed in the Saturday downpour. Zaccagnini was inert behind his marble-top desk in the Square of Jesus; Andreotti was at home in his apartment on the Corso Vittorio, and if he were following daily routine, he sat sometime that morning with a blanket around his shoulders, making coded entries in his secret diary. Everything that the government and the party would do in response to the ultimatum was done.

"This is Vatican Radio. The 'Four Voices' newsroom brings you a special edition. Paul VI has addressed an appeal to the Red Brigades. . . ."

In the forty-fourth hour, the Holy Father spoke. At 10:49 A.M., the Vatican began to transmit in twenty-six languages the Pope's message, which had come after long hours of total solitude. Ten minutes earlier, at a press conference in the former palace of the Holy Inquisition, in Vatican City, spokesman Monsignor Panciroli read and distributed photocopies of the handwritten appeal. The Pope had set it to paper, he said, between shortly before midnight and 1:30 A.M. Written in a small, easily read hand under the engraved papal coat of arms, it went by measured and mighty words farther than anyone in Rome had dared before. Said Paul:

I write to you, men of the Red Brigades: Return the Honorable Aldo Moro to his freedom, to his Family, to his public life.

I do not know you, and I have no way of making contact with you. This is why I write to you publicly, using the margin of time remaining before the expiry of the threat of death that you have raised against him, this good and honest man, whom no one can blame for any crime, or accuse of lacking in service to justice and a peaceful, civil existence.

I have no mandate on his behalf, nor am I linked to him by any private interest. But I love him as a member of the great human family, as a friend in study, and in a very special way, as a brother in faith and a son in the Church of Christ.

And it is in this supreme name of Christ that I turn to you, who surely do not ignore Him, to you, unknown and implacable adversaries of this worthy and innocent man, and I pray to you on my knees, free Hon. Aldo Moro, simply, without conditions . . . because true social progress, which I want to believe is a force in your conscience, must not be stained by innocent blood, nor tormented by superfluous pain. . . .

Men of the Red Brigades, allow me, interpreter of the faith of many of your fellow countrymen, the hope that a victorious sense of humanity still dwells in your heart.

I prayerfully, and loving you always, await the proof.

Paulus PP. VI

FROM THE VATICAN, *April 12, 1978*[1]

He had called them men. He loved them. They had a heart, a conscience, and perhaps some substance of humanity. Most important, they belonged to an organization with no less than the same qualities, and the organization had a name twice set down on an official paper already in the Vatican archives, and so, in human history. On his knees, supplicating, he had recognized in them all the things the men on the left bank of the Tiber had so jealously withheld, and though he had nothing to give them to negotiate, he stunned the men who did.

Zaccagnini's reaction was described as a drowning man's groping for the only thing floating, as he muttered, "if only they listen. . . ." Everyone began to reach for the same life preserver. It took two or three hours for the parties of the majority to recover, leaving only minutes to the ultimatum, but then, suddenly, the Pope's message was being universally projected as the highest concession *they* would give to the Red Brigades.

Paul VI had fought a lonely, private battle, and now behind the white silk on his shoulders stood the armies of the hard line. He had asked what he could do to save Aldo Moro, and had gone as far as a Pope could short of urging the intransigents to soften. But this, the Conference of Bishops had done, outflanking, as he had, the impassible Vatican. He instead had relied heavily on the recognition aspect, and what he could not give politically he tried to remedy by his prestige. If this was a battle fought on two fronts, it was twice lost. Those who favored the hard line simply ignored the bishops and rode the papal offensive as their own. The Pope had beckoned the Red Brigades to release their prisoner "without conditions," and this was the phrase, the only phrase, that echoed when the forty-eighth hour was gone.

Historians will have to wait half a century to learn what transpired overnight to make the Pope on Sunday withdraw his "recognition," calling but no longer naming the Red Brigades "self-constituted hangmen." Fifty years is the customary delay in the release of papers in the Vatican archives, but for those with less patience or time there is the testimony of Red Brigades lawyer Eduardo Di Giovanni. Consulted by the papal emissary, Father Curione, Di Giovanni was asked what effect the Pope's Saturday appeal might have.

"It would have been better without what he said afterward," the Sicilian replied.

"Ah, you know," said Father Curione, "the Pope is very old."[2]

By Sunday, after a night in which the death of the president was announced repeatedly by the spendthrift callers of televised phone numbers, it was all too plain to the negotiations party that the ultimatum had reinforced the hard line. The family's efforts to elicit an intervention by the United Nations had succeeded on Saturday evening when Secretary General Kurt Waldheim spoke out.[3] His "personal" message had less impact than the Pope's, but added to the great visibility of all the international appeals, there was an *appearance* that the Christian Democratic party was living up to its pledge to leave nothing untried. Yet the opposite was true. Nothing at all could happen without a reply from the party, and the only one given was null.

Sunday, then, with the sun breaking through and families out to stroll, was a day to wonder on. What would the Red Brigades do? Speculation ran wild, and when an early-evening network-radio program was crossed by a crackling interference and a voice that said, "The count is on his way to Yugoslavia; the family is in touch," this was seen as the start of secret negotiations. Some believed they were already over. The president, Reuters was rumored to have reported, had been exchanged for Renato Curcio. Panama announced that it would accept any prisoners released by the Italians for Aldo Moro's freedom.

It was like a bad dream ending for an hour or two that day, but in Turin, one of the triumvirs of Red Brigades lawyers, black-bearded Sergio Spazzali, declared himself a pessimist.

Christian Democracy's reply, he said, was a "pharisaical way of saying 'no.'" The telephone call-in service was "absurd."

Said Spazzali: "Monday will be an important day . . . big news."[4]

V

APPEAL

*I begin to understand
what imprisonment means.*[1]

19.

He began to prepare for his death. He had spent the ultimatum period watching the minute-by-minute developments with the tenacious attention to detail unique among the condemned. His notations on fleeting particulars and an outpouring of written response bear testimony to both the unflagging keenness of his mind and how complete and swift was his access to news. He had sent off letters, sometimes no more than a paragraph or two, which were already overtaken by events when they arrived only hours after dispatch. Moreover, he was filled with ideas yet untried, allies still to be won, and resources untapped. His adamantine refusal to accept the destiny his world insisted on and his faith that in the end his precious Reason would prevail were the irremovable boulders of these days. Yet the presentiment of death bored in.

In almost all of his letters until now, and throughout his interrogation, there were plaintive expressions of the pain he could not help spare his family, but having passed through the press of the ultimatum, he appeared to believe that their frailties could endure no more and that *much* more was on the way. Not that he saw his own end as theirs. Rather, he made death the lesser evil, as though it only concerned him peripherally, a bothersome diplomatic mission, perhaps, from which there was no return; heart-wrenching, however, were the thoughts that more and more obsessed him of a family ruined and forsaken.

"I accept what the Lord sends me," he wrote to his secretary, Nicola Rana, in a series of practical as opposed to political letters whose confidentiality remained intact. "What I'm left with are most bitter preoccupations about my family, who are deprived of guidance, and my anxiety about my beloved little one, whose vicissitudes you know. I never stop thinking of him and looking at him, as I do with all my dear ones in these hours of infinite sadness. Needless to say that in my tragedy, I still hope that you, with your wisdom and love, will continue to think of us, and among other things, counsel those who are extremely inexpert and fragile."[1]*

To his aide Sereno Freato: "This hallucinating affair leaves me with the impression that I am friendless. I know that isn't so. Even if some (or many) who could have, haven't tried. . . . But I don't want to lament. I accept my destiny from God. But the problem is not mine, but of a family, whom you, who have been so good and affectionate for so many years, know in all its complexities. . . . I have a thousand preoccupations, but aside from the poor health of my wife, there is the fate of my beloved Luca, of whose difficulties you're aware. . . . Keep my loved ones together, dear Freato, by the force of your immense good will."[3]

"One last urgent thing," he wrote to Don Antonello Mennini, the young priest who had been acting all along as a messenger. "Tell my wife that she should immediately cash some checks I left signed in the mansard. This is necessary to avoid inheritance complications."[4]

But such are also the thoughts and requests of men facing open-heart surgery or a great invasion, and by none but the strong are they dutifully tended. In the living, there is nothing less final than life, and he, in his sixty-second year, acted more revitalized than done-for. Over that ultimatum weekend, he wrote a cyclone, and when he was not writing, he watched with a mind's eye all that was happening outside. Shortly after his party's reply to the ultimatum, he wrote of what he had been thinking while the leadership was meeting, or as the case may be, dismeeting:

"I kept saying to myself: The situation is not mature and we had

---

* The "little one" was a perfectly healthy child. His "vicissitudes" concerned his parents, whom Moro felt to be "inexpert and fragile." In recent months he personally had taken up a large part of the role of caring for the boy. The hierarchies and culture bonds of southern Italian families did not halt at the presidential level. The mention Moro makes of "looking at him," repeating a similar phrase in an earlier letter, seems a reference to a snapshot he may have had with him when captured.[2]

better expect traditional Christian Democratic prudence. And I waited faithfully, as always, imagining what [the leaders] would be saying at the real meeting, after the first exchanges of ideas. . . . And, instead, nothing. Nocturnal get-togethers, full of anguish, intolerance, and the summoning up of reasons of Party or State. Then comes a very noble unanimous proposal, but unfortunately it evades the real political problem."[5]

He pounced on every shadow that seemed to be moving his way, rifling in the dark for its source so that he might put the force of life behind it. On the Friday of the ultimatum, for example, press reports revealed that the United Nations Security Council had rejected the request of its president, U.S. diplomat Andrew Young, to speak out on Moro's behalf. Moro immediately sent a message to his contact in the Foreign Office asking him to find out with urgency why Young's initiative had been blocked and if there was any way to get around it. "Keep the reply to yourself," he said hurriedly, "it'll be asked for at the right moment."[6]

As soon as he heard Waldheim's appeal, he got off two long letters, one to Waldheim's Italian relative, Ambassador Cottafavi, and the other to the Secretary General himself.

Waldheim's statement, he wrote to Cottafavi, was welcome though insufficient. Yet he had used a tone, Moro said, "giving the impression of being willing to go further when needed." Would he come to Italy? Moro asked, though he realized it would be no easy task overcoming "the resistance of the government, which hopes to resolve the matter in humanitarian terms (that is, paying nothing)."[7]

To Waldheim, after thanking him and repeating the same request about coming to Rome, he said: "Maybe this sacrifice on your part, with adequate pressure on the unreasonable position of the Italian Government, could perform the miracle. . . ."[8]†

As for Paul VI's appeal, Moro writes to Don Antonello: "Tell Cardinal Poletti . . . to implore the Pope to do *more*. . . ." He wanted Poletti to point out that "His Holiness's very gracious mes-

---

† This message, written in the people's prison on Saturday, traveled via Cottafavi to New York in less than twenty-four hours. On Sunday evening, Waldheim announced his availability to come to Italy. The invitation, however, would never be extended, and the Secretary General would soon come under fierce attack in Rome (see pp. 177–79).

sage, hedging on the question of a humanitarian restitution and an exchange of prisoners, unfortunately lends itself to being used against me."[9]

And he kept writing: letters placed in reserve, like missiles in silos, drafts repeatedly updated to be fired off if and when this or that development took place; different versions of the same theme, some to be discarded, others to be released, complete with explanatory notes to the strategic command ("Second letter to the party, as substitute to the first, to be sent—one or the other—according to how situation unfolds"; "The lines that follow are to be revised [before sending] according to possible usefulness of opinions expressed").[10]

He was dying hard. His new, postultimatum strategy, made of the gleanings of that weekend, consisted of publicly withdrawing his confidence in the party directorate, making a last-stand effort to break Zaccagnini, and appealing to the second echelon of party power as well as the grass-roots, from where family-inspired pressure was already being applied upward. In a word, to bring about a revolt in Christian Democracy.

The two most encouraging domestic events he had observed on that weekend were the petition of members of his own party, including ex-Chief of State Gronchi, and the calamitous defection from the hard line of Craxi's Socialists.

"There has got to be an alternative to the government's line that echoes the Socialist aspirations," he wrote to the family in advising how the second-echelon Christian Democratic group should be oriented.[11] To launch this new campaign spectacularly, he sent a letter to his press secretary, which captures in one paragraph all the sharply edged life-death facets of his mood in this moment:

> There has to be an appeal made by my wife and disseminated widely and quickly. Further, it is believed essential here that my wife go to the party (Zac + 5) and tell them clearly that the refusal of Christian Democracy to deal seriously, even in the minimum form proposed by Craxi, means my end, the responsibility for which the family must attribute to them. This is to be repeated on TV. I would be grateful if you were to accompany her and help her because it's the first time my wife would be doing something like this and she's terrorized. If they

don't receive her, have it said on TV anyway. At least radio, which should be easier. As for its usefulness, let me be the judge. Thanks.[12]

In a p.s. full of second thoughts about putting his wife under this strain, he says that if her health (or the state-owned radio and television) does not permit, it should be done by open letter. The important thing, he says, seeking collateral support for moves he himself was planning, is to publicize the break with the party directorate.

The next day he is wracked by doubt. Did his message arrive? Would his wife's appeal be transmitted by the media?

"The fact that my wife's appeal doesn't reach me," he writes Don Antonello, "alarms me about her health. Perhaps that's why I'm getting the impression that the family is closer to the official line than to me, which is false."[13]

And once, when he was neither writing, nor worrying, nor imagining what was or was not going on in Rome, he wondered—and we know this, too, from his papers—who would have thought this could be?

The Red Brigades wrote, too, drafting, typing, correcting, inking, mimeographing, collating, folding all day Sunday the news they planned for Monday. With Communiqué VIII, released at noon of the twenty-fourth, or forty-five hours after the ultimatum expired, no one could ever accuse them of faltering under the cold front in Rome. They raised the ante. Their judgment of events and the need to reconcile various strains of opinion in the strategic command had carried them to the conviction that after forty days the time had come to take a position from which there was no retreat. They were barely able to climb out of the credibility gap the ultimatum had thrown them into. They were forced to scrape up the Christian Democrats' one-sentence declaration of Friday evening, which had been cast away and forgotten by now, and use its "ambiguity" as a reason to renew the dialogue. But this could not easily recur.

"Equivocation is no longer possible," they said, and this was to be applied to themselves as well as the party. They had been asked on all sides to state their terms concretely, they said. While they would continue to fight for the liberation of all communist prisoners,

speaking "realistically," they were asking in exchange for the freedom of Aldo Moro the freedom of only a part of the whole prison
guerrilla population. This was followed by a list of twelve convicted terrorists, and for health reasons, a thirteenth "fighting communist," the wounded *brigatista* captured in the April 11 slaying of
a prison guard and awaiting trial.

"At this point," said Communiqué VIII, "our position is completely defined." There could be no double-cross as in the Sossi
affair, and an "immediate and positive reply" from the Christian
Democrats was now the only road open for the return of Aldo
Moro. If this was not to be, said the Red Brigades, "we will immediately draw the proper conclusions and execute the sentence. . . ."[14]

The most striking feature of Communiqué VIII was the exposure
of the Red Brigades' slavish attachment to the bourgeois culture
they professed so vehemently to despise. In discussing the humanitarian appeals of "some religious authorities" and other "renowned
personalities," they seemed almost on the edge of admitting having
been impressed, and when they asked them to appeal now to the
Christian Democrats in the name of the same humanity—to remove
their suspicions and prejudices that this was all a political trick—it
sounds near to a cry for help.

More revealing was that the Red Brigades believed that one Aldo
Moro, discredited, disenfranchised, and miserably degraded by his
peers to the level of a zombie, if not a zombie-traitor, was still
worth thirteen fighting communists. This attitude was not unlike
the myth of the great man's natural security that had been the
comfort of Moro's peasant bodyguards. There was a difference,
though. Not for one instant did the Red Brigades coddle a thought
that there was any coalition of forces between heaven and hell that
had the power and would use it to free these twelve men and one
woman who were in society's debt to the extent of three life sentences, plus 172 years of prison, and eight homicides. Not for an
Aldo Moro, anyway. Yet this was the list price they thought the
merchandise warranted, if only in the style of thieves-market
sellers who must ask for the moon to get cheese. They had taken
up the ancient role splendidly, loyally, expecting that the buyers
would assume theirs as well, that they would understand the
traditional, Mediterranean nature of the request, and then get
down to the business of the day, however tumultuous it might be.

The symbolism in the latest communiqué ran deep, but it was certainly understandable in Rome. First, it was issued on the eve of Liberation Day, a national holiday that celebrates the Resistance and the victorious insurrections in the North that ended fascism and routed the Germans. The spirit of *liberation* was making its annual visit to Italy, or at least it was thought to be on the way. Second, the Red Brigades' list of thirteen was nothing more than a totem pole of the Movement. It consisted of chronological representations of the Great Moments in Italian Political Terrorism on the Left since the 1960s. Only the last five were members of the Red Brigades, and they ranged from Renato Curcio to the captive of only two weeks ago, who was the only second-generation *brigatista* in police custody. The first eight places were shared in chronological order by members of precursor movements or less-articulated groups. The most obvious sign that the Red Brigades had no expectation of winning their freedom was that unlike their behavior in the Sossi case they gave none of the particulars common to such demands: the mode of release, transportation, destinations, money, security, etc.

True, Communiqué VIII signaled the decline of all schools of thought in the strategic command but one. There was to be no more talk of the prison or any other system. The Red Brigades had decided to adopt the approach Moro had taken and not veered from since the start. The president had gambled, and gambled still, on his powers to persuade, and the problem had now been reduced to its simplest terms. There was either going to be some form of prisoner swap or there was going to be one less prisoner. Yet even this was negotiable. They had avoided a new ultimatum and they had asked for no more than a "positive" reply. Obviously, there is a world of elbow room between a positive reply and a flat *yes*.

20.

A flat and resonant *no* is what they got, as the intransigent side seized the whole armory of shiny new weapons the communiqué had foolhardily handed over. Rome had no temper for subtle analysis. The prisoner exchange meant thirteen to one, period. Newspapers hauled out Liberation Day headlines such as "Atrocious Blackmail" and "They Ask the Impossible," and the government declared evident that the kidnappers had no intention whatsoever to free Aldo Moro. The Christian Democrats said that this time they *really* would not meet, the Communists made an admirable effort not to gloat and let the state's indignation speak for them, and even the Socialists, whose position was irreparably damaged, were forced to say that the Red Brigades were asking the impossible, though they like everyone else knew it was the starting price. On the other hand, the Socialists were the only ones in Rome whose shouts of "unacceptable" were cries in the market from an interested buyer.[1]

It had always been a battle of words, but on Liberation Day it became and remained an ugly war to the death. The president would not let up. In his final letter to Zaccagnini, he ran at him screaming between the lines:

We are almost at zero hour. We are counting in seconds not minutes. We are at the moment of slaughter. . . .

Zaccagnini, you were elected by the [Christian Democratic] Congress. Nobody can overrule you. Your word is decisive. Don't be uncertain, hesitant, acquiescent. Be courageous and pure as you were in your youth. And now, having said this, I repeat that I do not accept this iniquitous and ungrateful verdict from Christian Democracy. I repeat: I will not absolve and I will not justify anyone. There is no political and moral reason that will make me do so. . . .

Do not believe that Christian Democracy will end this problem by liquidating Moro. I will still exist as an irreducible point of contention, as an alternative, a barrier against Christian Democracy becoming what it is doing today.

For this reason, for our evident incompatibility, I ask that neither the authorities of the State nor the men of the party participate at my funeral.[2]

Zaccagnini had settled into a maudlin melancholia. In crying jags, slow-roll weeping, spastic sobbing, and wet-eyed stares, he alone shed more tears than anyone could have desired in those April shower days. By Liberation Day, however, the party's answer to the president's flagellating letters to Zaccagnini was ready and handed out in the Square of Jesus. The Christian Democrats had solicited what Leonardo Sciascia has called a "monstrous . . . uncivilized protest,"[3] a statement signed by about seventy-five men and women who presented themselves as Moro's truest friends. Among them were several high prelates, including a cardinal, university professors, and others who were in fact what they claimed: "friends from long ago."

They had two points to make: "The Aldo Moro whom we know . . . is not present in the letters directed to Zaccagnini and published as his." They were the handiwork of the Red Brigades, who were trying "to destroy Moro's image." Second, alluding to Moro's repeated admonitions that only his party could save him, his friends replied, "the irremediable guilt in the event of an absurd homicide will fall only on its actual executors and the organizers of it."[4]

For any other kind of guilt, such as guilt by omission, by silence, or by the cold eyes of a Roman family, presumably there was a remedy. Of this greeting card from his long-ago friends, Aldo Moro would remark, "I never would have believed it possible."[5]

Secretary General Waldheim had no trouble finding Aldo Moro present in the letter he had received from him. He was profoundly moved by Moro's plight, which he saw as representing a growing threat to the international community of statesmen and diplomats. He was, then, more than willing to accede to the president's request that he come to Italy as a mediator, but since he had announced his availability publicly and privately, he had had no invitation from Rome. Indeed, the Italians had asked nothing of him, which was the same as telling him to keep out.

Waldheim, however, had been in touch with Pope Paul, and he understood the underlying significance of the Holy Father's attempt at "recognizing" the Red Brigades. From his reading of Communiqué VIII, with its reference to appeals from renowned authorities, Waldheim now believed, it was learned later, that the Pope's and his own intervention had had a "psychological influence" on the Red Brigades. The situation, he felt, had reached the "decisive stage."[6]

The problem was, as viewed from the thirty-eighth floor of United Nations headquarters in New York, what within the limits of his mandate could the Secretary General still do. He was, some of his aides thought, already treading in the rough waters of interference in the internal affairs of a member government. Waldheim himself, however, decided that same Liberation Day to go even farther beyond those limits. In an unprecedented move, he did the next best thing to coming to Italy in person.

Surprising his staff—to begin with—he arranged for his likeness to be bounced by satellite TV that day into the homes of the Italians and first of all men of power. In what was to be considered in Rome as the highest effrontery of the negotiations party, Waldheim, speaking in Italian, addressed himself "to the members of the Red Brigades from the Secretary General of the United Nations"—which was precisely the same form of address he would have used had he been speaking to, say, members of the Italian Parliament or Andreotti's government.[7]

This was no more a personal appeal. It was a political message, containing political advice, in which words like *humanitarian* or *without conditions* were conspicuously eschewed. The Secretary General was fully aware that he was risking his reputation and his future effectiveness as an international civil servant. Nevertheless, he gave the Red Brigades three sensible, political reasons why they should free Aldo Moro immediately: They had attracted world attention to their position; the continued detention of their prisoner could only damage their objectives; and finally, Moro's release would be applauded by "all who dedicate their lives to seeking a world of greater justice and social well-being." It was almost as if the *brigatisti* were fellow travelers of such company.[8]

The teeth-gnashing and foot-stomping this caused in Rome ("We are not Lebanon"), which had not been pre-advised, much less consulted, lasted for days. Most furious were the Communists and their supporters. They saw every form of eely machination. It ranged from *fait accompli* international recognition of the Red Brigades as a sort of Palestine Liberation Organization to Washington arm-twisting at the United Nations in support of Craxi's Socialists to undermine the Communists.[9]

There was, as always, no limit to how many involutions a plot might have. But what seemed to bother the hard-liners most was that Waldheim had counseled the Red Brigades to release Aldo Moro so as not to damage their objectives.* But everyone knew, including Waldheim, it was said, that their infamous objectives were to rape Italian democracy. This was where the reasoning broke off, leaving the foul odor of insinuation. Here was a logic which, carried but two places farther, led to it therefore being a good thing to damage their objectives and hence a good thing to work *against* the release of Aldo Moro.

Waldheim, though he expected a barrage of criticism from Rome, was hurt deeply by the Italian reaction, and in fact he resented it.[10] But he made no retraction, and the matter ended in slurs about his lightheadedness, vanity, and bureaucratic count-for-nothingness.[11] Besides, there was much else to attend to, and when Liberation Day was over there were no fewer prisoners than before.

In a large apartment overlooking the Tiber and Rome's Queen of Heaven Prison, Giuliano Vassalli, the political prisoner freed in 1944 by the intercession of Pope Pius XII, celebrated his sixty-third birthday on Liberation Day. This was but the smallest of a series of

---

* In Italian he said *causa* (cause), which in carrying a somewhat positive charge made Rome particularly angry. In the English text, as provided by the UN, the word was a more neutral "purposes." Waldheim explained that he had read a slightly less than accurate translation and that there was nothing more to it, but Rome was implacable, until it moved on to the next thrust of the negotiations party.

coincidences that were to carry Vassalli to a crucial place in the Moro affair, altering the fortunes of men of power, including his own.

Gray and slender, a man with sharply lighted eyes, Vassalli had been contacted by Craxi a couple of days earlier. He was asked to be part of the expert group in formation to seek out a counteroffer to the Red Brigades, the intention being to make it irresistible to both sides, and Vassalli agreed.

Although the older generation of the political class in Rome contained an unusually large number of men and women who had spent time in the city's prisons, none better than Vassalli could understand the gift of political reprieve. During the Occupation, he was head of the military junta of the Proletarian Socialists, an armed underground organization. He was responsible for the prison escape of future Chief of State Giuseppe Saragat and was arrested soon afterward, tortured, and sentenced to death. He missed the mortal appointment when some forty-eight hours after his release the Germans began to withdraw from Rome, and the remaining political prisoners were taken out and shot.

No one but Pope Paul was aware that Aldo Moro had invoked Vassalli's case as a reminder of his own, but Vassalli had been chosen by Craxi for reasons that had little connection with the distant past. Vassalli, at war's end, had gone on to distinguish himself as a professor of penal law, an attorney of the highest renown, and a Socialist member of parliament during the Moro center-left governments. He was from an old Roman family that had always been friends of Popes, and Vassalli himself was close to past, and more important, present Chiefs of State.

The plan being developed by the Craxi task force was to hand both the government, or the Christian Democrats, and the Red Brigades a solution that would fall within the limits imposed on either side. This meant that it had to be seen as strictly political by the Red Brigades and as humanitarian and nothing but by Rome. It had to be carried out within the framework of Italian law, and yet, after Communiqué VIII, it had to provide for a prisoner exchange, which was theoretically illegal. Last, it had to be arrived at between the Christian Democrats and the Red Brigades appearing as negotiations to the latter and as nothing of the sort to the former.

It seemed an improbable balancing act at first, or like feeding the Four Thousand, but if the illusion could be created even briefly, it would be extremely difficult for the parties to the dispute to reject it, as it would disarm them all of every argument except the most dismal, stoniest kind.

Apart from Vassalli, the all-Socialist group consisted of six other men and one woman who were linked to the three branches of government, but mainly Parliament and the judiciary. It did not take them very long to come up with a pair of alternatives that met most of the requirements and offered the possibility of being extended to all.[12]

The first alternative was an "autonomous" act by the state granting a pardon to an as yet unspecified number of prisoners whom the Red Brigades considered as fighting communists and the state as common criminals. They would include persons, not necessarily on the list of thirteen, who had been convicted of nonviolent or relatively minor crimes and who were presently afflicted with some sort of health problem that could justify their release on humanitarian grounds. In other words, Moro's freedom was to be obtained, depending on how one cared to view it, either by a prisoner exchange or by a unilateral act of clemency, and the less said the better for all.

Such pardons, according to the Italian Constitution, are the exclusive prerogative of the Chief of State. At the request of the Minister of Justice, he may or may not issue the necessary presidential decree. One of the first moves of the task force, then, was to test the idea on President Leone. This was left to Vassalli. He was the lawyer for the principal defendant in the Lockheed bribery case, a mutual friend of both Vassalli and Leone, and if anyone in these days of Leone's corollary troubles had the Chief of State's famously flappy ears, it was Vassalli. Besides, Leone was approached by another of Vassalli's friends, his comrade-in-arms ex-President Saragat, and, by way of the family's urgings, Amintore Fanfani called, too.

"The President of the republic was very receptive," a member of the task force said later. In fact, Leone let it be known that he would offer no resistance at all.[13]

The second alternative provided for the "spontaneous" abolition of the special antiterrorist prisons, or at least some major relaxation of their worst features. This required mere administrative action and was as far from violating any law as repenting sin. One of Craxi's experts, a renowned jurist, had inspected these internment centers and reported "aspects of illegality and outright unconstitutionality."[14] Although relief in this area would not mean a prisoner exchange, it would be a far greater achievement for the Red Brigades than the release of some ailing comrades, and hence almost impossible to turn down. The government could keep all its criminals and proclaim that the hard line and humanity in general had won.

These were the premises from which Vassalli and his colleagues proceeded. Whether there were any fighting communist-criminals who might fill the order, whether the disputants would accept one of the choice of two, and whether it could all be made to happen in Aldo Moro's predictedly limited lifetime were the questions that throbbed for them now.

The woeful, disheartening news that Papà was beginning to have thoughts of his family being nearer the hard line than to him reached home on Liberation Day. His consternation had also appeared in a laconic phrase about his family contained in the last letter to Zaccagnini: "I hope they can speak autonomously." Taken with the fears he had expressed privately to Don Antonello about not hearing anything of the television appeal he had asked of his wife, they appeared as signs that Moro had been struck by an agonizing crisis of doubt. He seemed terrified that his abandonment was now complete, or at best that his family had been silenced by the government, his party, and the media.

The latter, as has been seen, was not very far from the truth. The idea of Eleonora Moro going on state television was regarded as impossible by the family. Mrs. Sossi had tried to make a televised appeal when her husband was a prisoner of the Red Brigades, and she had been turned down by both networks. In the present situation, Italian television had not even been reporting the contents of Moro's letters, though there was no lack of prime time for panels of experts to delve into how they had been pried from what was left of the president's mind. Furthermore, after the unwelcome surprise in the contents of Kurt Waldheim's satellite telecast, there would be less TV time than ever for the negotiations party.

Moro's instructions, however, were being followed faithfully by the family, and they were receiving all of his messages. They were, as he had asked, planning a dramatic break with the party, but it had to be carefully timed lest it go more or less ignored. No one could contest Moro's claim to the family that he knew best what forms of support he needed from the outside to advance what he alone knew as the reality on the inside. But there was much he was unaware of about the reality in Rome.

Apart from the Socialist alternatives, which were not yet clear in the people's prison, the family had two other hopefuls. The first was the continued willingness of Senator Fanfani to step in at the "right" moment, which was rather like the right chamber in Russian roulette, but the family could do no more than urge him, and his power could prove decisive. Second was the Geneva Convention idea, now fully developed by the good scouts of February '74.

Giovanni Moro, group leader Giancarlo Quaranta, and others had gotten their own expert counsel. A memorandum had been drawn up explaining that Article 3 of the 1949 treaty, to which Italy had adhered in 1951, provided for situations such as the one at hand. According to this international law, in cases of internal conflict in signatory states, the government may request the intervention of the International Red Cross to mediate an exchange of prisoners. The exercise of this article specifically excluded any juridical recognition by the state of the insurgent forces. Quaranta, with the family's approval, was preparing to submit this memorandum to Andreotti, but for the moment it was being held in reserve just behind the Socialist salient.[15]

The family were unable to communicate the vast amount of information being amassed daily and much less could they transmit nuance to the people's prison. But the latest message, coming via Don Antonello, asking him if he could get someone at home to write a few words about how they were feeling—to be retrieved "when it will be possible for me to ask you"—prompted them to seek words that might make magic.

They composed a letter immediately and arranged to have it published like last time in *Il Giorno,* where it appeared the next day on the front page:

Dear Papà,

We feel the need after many days to send you these few lines as a sign of our affection.

We think of you every moment with new love and an awareness that grows day by day of what you are and have been to us, and not only to us. We are seeing the affection that so many different kinds of people have for you: from your associates and friends to the young ones, to the persons who every day write us dear things for you.

In this tragedy we have discovered, each in his own way, that you have given us unsuspected resources of moral force and love. And this is why, even in our great weakness, we are today immensely strong and united.

We nourish the hope, with prayer and deeds, of having you with us, in our arms once again. Anna is fine and she thinks of you with a special love, remembering all the beautiful things she has received from you.

We love you profoundly.

Your family[16]

This letter would be read in Rome with the fastidiousness of a cryptologist's eye in search of a hidden message. A sense of uneasiness was creeping about that the family was up to something that might disturb or even overturn the affairs of state. The Waldheim incident was one of many, if not all, family initiatives that were regarded as unfriendly operations.† Now the letter to Papà was going under scrutiny to divine, if one could, what the future held in store. Indeed, the more one read it, the curious reference to Anna came to appear as a possible signal to the Red Brigades that the mysterious "beautiful things" had been received.[18] Did the relentless president have a secret weapon that would now, as the inevitable climax drew near, be turned on Rome?

† Earlier in the month, to cite another example, Sereno Freato made a hurried but not unobserved trip to Geneva to consult on behalf of the family with the head of the League of Human Rights, Denis Payot. Payot had acted as a mediator between the West German Government and the Red Army Fraction in the Schleyer case. He was prepared to repeat the role, but Cossiga's Under Secretary, Lettieri, intervened with surgical promptitude, inviting Payot to keep out.[17]

21.

Aldo Moro read the message from his family for what it was: "a tender letter of love," he said, "from my wife, my children, my beloved grandson, and the one I will never see."[1] Anna had been in the sixth month of her worrisome pregnancy when Papà had last been home, and now she was entering her eighth. She was fine, the letter said, and he knew that the beautiful things he had given her were long days on the beach at Terracina, nights when he calmed her fears, and tiny adventures in which father and daughter mischievously disappeared for two hours or so at the movies.

The letter in *Il Giorno* had been brought to him by one of his captors, who out of "sympathy," Moro said, "had cut out what was around it, which spoke of my death sentence."[2] If this gesture enhanced his interlude of relief and reassurance, the message as a whole made it even more complete. In spite of the "great weakness," about which no one any longer had illusions, the family appeared to be saying that there was unity and order in all the external supports down to the "young ones," which could be read as the newcomers, or the Socialists. By prayer, yes, but also by *deeds* did the family dare hope for his return. Moro's doubts were rested by his letter from home. Deeds were what he turned to.

It was Wednesday, April 26, the forty-second day of his imprisonment. He had no secret weapon. He did have, he said, "a very slender optimism."[3] It was based on what he was being told by the Red Brigades about their minimum terms and his judgment of the shifting alignments of forces on the outside. He also had a prodigious reserve of energy. Between now and Saturday, he would release it in an exquisitely orchestrated, impassioned, final assault on Rome. It was now or never, do or die, home or bust, and every other cry raised by human beings when they touch the bottom of their soul.

Everything done before seemed only preparatory now, the necessary groundwork for what he sought to do. To his strategy of bringing about a revolt in his party, which he planned by *coup de main* at week's end, he had an entirely new element to add. Perhaps he had been saving it all along, but it seems more likely that in a moment of recent reflection, he was suddenly struck by a half-forgotten memory of a case in 1974 in which he himself had initiated the negotiated release of terrorists in Italian custody. He had been arguing that the release and expulsion of political prisoners had been practiced by many countries. Now, not only could he cite an undeniable Italian precedent where formal legality was stretched, it also proved the continuity of his thought. Not one critical word had been uttered then, and furthermore, Moro recalled that there were other cases of the same kind.

The incident involving Moro himself originated in September 1973, when three Palestinians living in Rome were arrested by the Italian Secret Service. The Palestinians were found to be in possession of a powerful ground-to-air missile and had rented an apartment under the air-traffic pattern near Leonardo Da Vinci International Airport. They were accused of planning to destroy an Israeli passenger aircraft flying low over Rome. Tried and convicted, they were sentenced to five years in prison.

Soon afterward, a colonel in Italian intelligence stationed in the Middle East was approached in Beirut by the Black September organization, then the terrorist arm of the Fatah. The group that had been responsible for the recent massacre of Israeli athletes at the Munich Olympics "requested" the release of their three comrades. This was a request that the colonel, returning with alarm to Rome, advised his government to grant. Black September had raised the threat of carrying out operations in Italy, and the matter fell to the Italian Foreign Minister, at the time Aldo Moro.

Moro's part was unknown or unremembered by April 1978, and the details would not come to light until months later, since the president chose a more generic method of calling the case to mind.

What had happened, however, was that Moro dealt personally with the problem. ("Let's face it in realistic terms," he said then.) With the help of the colonel and the Ministry of Justice the "state of necessity" was explained in a judge's chambers and the Palestinians were released on the equivalent of one hundred thousand dollars' bail. This money had apparently been posted by the Secret Service, which in any event arranged for the three terrorists to fly to Lebanon, never to be heard from again.[4]

This may not have been the best way to protect Israeli aircraft,* but it was certainly good for the security of the domestic population, whose interests governments rarely pretend not to be No. 1. There is no state in the world that does not expel undesirable aliens.

"In all, about ten Palestinian terrorists captured in our country were freed on three occasions," an intelligence official said later. "These were decisions taken by the Italian Government, carried out by the Secret Service with a judicial cover."[6]

When the group of three was expelled in the fall of 1974, far from causing an outcry, Moro was in the process of forming his fourth government. Furthermore, the Sossi affair had taken place in the interim, and the new chief executive removed hard-line Interior Minister Paolo Taviani from his office of many years' standing. Unfortunately, Moro replaced him with his own protégé, giving the first ministerial portfolio of his career to Francesco Cossiga.

With an air of electric urgency, Moro on Wednesday or early Thursday, and probably both, wrote four long, private letters to recall the Palestinian case to men he hoped would back him up in different ways. He was planning to underscore this precedent, among other tactics, in a public letter timed for the weekend. Now, he wrote first of all to the former Under Secretary in the Ministry of Justice who had worked closely with him in obtaining the release of the three terrorists. His name was Erminio Pennacchini, presently a Christian Democratic member of Parliament. Moro asked for his help ("which consists simply in telling the truth") in publicizing the case and in locating the colonel who had dealt with Black September ("I would like him to be on the scene").[7]

---

* In a mysterious epilogue, the Italian military plane used to transport the Palestinians on the first leg of their journey, to Algeria, exploded in flight a short time later. Suspicion fell on the Israelis.[5]

Letters were also dispatched to two other Parliament members, Christian Democrats carefully chosen for their political leanings and their potential influence in the party and the government during the moment he was seeking to create.[8] The fourth letter, in a packet containing the others, went to Don Antonello with frantically vague instructions, with every minute counting, about where in Rome the others might be tracked down. Of one man, he wrote: "He may be at the Hotel Minerva (I think that's the right name and it's in front of the church) or he's at the Ministry of Justice or finally at the offices of the Christian Democratic group in Montecitorio. If for some damn reason I'm wrong about the name of the hotel, remember that the two buildings are like this: church-Minerva." The letters reached their destinations the same day.[9]

On Thursday and Friday, Moro composed his final letter to the party, a carefully articulated document with which he hoped to bring down the leadership, or at least bend them to his will. It was an effort to exert Samsonian pressure on the hard line, and during the same two days, he wrote six other letters. These were addressed to President Leone, Andreotti, Craxi, the presidents of both houses of Parliament—Fanfani for the Senate and Communist Pietro Ingrao for the Chamber of Deputies—and finally, a Christian Democrat whom Moro saw as the possible leader of his revolt.[10]

This man's name was Riccardo Misasi. He had never been especially close to Moro, nor part of the Moroite group. He was a leader of the grass-roots faction of the party and the chairman of a parliamentary justice committee. By some undisclosed route, Moro had learned that Misasi in confidential meetings with the party directorate had been supporting his cause. In Moro's last letter to Zaccagnini, he had twice mentioned Misasi in a flattering way, and many had found this puzzling. Now, trying to insert him into the key position, he wrote: "If you grab the legalists by the collar you'll win."[11]

The letters to Leone, Andreotti, and the presidents of Parliament were more or less formal appeals for "fair negotiations." Only with Andreotti did he refrain from using that phrase, warning him instead of possible political repercussions. "I know well that by now the problem is in your hands," he said. Now that the Socialists had come out with a "humanitarian orientation," his death would not go well for Andreotti. In the long run, he was playing a losing game by betting all on the Communists and Moro's own political design. Moro could not resist reminding the Prime Minister that he had given him his job in spite of opposition. "The only thing I can do in my present circumstances is to wish your efforts well," he said, referring to decisions Andreotti alone might be called upon to make regarding Moro's fate.[12]

In almost all of the letters of these days, he had been urging support for the Socialist line, and to Craxi, sending him "infinite thanks," he wrote:

> I am here to implore you to continue, rather, accentuate your important initiative. It must be made clear that this is not a matter of making appeals for an act of humanity, appeals that are completely useless, but of opening serious and balanced negotiations for the exchange of political prisoners.
>
> I have the impression that this is either not understood or is pretended not to be understood. This is the reality, however, urgent, with a minimum of breathing space. Every hour that passes may make it all in vain. . . . Believe me there's not a minute to lose. . . .
>
> It all seems to me a little absurd, but what counts is not to go around explaining, but, if something can be done, to do it.[13]

For the first time, in speaking of the prisoner exchange, he used the qualifier *balanced*. This would not go unnoticed by Craxi, but none of these letters would leave the people's prison until Saturday —the day he would make Rome tremble.

On Wednesday, Thursday, and Friday, Craxi had thoughts that Moro was already dead and that his efforts were time wasted. These feelings may have been due less to the days of tight silence from the people's prison than to the thundering rage of the other parties for what the Socialists had so meddlesomely proposed.

Vassalli and his group had made no great try about keeping their work secret. They were using the computer in the Ministry of Justice—the department of the executive in charge of the nation's prison system—to screen hundreds of candidates for a prisoner exchange, and as early as Wednesday the Socialist alternatives were fairly well known to all. Craxi and his aides were also meeting with all the majority parties explaining what they had in mind and seeking support, but apart from the old adherents to the soft line, no one joined their side, and Craxi was unable to hold his own party above back-stabbing ploys here and there.

The Christian Democrats made a daily ritual, sometimes twice daily, of confirming their immutable agony, which was becoming visually convincing, but the other majority parties threatened, insulted, slighted, and otherwise pawed the Socialist plan. When its authors were not vulgarly attacked *ad hominem*, it was considered as "strange," "not understandable," "truly disconcerting naïveté," and so on, as if the Socialists had suddenly come down with the same brain disturbance attributed to Aldo Moro.[14]

There were no political prisoners to free, not in Italy, said the Social Democrats.[15] But if they were freed, there *would* be, ran the Communist argument, since that would constitute an incentive for "the political conversion of common criminals."[16] The Republicans saw the Socialist project as representing *the* most deplorable surrender to the Red Brigades and "the definitive ruin of democratic institutions in Italy."[17] The Vatican harked back to the family's appeal in *Lotta Continua*, saying that its purpose was "to promote the yielding of the State," and it pronounced its own *no* to negotiations.[18] Only old Pope Paul had been left to wonder at his public audience on Wednesday how the world and the city of Rome could look on as "passive observers" while Aldo Moro's life was at stake. This seemed like only one question mark away from calling for negotiations, but the remarks of the Holy Father were now under careful surveillance by the Curia and there was to be expurgation in *L'Osservatore Romano*.[19]

"I'm terrified," said Craxi after three days of making his rounds of the majority parties. "I may be naïve, but what's happening is incredible. There's a great number of people—politicians and media executives—committed to present the Moro problem as insoluble. Maybe it is, but the attitude should be otherwise."

The aspect of the affair that distressed him most was the way Moro was being treated, he said. "Moro is alive, in the prey of alteration, which has not, however, obscured the central thread of his reasoning. But in this period he has been subjected to psychiatric analyses to demonstrate that he is not himself. Authoritative political voices have invited him to commit suicide. They are abusing him and making him out to be a coward.† May God forgive them!"[21]

Craxi declared this publicly. Privately, he said, "Someone wants blood. Moro's will justify a hemorrhage."[22]

Giulio Andreotti went on television Friday evening to deny that there was anything wrong in Rome. Appearing on a press-conference-type program called "Political Tribune," the Prime Minister said there were neither hawks nor doves in the new majority. Only "absolute solidarity" prevailed. Woe, he said, if the enforcers of law and order "were to suspect that behind their backs the government —violating the law—was negotiating with those who truly ran havoc with the law and continue to do so."

Looking solemn but otherwise inscrutable, he gave the impression that while the waters were troubled, Italians were all on the same ship of state; it was proceeding on course with a sure hand at the helm. Since the events that began on March 16, he said, "everything has continued to move along at a normal pace." He advised everyone to labor so that "this ugly season can be forgotten."[23]

If in the television hinterland anyone wondered what happened to Aldo Moro, he wondered still. Andreotti never mentioned his name.

Later that night, at 1:30 A.M. on Saturday, when there was nothing but porno TV on the airwaves, a telephone rang in an apartment not far from the east wall of Vatican City. It was answered by Fabio Isman, a reporter for *Il Messaggero*. In the past few weeks, Isman had become his newspaper's expert on the messages from the people's prison. His day's work had included writing a piece for the upcoming morning edition forecasting the imminent release of Communiqué IX with the announcement of Aldo Moro's death. Such was the latest opinion of Cossiga's think tank, with which he

† These obnoxious sentiments would travel and return to Rome fattened. *Il Messaggero* on May 7 would give an account of William F. Buckley's New York *Post* column of the day before in which he called Moro an "anti-Christian" because of the difficulties he was creating for his party. It was Moro's duty to take it all stoically, said Buckley, who urged the Pope to appeal to Moro "to die with courage."[20]

had consulted, and the estimated time of arrival was seen for this very Saturday, since newspapers had their largest circulation on Sunday and people had more time to read. His own view was that whatever might come "will be another hard blow to the State."[24]

Now, the nameless late-caller at the other end of the line told him that a letter from the president had just been slipped into his car. It was being given to Isman exclusively. It was highly unlikely that his home phone was tapped, and the risk of police interception was almost nonexistent. On the street, the reporter found the ten-page missive in the designated place. It was the original copy, and as the Moro papers were his beat, he immediately recognized the handwriting, though he judged it to be more "indicative of a state of tension and sometimes of dullness" than the penmanship in any of the earlier letters.

He drove directly to the *Messaggero* building across the Tiber, a ride of a few minutes that time of night. The paper was already on press. Pages one and three were recomposed, while Isman wrote a spot analysis: There was nothing left of the president of Christian Democracy, he said, only the tremulous hand that had written these lines for the Red Brigades, and had written them with clumsy error. "In reality, he is a man, undergoing who knows what, who is afraid to die."[25]

Rome had become a city of analysts.

22.

When the morning pinkened and the sun climbed, Aldo Moro's "Letter to the Party of Christian Democracy" looked somewhat different from the way it had been presented by night light. Among the men of power, some believed that the president had provided the answer to the wretched problem. He had turned loose forces that would be difficult to withstand. What the reporter had taken for a decline in Moro's hand (downhill writing, poor spacing, and the like), was later recognized (by the reporter, too) as the result of intense rewriting: updating, insertions, and last-minute editing. The result was a construction that was eminently limpid, as he moved from his last defense of his sanity, to his proposals, to his last testament on earth.

The finality of it was chilling. He was spending his all, and there was nothing more he could say afterward. There could be no more letters to the party from the people's prison.

He began straightforwardly, remarking that as far as his party was concerned nothing at all had happened since his last letter. Not that there was nothing to discuss, he said. There was much. What had been lacking was "the civil courage to open a debate on the theme proposed, which is the salvation of my life and how to attain it in a balanced framework."

There was the word *balanced* again. He went on:

It is true: I am a prisoner and I am not in a happy frame of mind. But I have not been subjected to coercion. I am not drugged. I write in my own style, however bad it may be, and in my usual handwriting. Yet, it is said, I am *someone else,* and I do not merit being taken seriously. So my arguments are not even answered. And if I make the honest request for a meeting of the directorate or some other constituent body of the party, because the life of a man and the fate of his family are at stake, what I get are continuous and degrading secret confabs, which means fear of debate, fear of the truth, fear of signing one's own name to a sentence of death.

He spoke now of how deeply saddened he was by the statement of some of his old friends, "who without either knowing or imagining what I am suffering, not unconnected with lucidity and my freedom of spirit, doubted the authenticity of what I was saying, as if I were taking dictation from the Red Brigades."
He seemed to be berating his friends, and by extension everyone else, for not having paid closer attention to his messages and the context in which they were being written. Yes, he was a prisoner; there were certain things he could say and others he could not say. The implication was clear—listen.

Why, there is not even a minimum of views I hold in common with the Red Brigades. And there is certainly no identity of views about the issue I have been sustaining from the outset (and, as I've shown, many years ago) that I believe to be acceptable, as happens in war, an exchange of political prisoners. And all the more so, when, by not exchanging, somebody continues to suffer seriously but remains alive and the other person is killed.

From a *balanced* exchange, he had gone now to the image of one man dying, himself, and *somebody* remaining alive but in prison. Then he recast the same image positively:

In concrete terms (and in all humility this is a point I permit myself to put before the Holy Father) an exchange benefits not only he who is on the other side, but also he who is in jeopardy of being killed, on the noncombatant side, in short, the common man like me.

Twice he had used the *singular* for the prisoners on *both* sides. And now, in the next two sentences, on the forty-fourth day of his imprisonment, Aldo Moro revealed in the only way he possibly could the rock-bottom terms for his release:

> By what manner of reasoning can it be deduced that the State would be put to ruin if, in this situation, an innocent man survives, and as compensation, another person, instead of prison, goes into exile? That is the long and the short of the matter.

Somehow, after all the blood schemes and heartbreak, after all the fear and anger, the bombast and swagger, the petty acts of selfishness, cowardice, and apathy, the great negotiator had succeeded in reducing the long and the short of it all to the biblical formula. One for one. The negotiations, so abominated in Rome and so yearned for by the Red Brigades, were in fact virtually complete. They had been conducted in the people's prison without surcease, and now Moro had emerged with all the magnificent pretensions of the Red Brigades pared to one dry bone.

The Red Brigades could go on everlastingly calling him a man guilty of crimes that had merited a death sentence; they could persist in saying that his release was worth thirteen fighting communists. But they had not stopped, and rather, had risked their lives to transmit his own description of the reality of his relationship with his captors. He was an *innocent* man whose release was contingent on the expatriation of *another person,* one noninnocent person who must continue to pay for his or her crime by expulsion from the motherland, ostracized from the culture and far from his or her family and friends, language, and mores.

What a long way from the judgment of the people's tribunal and the demands of the Red Brigades! But he could say this only by insisting, as they had in their communiqués, that his views were distant by one or two infinities from theirs. This was the face-saving ladder by which they could come down from on high. They could be as "humanitarian" as the next fellow. They had permitted him from the very first to speak of a prisoner exchange, and if after six weeks they had let him announce that he had reasoned it out to one for one, or even one for something less than one, evidently their cautious component could be placated and their trigger-happy comrades were still at bay.

Only the choice of the pariah person to be exiled remained to be negotiated. But Moro had not a shred of confidence that the party leaders would respond to the final offer with anything but the obstinacy he accused them of now. They, like the government and all the majority parties save the Socialists, had become entrenched, which was why the latter's role could be decisive, he said.

"But when?" Moro asked. "Grief, dear Craxi, if your initiative fails."

Craxi was on the right track, and he needed cheering, but he was running slow and too lamely for comfort. Moro was not counting on Craxi alone. Having given the formula for his release, he moved from the general to the specific.

The legal problem of expelling a prisoner of the state was reapproached by recalling the Palestinian precedents. "Then, the principle was accepted," he said. "The necessity of departing from the rule of formal legality (in its place there was exile) had been recognized." There were witnesses who could explain the details, he said, hoping the letters he had sent in this regard would have a positive effect.

These were the things that should have been discussed in the Square of Jesus, he said, and charging the leaders with neglect, he proceeded with his move to overturn them:

> For my part, I have said and documented that the things I say today I said in the past in completely objective conditions. Is it possible that there is not to be a formal and statutory meeting to show this? Is it possible that no one has the courage to ask, as I ask for it in the full lucidness of my mind? Hundreds of members of Parliament had wanted to vote against the government.* And now has no one a problem with his conscience? And all this from the comfortable excuse that I am a prisoner. . . .
>
> I ask Craxi if this is just. I ask my party, those who were my most loyal in the glad hours, if this is admissible. If further formal meetings are unwanted, well, I have the power to convoke at a convenient and urgent date the National Council [of

* In the period prior to the formation of the new majority, a bloc of Christian Democrats had organized against the Moro design. They called themselves the Group of 100 and said before yielding, they could not vote for a Communist-supported government as a matter of conscience—a matter Moro hurls back at them in the next sentence.

Christian Democracy] having as its purpose the theme regarding the ways to remove the impediments of its president. Ordering this, I delegate the Hon. Riccardo Misasi to preside.

He had used his last. Calling the highest governing body of his party into session, the president had exercised the chartered right of an office to which he had never aspired. He had gone over the heads of the directorate, whose powers derived from the council. By designating grass-roots leader Riccardo Misasi as chairman, he had sounded the bell of revolt. As for who would answer the summons, that was out of his hands and he knew it. He was done. He had only to make his last will:

It is known that my family's very serious problems are the fundamental reasons for my fight against death. Over many years and many events, my ambition has fallen and my spirit has been purged. And, in spite of my many faults, I believe that I have lived with quiet generosities and good intentions. I die, if this is what my party will decide, in the fullness of my Christian faith and an immense love for an exemplary family whom I adore and hope to watch from above. . . .

I repeat, I do not want the men of power around me. I want near me those who truly loved me and will continue to love me and pray for me. If all this is to be decided, let the will of God be done. But let no one responsible hide behind the fulfillment of a presumed duty. Things will be clear; they will be clear soon.

Aldo Moro[1]

Thus had he used up all his own earthly power, and being powerless now, in the hands of God and the Deciders, he acknowledged that he was no more the man he had been. He had repeated his will as to who might and who might not attend his funeral, but he restated it in a way that would not pass unnoticed in Rome. He had called them "men of power," not "authorities of State" or "men of the party," as he had before. He was no longer one of them and he could call them nakedly, for what they really were.

"For power and by power had he lived until nine in the morning of March 16," Leonardo Sciascia was to write. "He had hoped to have it again, perhaps to return and assume it fully, certainly to avoid having to confront *that* death. But now he knew that it was the others who had it, and he recognized in them its repulsive, ferocious, and stupid side; in his 'friends,' in those 'most loyal of the glad hours.' Those macabre, obscene, glad hours of power."[2]

23.

The series of confidential messages Moro had prepared in support of his open letter to the party were delivered all day Saturday, which came to be known as "The Day of the Post," in apparent recognition that if nothing else the prisoner was prolific. In the meantime, reactions began to seep from the Square of Jesus, and some unofficial or unattributable comments indicated that at the edges of the leadership Moro had broken through.

There were those who believed that Moro's call to assemble the National Council had to be respected. Riccardo Misasi, wearing a checkerboard tie, went to party headquarters. He refused to express any opinions publicly. The dark-eyed Calabrian was tormented by a fear, he would say later, that the image of a party openly divided into hawks and doves could furnish the reason to kill Moro, it being to perpetuate the split. Nevertheless, he felt the party had to go farther, and he was prepared to press ahead.[1]

At least one member of the directorate, cornered by two reporters in the oval elevator of party headquarters, admitted that Moro had lost none of his persuasiveness. The letter was filled with subtleties, he said anonymously, that could only be appreciated in the inner circle of party power.

"But there was one thing that struck me hardest of all," he said, "and I'm on my way to Zaccagnini to show it to him."

"What?"

"The fact that Aldo Moro refers to exile for one person only. Without doubt this is new. It's one thing to free thirteen *brigatisti* assassins, especially in view of public opinion. But when it's one, one person only, there are many roads open. There's the possibility of a stopgap solution, as has been done before."

"Like the Palestinians Moro refers to?"

"In effect, it happened the way he wrote it."

"So what are you going to do? . . . Convoke the National Council?"

"It certainly is an embarrassing request. . . . Now it's a matter of refining our line, and I think Moro has once again given us some useful indications when he speaks of one person in exile, if it's true."[2]

Craxi's letter from Moro was left at the desk of the Raphael, an elegant Rome hotel where the Socialist lived among a clutter of antiques. Picking out the word *accentuate* from the note, he immediately made a statement to the press, saying, "We will accentuate our efforts . . ."[3] which was his way of telegraphing the prisoner that his letter had been received and agreed to.

Craxi had no difficulty in reading Moro's one-for-one proposal correctly. He consulted with Giannino Guiso, who confirmed, as the *gola profonda* said later, that it was a "clear message" of what the Red Brigades would settle for. Craxi decided to concentrate on the first alternative, the "autonomous" prisoner exchange. The Vassalli group met that same day. From a computer-generated list of 147 possibles, the search began for one.[4]

All through The Day of the Post, the Moro strategy continued to gnaw at the hard line. This could be seen in how the centers of intransigence returned to the defensive with still more enfeebled reasoning power behind them. The Republicans said that if the government gave even the tiniest concession, "its domestic and international credibility would be reduced to zero."[5] The Social Democrats said the best way to save Moro was to post "very high rewards" for the capture of the kidnappers.[6] Communist Senator Pecchioli accused the courts of being soft on nonparty Communists and others who were attacking the government's position; the magistrates, out of fear or dereliction, he said, were not issuing any arrest warrants for "instigation against the powers of the State."[7] The Vatican said it was certain that Moro "does not want his own freedom at the risk of losing the State, the nation, and its citizens,[8] and one of the signers of the old-friends document, whom Moro had singled out by name in expressing his dismay, said the latest letter was "further proof" of what the old friends had known before.[9]

The rationality leak that had been sprung at the beginning was probably beyond plugging now, but there was on that day, or the weekend, a strong sensation that the collapse of the intransigent front was an any-moment affair.

The family added a well-timed shove by turning loose February '74. In the late afternoon on Saturday, a delegation showed up at the Prime Minister's palace with the memorandum to Andreotti asking that the Geneva Convention be applied. All that was needed was an official request to the International Red Cross, which was alerted and ready. It would then be up to the Red Brigades to accept mediation, which of course they already had. The delegation was received by the Prime Minister's press secretary. He promised to pass the word to the top.[10]

Andreotti was in the Square of Jesus, consulting with Zaccagnini and the other Deciders. Christian Democracy had to respond once more, and the matter had gotten down to last words.

Caught at the oval elevator after ninety minutes upstairs, Andreotti was "noncommittal."

He said, "Practically every evening we pass by Zaccagnini for an exchange of ideas and to see if there's any news. Today there's none."[11]

Unlike Papà, the family still controlled exclusively one power all their own: a formal break with the party. In spite of the urgings from the people's prison, they had been reluctant to use it. Over the past few days they had operated on the premise that the *threat* of a break could be equally as effective, while the power itself remained intact. It was not exactly a doomsday weapon, but now, coming along with Moro's call to arms, it was greater leverage than ever. It would peel away additional credibility from the party directors, encouraging any proponents of a meeting of the National Council. On the other hand, perhaps now the leadership would move on its own accord. Certainly, the pressure was already enormous, and the Saturday signs from the Square of Jesus had been generally positive.

The family's last resort might thus be better applied at some even more decisive moment.

This was not the thinking in the people's prison. In an unprecedented move, on Sunday afternoon a member of the Red Brigades made direct telephone contact with the Moro household to tell them so.

The caller, as revealed in an unusually clear wiretap recording, is a man intent on allowing no discussion of a message he has carefully rehearsed. He speaks with an authority lacking in the routine couriers. His voice is charged with tension, and his message is an arrow drawn on a bow. By chance, Mrs. Moro has answered the phone. The caller mistakes her for one of her daughters, perhaps misled at first by the vigorous timbre of her voice, but as likely, since she states her name, out of his race against time and a compulsion to regurgitate the information he is primed to convey. It is 4:32 P.M., April 30. The *brigatista* speaks first:

"Hello. Who is this?"

"I am Nora Moro."

"Listen. I'm one of the ones who have something to do with your father. I must give you a final communication."

"Yes," says Mrs. Moro, neither correcting his error nor betraying any emotion.

"We're making this last phone call out of pure scruple."

"Yes."

"Because your father insists in saying that you have been somewhat deceived and are probably reasoning on a misunderstanding, you see? Up until now, all the things you've done are—they have absolutely no value."

"Yes."

"We believe that by now nothing—the games are over and we have made a decision. In the coming hours there is nothing else we can do but carry out what we said in Communiqué VIII. So we ask only this: an immediate and clarifying response in this sense, if possible, by Zaccagnini. If that doesn't happen, you have to know that we can't do anything else but this. Understand? Have you understood me exactly?"

"Yes. I understand very well."

For some reason, maybe because he has gotten it all out and the woman upon whom he has heaped it stands passively, dripping injury, the *brigatista* feels a need to "explain" and has trouble finding the words:

"Look, this is the only possibility, and we're telling you simply out of scruple. In the sense that, you know, a death sentence is not something that can be taken lightly, not even by us. We're ready to bear the responsibility that falls, that falls to us, and what we would like, since—among us there are people who believe that you have not intervened directly because you've been badly advised—"

At this second reference to the family's failure to use its final hold on the party, which sounds almost like an admonition from Moro himself, Mrs. Moro can no longer restrain herself. She breaks in:

"We've done everything we could do and what they let us do, because—"

"There's the problem," says the *brigatista,* drowning her out. "The problem is—"

His voice runs on but Mrs. Moro cannot be stopped either, as she reveals a stark reality under the rush of his words:

"—they are really keeping us prisoners."

"—But the problem is political," he goes on, doubtless without having heard her. "That's why Christian Democracy must intervene on this point. We're very insistent on this because it's the only way to get to an eventual negotiation. If this doesn't happen in the coming hours—"

"Listen to me—"

"I can't discuss it. I'm not authorized to do it. I have to—"

"Forgive me."

"—merely give you this message. Only a direct response from Zaccagnini, immediate and clarifying and precise, can alter the situation. We have already taken the decision. In the coming hours, the inevitable will happen. We cannot do otherwise. I have nothing else to tell you."[12]

He hung up. The window on the Moro family, which newsmen scaling roofs had hoped to peep into, had been thrown wide open, if only to the electronic spies in Rome. Now it was slammed tightly shut again.

In the coming hours. Three times had he said it. He had wanted to be understood, to leave no space for illusion. In that he had succeeded. *Even* the Red Brigades had to take the death sentence seriously, as if it had been flung down frivolously. They were all in it together, the family, the killers, and the universe of "passive observers" so bewailed by Pope Paul. The inevitable was going to happen, despite the will of men, *in the coming hours,* and only broken-down, old-mareish Zaccagnini could save them.

The family was momentarily bewildered. Giovanni Moro grabbed the telephone and called Zaccagnini. Of this conversation, no tape exists, it is said, but young Moro spared the party chief none of the details of both the "final communication" and the family's alarm.

"Do something," he demanded, "otherwise they're going to kill him!"

Zaccagnini said all was not lost.[13]

An hour or so later, the family broke with the party leadership. Moro's press secretary, Corrado Guerzoni, came down to the lobby of the building in Via Forte Trionfale and read a statement to the press corps.

"The family," he said, "retains that the attitude of Christian Democracy is totally insufficient to save the life of Aldo Moro." Citing all five directors by name, and Zaccagnini first, the statement began to sound like an indictment:

> With their immobile behavior and their refusal of every initiative no matter where it comes from, they are ratifying the death sentence of Aldo Moro. If these five men do not want to assume the responsibility of declaring themselves disposed to negotiation, let them at least convoke the National Council of Christian Democracy as formally requested by its president.
>
> Our conscience can no longer remain silent in view of the attitude of Christian Democracy. We believe that with this appeal we are interpreting the will of our loved one. He is unable to express himself directly without being declared substantially mad by Christian Democracy and parallel groups of so-called "friends" and "acquaintances" of Aldo Moro.
>
> To avoid a long season of pain and death, there is no use denying the hard reality; it must be confronted with clear courage.[14]

But in a universe of passive observers, in which even the Red Brigades make appeals of their own kind, where was courage now? *Il Popolo,* Moro's own party newspaper, had not even the courage to print the family's statement.

A thousand miles away, in another European capital that same last day of the cruelest month, François Mitterand, head of the Socialist Party of France, made an entry in his diary that caught the courageless moment in Rome like a photograph. He was in Madrid attending an international Socialist conference, and as Craxi had flown in, too, the two men had talked of Moro privately. Mitterand wrote that his Italian counterpart had explained to him the reasons why, in spite of everything, he still believed in the possibility of saving Aldo Moro.

"He received a letter from the prisoner yesterday," Mitterand said, "and he is awaiting the combined efforts of Paul VI, Fanfani, and Saragat so that the President of the republic, Leone signs a pardon decree and the government decides on a limited exchange, one for one. . . ."

Craxi had spoken "terrible words" about the Christian Democrats, Mitterand said, quoting Craxi directly: "Many of them are finished with Moro. At the beginning they were saying, weeping, 'he's dead'; today, they're saying, weeping, 'he's mad.' If he returns there will be one too many."

"According to him," Mitterand went on, "the political chiefs of staff are thinking only of the coming local elections. When, believing that the State would not be dishonored if it were to negotiate, Craxi made a proposal in favor of Aldo Moro, the Demo-Christians accused him of seeking the Catholic vote."[15]

At midnight, all the world's Socialists, all the world's Communists, and many Christian Democrats began a long day of rest. It was May 1, the workers' holiday, and though there were no more illusions in Rome, there were prayers that even fighting communists might take the day off.

VI

IL GRAN RIFIUTO

I was not the uncontested chief of Christian Democracy. You can only say that I was present in it and I played my game winning or losing, rather, more often losing than winning. . . .[1]

24.

Paola Besuschio, at thirty-one, was a slender, dark-eyed woman from Verona with long black locks of hair she twirled repeatedly with an edgy finger. She had a degree in sociology from the University of Trent and was a former employee of the Siemens electronics plant in Milan. In 1975, according to her police record, she began her career as a political terrorist. It was a short career. On September 30 of the same year, she was arrested, and by May Day 1978 had been in prison ever since.

The reason for her arrest was that not surprisingly she was noticed by a young Carabiniere on a street in a small town of Tuscany. He had watched her get out of a car, and not only had this strikingly attractive stranger caught his eye, but also the model and number plate of her Fiat 124 were on a short list he had just received of vehicles stolen in the province during the night. He asked her to accompany him to the station, a few blocks away. She offered no resistance and they went off by foot. Suddenly, however, she darted down a side street, and was escaping handily when a second Carabiniere saw her running and took up the pursuit. She drew a pistol and fired at him. She missed. He fired in return, hit her in the right leg, and a few moments later, she was being lifted from the sidewalk in handcuffs.

"I am a political prisoner," she said when asked to identify herself beyond the false documents in her possession. "I appeal to the Geneva Convention." Later, she admitted that she was the Paola Besuschio wanted by the police in Milan for unspecified crimes but as a member of the Red Brigades.

These accusations remained in abeyance. On the charges of

weapons possession and having shot at a law officer, she was tried
and sentenced to fifteen years in a special antiterrorist prison of recent construction in Sicily.

A graceful woman of vivacious movements, she had a limpid
beauty, which was lost in her police photographs and would not endure very long in life. In prison, she had lately manifested a spinal
arthritis, an incurable, particularly crippling form of the disease
and a bane of heavy smokers, of whom she was one. Whatever had
been the threat she posed to the state in 1975, it was by natural
causes diminishing rapidly to none. On the Vassalli list of possibles
for an exchange of political prisoners, Paola Besuschio was one of
the names underlined now.[1]

Aldo Moro had given the uncluttered one-for-one equation, but
the choice of the other person, according to Red Brigades' lawyer
Guiso, "could not be symbolic or simply anyone; it had to be put in
terms of a real proposal."

This was the point he made at a meeting on May Day in Craxi's
small apartment in the Raphael. Guiso had just arrived in Rome
after a long consultation with Curcio and comrades in Turin. Craxi
had begun the meeting, attended by members of the Vassalli group,
with an exposition of the political situation, and this hardly differed
from what he had told Mitterand in Madrid.

Guiso reported that when he had asked the Red Brigades what
they thought should be proposed, the reply was, "Real things. Prisoners of war are real things. One prisoner of war for another. Nothing else." Such an offer corresponded perfectly, he said, to their
request for a political response. The Red Brigades were uninterested in the autonomous, legal procedure to be used, but cared
only about the result. Thus all parties could be satisfied. But one
had to bear in mind the "quality" of the proposal, said Guiso. "The
more you reduced the number, the more you had to think of quality. Paola Besuschio . . . was quality."[2]

Few people had paid any attention to her at the time of her trial,
and not much more was said when her name appeared twelfth on
the list of thirteen being asked in exchange for Moro. She was the
only woman of the group, the least criminally compromised, and
the least known publicly. She was, however, an important figure in
the Red Brigades' thirteen-totem representation. From her ideolog-

ical origins in the School of Sociology at Trent through her proletarian experiences in a Milanese factory, she had, going clandestine,
fired her first shot as a fighting communist, and she was the last of
the old breed.

And she was seriously ill. "To us, it seemed a humanitarian case,"
said Maria Magnani Noya, the woman member of the Vassalli
group, who was present at the May Day meeting. "Who could have
been scandalized if she were to have been let out?"[3]

Guiso and everyone else agreed, but the Sardinian lawyer
worried about another matter and said so. Rome moved at one pace
and the Red Brigades at another. In underground life, he had been
reminded in Turin, decisions had often to be taken with the
quickness of hunted prey, while the tempo of conventional political
motion was usually wait-and-see. Moro, perceiving this early, had
continually harped on the need for swift action, and now Guiso
recalled to the Socialists the peril in delay. Craxi's party alone
could offer nothing. There were doors to be knocked at, some to be
battered down.

"Craxi was an optimist," Guiso was to say. The party chief was
scheduled to make his proposal to the Christian Democratic directorate on the very next day. The support of Fanfani, Saragat, and
the Pope appeared as a guarantee that the pardon would be se-
cured, and the more complicated matter of exile would thus be
avoided. "That evening," said the lawyer, "it seemed to us that we
had resolved the problem of saving Aldo Moro."[4]

The *first* test came the next morning, Tuesday, May 2. Craxi,
tête-à-tête with Enrico Berlinguer in the private-club atmosphere of the old building that houses the party delegations to Parliament, gave a full accounting for his optimism. Doubtlessly unknown to Craxi, the Communist leader had, or would have
during the day, a secret message from Moro.* Berlinguer was being

---

* Moro is said to have written directly to Berlinguer, but the Communists deny
it. In any event, on May 2, Moro's long-time liaison with the Communist Party,
Tullio Ancora, received a letter from the prisoner asking him to intervene with
the above message in the Street of the Dark Shops. This brief note, a sort of
afterthought to the epistolary storm of the week before, was Moro's final political word on the matter, and contains this bitter remark: "I receive as a reward
from the Communists, after the long march, the death sentence. I make no
comments."[5]

asked by the prisoner that if he really believed in the hard line as a principle and not merely an ad hoc political expedient, let the Communist Party declare its position as a "point of reference" but lift the obstacles it had placed against his freedom.[6]

The only possible way Berlinguer could answer this challenge was by his reply to Craxi's proposal, and the press was the only way he could communicate his answer to the people's prison. Of his hour-long meeting with Craxi, *Il Messaggero* would report that afterward, Berlinguer "appeared sadder and more taciturn than usual." He said he hoped to see Craxi again. He was "unconvinced." Craxi, who had already been told by a high Communist official that Moro had forgotten the lesson of Socrates, said nothing. He looked like he had been given the hemlock.[7]

The *big* test was in the evening. At 7:30 P.M. Craxi and five or six of his closest aides met with their counterparts in the Square of Jesus—the five men whom the family had accused of ratifying the death sentence by inaction.

This hyperheated encounter, which went on past midnight, produced almost as many different first-hand versions as there were participants, though in the end very few points remained contested. According to a composite reconstruction, the meeting started with a fog-shrouded Zaccagnini saying a few words of welcome, whereupon he fell into a mute torpor that lasted through the night.

Craxi began with an exposition of his plan for the prisoner exchange. He said that he had the backing of the family, and they, along with the lawyers for the Red Brigades, were convinced that Moro's reference to a one-for-one deal had all the authority it implied. Warning that Italy, by rejecting the concept of negotiations, was unnecessarily limiting its future options and would suffer the consequences, Craxi turned the presentation over to his colleagues, who explained the work of the Vassalli expert group. The Socialists had come prepared with a file of precedents, international and domestic, for both negotiations with terrorists and the release of prisoners. Apart from the home case of the Palestinians, they had come up with several others, including an incident in the 1960s, when an Italian Communist, serving a life sentence for political homicide, was released and expatriated to an eastern European country by presidential action.

The Christian Democrats listened dutifully in silence, some taking notes of all that was being expounded. Thus far, all accounts of what happened concur. When a period of questioning was opened, however, they begin to differ.

The Christian Democrats, by their own version, asked the Socialists what proof they had that the release of Paola Besuschio or anyone else would assure Moro's return.

One of the five, Giovanni Galloni, said to the visiting group: "We cannot negotiate in the dark, otherwise we would be handing over the State lock, stock, and barrel to the Communist Party, the only one firm on the no side."

Flaminio Piccoli, another one of the five, who had been making more notes than anyone else, said he agreed with Galloni. "Before giving a definitive no," he observed, "we want to know what the concrete possibilities are. Through what channels has Honorable Craxi come to believe that, if we accept, Moro's life will be saved?"

At this point, Craxi stood up, gathered his papers, and led his group out the door, saying, "But these people have gone mad. How can anyone trust them?"[8]

So much for the Christian Democratic version.

The Socialists agree that they were asked to furnish proof that their line would obtain the projected result. They are also in accord that Craxi, who had just passed five hours of his life making the case being asked for stormed out in anger. But their telling of the clash is richer in detail.

"They looked at us," a member of the Socialist delegation said later, "as if to ask what we were up to, what did we want politically."[9]

Flaminio Piccoli reportedly said: "I'm ready to do whatever is possible to get Moro out, but you Socialists have not given me much encouragement to work with you."[10]

To the Socialists, this sounded like an offer for a secret political alliance, and the reason was that Piccoli had already been prospecting it privately in recent days. His plan was that if the Socialists were to reject the new majority and support a bilateral center-left (Christian Democracy-Socialist Party) government, with himself as

Prime Minister, he was prepared to do battle with Andreotti and Berlinguer, coming out for negotiations with the Red Brigades.[11]

Moro had called Flaminio Piccoli error-prone, but no one had ever said that his ambitions were aimed low. Sometime after midnight, he is said to have made it all perfectly clear, declaring: "In the end, what you're asking is that we negotiate. But what are you giving us in return?"

This was the moment, it seems, that Craxi got to his feet in a rage.

"There is someone in this room," he railed, "who wants Moro dead, and I'm going out and cry it in the streets!"[12]

It was no wonder that a meeting of this nature was retold according to what seemed to this or that person as emblematic, and political men are like fishermen when it comes to description. More striking, however, is that no one seems to have gotten around to discussing the great democratic principles being paraded like saints in public. In the back room there was no peril at all to the state and the republic. There was only the eternal heaving of the drowning sea of power. This, not one side or the other disputed.

25.

May, as always, was trying to be beautiful, primping a green bonnet and smiling at a mirror-blue sky. But this year the appointment with spring was late. It was a cheating, niggardly spring in 1978, eluding just when it seemed in hand. Artichokes were rare. The blossoms in Via Fani had fallen, but the leaves, like leaves everywhere in Rome, were stunted. The flower man's prices rose, though he sold more flowers than ever, mostly white carnations for the shrine of the men fallen there. The furry buds on the grapevines had been hammered by hail, at least those that would make Tuscan wine, and on many hills they would fail to recover; it was going to be a low-grade year.

Craxi was being hurled against his limits. In truth, the leader of a party with less than 10 per cent of the vote had little to offer the ruling party "in return" that was not mere vassalage. Craxi, alone, could make a stand for the inviolable dignity of man, but not a last stand. He could gamble. He could risk isolation, lay frosty calculation by the fire, and cry tough in the streets, but only if he was a certain victor. The one thing he could not do was cut the rope of retreat, and the Deciders, those in the 30 per cent bracket, knew it. Elections were not a fortnight away, and if Craxi had criticized the Christian Democrats of thinking only of the voting, he would not be a party secretary very long thinking of it less.

In the morning, May 3, as though to be certain he could not forget this, forces in his party were organizing to come out against him

publicly, and they would on that as well as the next day. The very
first was the old Resistance leader Sandro Pertini, a power unto
himself in the party (and now Italy's Chief of State). He said negotiations would mean the end of law and order. Recalling his presence at Mussolini's takeover more than half a century ago, he
added what seemed to many the Voice of History, saying, "I do not
intend to be forced a second time to go to democracy's funeral."[1]
Against this was the Socialist Party paper's lame defense of Craxi's
position, whimperings about the danger of further delay. By nightfall, the Socialist thrust seemed near exhaustion.

Yet it was more the result of snarling, tail-thumping cat strutting
on a roof than outright rejection. Nobody was ready to take responsibility for a no without dimensions. The penetrating point in
Craxi's plan—the point that made the end-of-democracy crowd
look panicked—was that only one crippled Communist need be
set free, and this was the point the other majority parties sought to
blunt.

Early in the day, one of those godsent stories was carefully
sprung, in which an unidentifiable high official of the Christian
Democratic party received an unmonitored telephone call from
"one of the widows" of the police officers slain in Via Fani. "If you
free even one of those assassins," she was reported as having said,
as if from a presence at the meeting the night before between the
Socialists and the Christian Democrats, "I swear to God I will burn
myself in a piazza in front of my two children!"[2]

While this not-even-one image hung like a flare on the horizon,
the Communists let it be known that they would bend "not one
millimeter" and favored "not one concession,"[3] though they would
look with attention at precise proposals. The Christian Democrats,
far from turning down their Socialist colleagues, asked the government to examine Craxi's proposal.[4] The government an hour or so
later said it would, but out of respect to the law and the families of
the men killed by the Red Brigades "not even the minimum departure" would be made from the government line. Nevertheless,
Craxi's proposal would be reviewed by the Interministerial Security
Committee, which would meet "in the coming days."[5]

In a turn of a midday sun, Craxi had been redrawn by the major
political powers as a man who thought little of police widows and

perhaps nothing at all of the law, and the minor powers were immeasurably less restrained. By the end of the day, Craxi could do no better than issue a statement that everything was "moving in the right direction," but there was talk at party headquarters of an "honorable retreat."[6]

All this would not get very far until the evening print and television news, and not until morning would it appear in the authoritative newspapers. If the Red Brigades were still waiting for a final word from Rome, Aldo Moro might see the night through.

They of course had said they would kill him in the coming hours. Seventy hours later, the government had said its interministerial committee would meet in the coming days. By the morning, it would become known that the committee would in fact decide on May 5; the Christian Democratic Party directorate would take up the matter of whether or not to convene the National Council at a meeting announced for May 9, and Parliament would debate the Moro dilemma on May 18—nearly five hundred hours after the terrible call last Sunday.

When somewhat more than one hundred of those hours had passed and Craxi had begun his retreat and the Paola Besuschio possibility had been picked apart to the marrow and the interministerial committee had said *no* but had asked for fresh ideas, and the family, waiting by the telephone, had locked themselves up in shutter-drawn darkness, the Red Brigades, on Friday, May 5, issued Communiqué IX, the last of a book of pain.

TO THE FIGHTING COMMUNIST ORGANIZATIONS,
TO THE REVOLUTIONARY MOVEMENT,
TO ALL PROLETARIANS.

Comrades, the battle begun on March 16 with the capture of Aldo Moro has reached its conclusion.

. . . Insofar as his cronics in Christian Democracy, the government and the accomplices who support it asked for his release, we furnished a possibility, the only one feasible, but at the same time concrete and real: . . . FREEDOM IN EXCHANGE FOR FREEDOM. In these fifty-one days the reply of the Christian Democrats, its government and the accomplices who support it has been given in all its clarity, and more than in words and official declarations, they have given it by deeds, by the counterrevolutionary violence that the clique in the service of imperialism has flung at the proletarian movement.

The communiqué then went on at length about the hundreds of preventive arrests, special laws, and the "political genocide" undertaken by the government with the "lurid collaboration" of the Communist Party since March 16. In that period, the state of the multinationals had been stripped of its "grotesque mask of formal democracy" and had revealed itself as nothing but an instrument of imperialist counterrevolutionary terrorism. Thus no amount of antiguerrilla psychological warfare could conceal, according to the Red Brigades, that the fifty-one days (which in fact had been miscounted) was a victory for the revolutionary movement and a "burning defeat of the imperialist forces."

Craxi's proposals, the communiqué said harshly, were worthless. They failed to come to grips with the problem of a prisoner exchange—which was true, since they had obtained the release of no one—and his references to the inhuman conditions in the special prisons were the proof of what had always been denied. Craxi was accused of simply jockeying in the game of power and hustling for votes. His position on the prisoner exchange was no different from the others, "and that is enough for us."

Finally:

In words, we have nothing more to say to Christian Democracy, its government and the accomplices who support it. The only language the servants of imperialism have shown themselves to understand is the language of arms, and that is what the proletariat is learning to speak.

Thus, we conclude the battle begun on March 16, executing the sentence to which Aldo Moro has been condemned. [Emphasis in original.][7]

Grammatically, there was but one way to read the communiqué. The battle was over. The possibility of obtaining the prisoner's release no longer existed. By the use of the present participle *executing*—given the time difference between the transmission and the reception of the printed message—Aldo Moro was either already dead or would be as a result of an action taking place now, such as pulling a trigger.

Read politically, none of this was true. Aldo Moro was alive. His release could still be had but only an act *in extremis* could stay the trigger hand. In the previous communiqué, the future tense had been used ("we will execute"); now they had gotten to the present, and as there is no tense more final than the present that is not a form of the past, the next communiqué, should there ever be one, was highly predictable. The threat issued by the Red Brigades was a rare political phenomenon. As there was no way to back down, it proved that an irrevocable decision had been taken. This was a threat that had 100 per cent credibility.

Communiqué IX had come eleven days after the eighth. It was extremely unlikely that another eleven days would be allowed to pass, since those were the days in which Moro's and the family's powers had been completely burned out. They were impotent now, as impotent as a *brigatista* without a gun, and they had already had a hundred hours. It was Friday afternoon. They had almost always released their communiqués on Friday or Saturday to let their message ripen over the weekend. Would they give Moro the weekend, say, until Monday, when all the reactions would be in? But the party directorate would not meet until Tuesday. Surely, they would want to know if the National Council was or was not to be convened. Or, would they?

The true, open-ended ultimatum was on. It was no more a question of do-or-die, for even the thing done might come too late. The time of the gun had arrived.

Rome fussed and fretted over the "excruciating gerund" named *executing*. The men of power chose a grammaticopolitical interpretation. Moro for at least the fourth time since March 16 was dead with a question mark, but all was not lost, for nothing would be left untried. The credibility of this position had been reduced to zero, though the durability of the hard line seemed everlasting.

In the darkened penthouse on Via Forte Trionfale, the family had slightly more to go on than the outside. It augured poorly. Eleonora Moro that afternoon received a letter from her husband,

a letter of *addio*. There was no more politics in Papà; only a few
regrets and a simply said farewell:

My sweetest Noretta,

After a moment of very slender optimism, owing perhaps to a
misunderstanding of what was being told to me, by now, I believe, we're at the conclusive moment. I don't think it's worth-
while discussing the thing in itself or the unbelievable sanction
against my mild and moderate ways. Certainly, aiming for
good, I made a mistake in the way I defined my life. But by
now nothing can change. One can only recognize that you
were right. One can only say that perhaps we would have been
punished in some other way, we and our little ones.

I would like the full responsibility of Christian Democracy to
remain very clear, with its absurd and incredible behavior
[phrase illegible]. It's also true that many friends perhaps
made no move because they were misled by the idea that
speaking out would have harmed them, or, worried about their
own personal positions, they did not move in the way they
should have. Only a hundred gathered signatures would have
forced [the party] to negotiate. But this is all in the past. . . .

Now unexpectedly, just when some slender hopes were shining
through, comes the incomprehensible order for the execution.
Sweetest Noretta, I am in God's hands and yours. Pray for me,
remember me gently, caress all the sweet little ones. God help
you all. A kiss to all of you.

Aldo[8]

Although he seems to have meant the care of the memories of
him, rather than his earthly existence, he had placed himself in her
frail hands, and now she held him and did not surrender. She was
convinced that he could still be rescued by means that had not yet
been tried. The Red Brigades knew, more than anyone else, perhaps, that the hard line could no longer be broken by the methods
used or still being used. If Zaccagnini was the weakest link, it was
evident now that inertia was on his side and he was no more mova-
ble than the strongest. Yet they had not killed their prisoner. Their
guns were clean and loaded. The order had been given. Moro had

testified to that. Yet they were waiting. But everyone's position had been rendered transparent by now. They were waiting for the *deus ex machina*. Everyone's but one. They were waiting for Fanfani.

Eleonora Moro telephoned. By the power of her voice alone, for she was otherwise powerless now, she brought Amintore Fanfani to her home.

Craxi had been left "with the lit match in his hand," as the Italians say when we might use "holding the bag." He had been made to appear by the majority parties as some sort of subversive, an underminer of the republic. Even the tiny opposition parties who favored negotiations accused him of vulgar politicking. His own party was in open rebellion, his ancient protector, Pietro Nenni, was said to be "perplexed." Now the Red Brigades, too, had called him an "illusionist" as well as an opportunist, which might have been a commendation if it all did not look so true. He had begun his retreat, but apparently not soon enough. The leader of the strongest minority faction in his party, who controlled 25 per cent of the membership, had broken the pact of silence. He had given an interview to the newsweekly *Panorama*, due to be out in a few days, launching an ultimatum of his own to Craxi.

Craxi's retreat, unless he wished to retreat to obscurity, had been cut off by a mutinous rear guard. He had only one course to follow now, one goal to pursue. He had to bring home Aldo Moro.

To the whittled-down group that remained loyal to Craxi, it seemed odd that a whole quarter of Communiqué IX had been given over to a critique of the Socialist proposals. Was there a message within the message? One phrase in particular leaped from the page. In repeating for the third time that Craxi had not faced the "real problem," the prisoner exchange, the Red Brigades had written, "and that is enough for us," meaning enough to fault him. In other words, there was really only one element lacking in his plan, so the reasoning went, for if he had succeeded in getting someone out of prison, there would not have been enough cause to reject his proposals. The Craxians saw a glimmer of encouragement from the Red Brigades. Give us real things, they had said. Now, they appeared to be saying get someone out and Moro will live, though there was no nonviolent way for Craxi and his first team alone to spring anyone but an unruly drunk or a hooker. And perhaps it was all wishful thinking. The Red Brigades' lawyers would know, they hoped.[9]

By Friday evening, very little optimism could be scraped together from a sounding of the three exegetes of *brigatismo*. The main reason was the time factor that had already been underscored by Giannino Guiso. Now that the decision to kill had gone operational, the slow-moving gears on the outside all but eliminated any chance that they might in some way be made to mesh with the high-speed ones inside. Furthermore, under the present conditions, the effectiveness of the triumvirate of lawyers as interpreters had fallen very low. Their sources of information were suddenly made useless by their intrinsic roundaboutness and filtration. Even Renato Curcio admitted to Guiso that these were tactical moments understandable only to those at the core. For everyone else, it was sensory guesswork now.

Gloomiest of all was Sergio Spazzali. "The Christian Democrats," he said, chain-smoking after reading Communiqué IX, "had to say something, not send Bettino Craxi around. And that something had to be a signal in the area of an exchange of prisoners, that is, their willingness to let somebody out. This signal had to be given. They didn't give it. For me, it's all over."[10]

Eduardo Di Giovanni believed that if the signal were strong, authoritative, and immediate it would still stop the execution.[11] Guiso thought the signal could come from any high official of Christian Democracy, not necessarily Zaccagnini or any of the five directors. It had to show an inclination to negotiate and need not go into details. This would suspend the sentence, he hoped, and the prisoner exchange could proceed with the death threat lifted.[12]

Such, anyway, was the premise from which Craxi began anew. At first, the Socialists thought of Riccardo Misasi as their Mayday signaler, but on Saturday they thought bigger, calling on Senator Fanfani.

26.

"A man with a certain old-fashioned flair for the great break-through."

That was how Aldo Moro described Fanfani during his interrogation. In his deposition to the Red Brigades, in which he had trimmed no criticisms of his peers, he had spoken only praise of the "sometimes freakish" traits of Fanfani, for whom he used the word *great* twice more ("great chief," "great ambition"). Fanfani, said Moro, was of the rare species of De Gaulle, impulsive, dynamic, and capable of realizing what others are capable of only dreaming.[1]

Nearing seventy, Amintore Fanfani, ex-Boy Scout, ex-Fascist, ex-zealot of the left, right, and center, had lost few of his virtues and had added prudence to it all. Had he blown his cover sooner, who would be left to save Aldo Moro? The old Tuscan senator was probably second only to the prisoner himself in bitterness felt toward men in his party. He had held every office his ambition desired save one, the presidency, and twice when it had been in easy reach the incorrigibly caballing Christian Democrats had bartered it away. Not that he shied from the marketplace of power. Fanfani had a front bench. As an opponent of the new majority, he was at this moment as far from becoming Chief of State as his old rival Aldo Moro, but now Fanfani was in a perfect position, empathetically and politically, to rescue the prisoner stylishly.

By Saturday afternoon, Fanfani had met with Eleonora Moro and a Craxian envoy. He had agreed to redeem his promises to the family and bring his support for negotiations out into the light of day. The signal was in the making. A plan to back it up with deeds was approved by all.[2]

The situation on Saturday afternoon, May 6, from the point of view of the improbable trinity of Fanfani, Craxi, and Eleonora Moro was as follows:

Twenty-four hours had passed since the receipt of Communiqué IX without a word, public or otherwise, from the Red Brigades. Presumably, Aldo Moro was still alive.

Rome had been temporarily emptied of power, as the leaders of the parties spread across the country campaigning for elections only eight days away. This was creating the impression, purposefully, of business as usual, and coming at this moment was a near equivalent of yet another *no*.

Zaccagnini, who seemed to be making a remarkable recovery from the bottom of his despair, had let it be known that the party would set a date on Tuesday for convening the National Council sometime around the *end* of May. The topics to be discussed would be the results of the elections and modifications of the party's statutes. Naturally, no matter how many people in the interim might be killed and maimed by the Red Brigades, a meeting of this kind could not avoid some mention of Aldo Moro, but this was de-emphasized.

Andreotti, in a surprise announcement, had said that the government would not object to a request by Amnesty International to examine the conditions in the special prisons. Even this, however, was being attacked acridly by the Communists and the Republicans, and whatever influence it might have on the decision of the Red Brigades at this stage could hardly be less than negative.[3]

Discouraging and giving cause for reflection to all *brigatisti,* however, was the result of an assembly of autonomists' groups in the Movement, held at the University of Rome. They unequivocally condemned the impending threat. The execution of Aldo Moro "would be a gross political and strategic error," said an assembly leader. "The proletariat, communists, do not kill political prisoners." The meeting passed a motion warning the Red Brigades that Moro's corpse would be used by a reunited and reinvigorated establishment as the "mystical body" by which the state would be made stronger than ever. It would offer the pretext "to unleash the first true attempt to suppress and disperse the revolutionary sectors of the movement."[4]

To the additional twenty-three alleged ultraleftists rounded up and arrested preventively that morning, the autonomist line may have appeared more politically astute than the Red Brigades.

Such was the public information feeding back to the strategic command.

On the confidential side, which was not necessarily beyond the realm of Red Brigade infiltration, some steps were, or appeared to be, in motion.

A decree providing for the release of Paola Besuschio as an act of clemency in consideration of her poor health had reached, or was on its way to the desk of President Leone. The Chief of State had reassured both Fanfani and Mrs. Moro that he would sign it ("Donna Eleonora, my pen is in my hand"),[5] but there were maddening complications.

While Article 87 of the Italian Constitution grants the power of pardon and the commutation of sentences exclusively to the President, the normal practice was that he did not act unless solicited by the Minister of Justice. Leone was reluctant to break with procedure.

On Friday, Mrs. Moro had called the minister, Francesco Bonifacio, and he said, "We are going to pardon a *brigatista*, but we can't do it too hastily." On Saturday, Mrs. Moro called again. The minister could not be reached. She would keep on trying.[6]*

Foreseeing the possibility of this predicament, the Vassalli group had prepared an alternative. Oddly, under a recent antiterrorist law, a prisoner may be released on parole by a simple court order if it is decided that his or her health is endangered by the rigors of prison life. This meant that even prison hospitals had to be considered by a judge as unequipped or unable to treat the prisoner's illness, and a very sick *brigatista*, indeed, had to be found.[7]

A decision by the judiciary to parole, which could impose any limiting conditions it deemed wise, could not be overruled or unabided by any other branch of government or state institution.

With the unofficial co-operation of personnel in the Ministry of

* Besuschio's case presented some further technical difficulties. A potential substitute was found in a woman terrorist, Franca Salerno, who had just given birth in prison.

Justice, the Vassalli group had, under secrecy, selected a twenty-five-year-old man who seemed to meet all the prerequisites, though he was not in the Besuschio class. His name was Alberto Buonconto, and without his knowledge, the process of procuring some measure of his freedom was already well advanced.

Buonconto was not a member of the Red Brigades. Nor was his name on the list of thirteen. But he had declared himself a political prisoner, and the guerrilla organization in which he had participated was represented by three persons on the Red Brigades' request. Buonconto was in a special prison near Naples, and had been in custody since 1975.

Arrested in October of that year, he was convicted of relatively minor crimes: possession of false documents, a stolen pistol, and some banknotes belonging to a ransom for a kidnap victim who was released unharmed. For this, he had been sentenced to 13 years, which an appeals court had lately cut to 8½ years. His case was under review by the Supreme Court, and with time served and reduced for good behavior and poor health, he could look forward to being released in any event before getting much older.

Buonconto, according to medical examiners, was seriously ill. Apart from a chronic liver disease, he was in a state of depression with loss of speech and locomotion. By that same Saturday afternoon, the second-ranking authorities in the Ministry of Justice working with and solicited by Vassalli and Buonconto's lawyer had ordered the transfer of Buonconto from the antiterrorist prison to a public hospital, where, kept under guard, he was to be treated.

He was due to be moved on Sunday. On Monday morning, since the bureau concerned would be opened no sooner, a legal brief requesting his parole would be filed with the Court of Appeals of Naples. Normally, in a judicial district with only seven magistrates to handle the affairs of four thousand prisoners, it would take weeks for a decision, but perhaps the circumstances might merit a speeding up of the process.

All this was known to Fanfani, the Craxian Socialists, and the family. It formed the backdrop to the last of a tragic play.

The signal was set for Sunday afternoon. It would be filmed for the evening television news and sent as a bulletin by press wire. It would be unmissable. It would not be given by Fanfani himself but by the Fanfanian presence in the party directorate, Giuseppe Bartolomei. Bartolomei, head of the Christian Democratic Senate delegation, was one of the five men whom the family had accused of lethal inaction. His voice raised now might in some ways be even more effective than Fanfani's, but the president of the Senate was choreographing more than a simple signal.

The plan was for Bartolomei to give an execution-staying high sign that something big was abrew. Fanfani on the following day was to go on the attack against Interior Minister Cossiga. He would charge him with gross inefficiency. After seven weeks of massive police operations without the slightest progress, the government had to own up to its failure, Fanfani intended to say. Rome had been incapable of rescuing the prisoner *manu forti,* and it had now to use other means. Aldo Moro must not be made to pay the price for the ineptness of Cossiga and the police forces.[8]

The scapegoat method, as always, is the all-purpose solution for everyone except the scapegoat. But it is no easy matter in any country to offend its law-enforcement services, and it was extremely risky in this circumstance with policemen being shot dead in the streets. If, however, anyone could do it and survive the experience it was the durable senator from Tuscany. Two years earlier, he had conducted a vigorous law-and-order campaign and had been criticized as being authoritarian. Now, in a moment when law and order had reached a state of blind veneration, he could pass every loyalty test. Yet he prepared his move with utmost and tortured caution.

A little past nine o'clock on Sunday morning, Eleonora Moro came outside in a driving rain. The police had recently prevented all unauthorized access to Via Forte Trionfale 79, and even newsmen could get no nearer than 150 feet to the building entrance. There were unhappy symbols in the way the family had been cordoned off, and it was difficult to see her as she got into her chauffeur-driven car and went to a nearby church. She was back in an hour, home again with the family.

She made telephone calls that day. The Minister of Justice was still unreachable. The Chief of State's pen was in his hand. She received no visitors. Only one telegram came. It brought the well wishes of Colonel Gaddafi.[9]

The rain let up early and the day brightened, but in Rome there was a rainy-day feeling that Moro was surely dead by now, so long after the last communiqué. It seemed that time had outrun hope and it was almost not indecent to get on to next things. Italy, everyone was reminded on soccery Sunday, would be in the World Cup competition in Argentina. And that was but a few weeks away. The Pope at noon had nothing more to say about Moro. Some newspapers published excerpts leaked by government sources of the prisoner's farewell letter to his wife. They were inaccurate textually, but conveyed an apparition dressed in mourning. The Red Brigades were closing down, some said, looking only for the "strategic moment" to announce where Aldo Moro's body lay.

Aldo Moro's body still breathed, and the broken heart inside it pumped regularly. He waited.

In a Tuscan town called Montevarchi, which lay flat in the valley of the Arno, Senator Bartolomei gave the signal to the Red Brigades. Speaking in Fanfani's home province in the context of the campaign speeches being made all over the country, Bartolomei ended a long and meandrous address, saying, "Christian Democracy has urged the government to examine the feasibility of the various initiatives prospected for the liberation of Moro."[10]

A weaker signal could scarcely have been devised. It was a cry from the wrong side of an ocean or a whistle blown in a vacuum. The only noteworthy feature was the attention given to its publicity. It made newsmen wonder why anyone had bothered and they reread what the Fanfanian had said. But these were aspects that would not go beyond the newsroom. The message itself was ambiguous, to say the least. It contained its exact opposite in an equal measure, like in one of those optical illusions where a cube can be seen as a height or a depth depending on the will of the beholder. By the time the Monday-morning newspapers came out it was hurtling back to obscurity.

Il Messaggero, for example, buried it in a larger story about the "extreme attempts" to save Moro. "Why does Bartolomei insist on relaunching 'the various initiatives,'" it asked, "which consist mainly of those of the Socialist Party?" The government's reply was already known, it pointed out. "Something may be moving," said the paper.[11]

The Craxians on Monday morning were convinced that this was not enough. In fact, the signal had misfired and the lack of space its true significance had received could become the determining factor, they believed. Fanfani met separately with Craxi and Mrs. Moro. He said that before this day was out he would speak in no uncertain terms.[12]

Early that Monday morning, lawyers for political prisoner Alberto Buonconto, who had already spent a whole day in the relative freedom of a public hospital, deposited the legal request for his parole. The chief justice of the Court of Appeals in Naples, Ottorino Longo, received a telephone call from the Ministry of Justice explaining the true nature of the lawyers' brief. No one was attempting to influence his decision, Longo was told, but it could make the difference between life and death for Aldo Moro. Precisely who the caller was and whether the "noninfluence" was meant to be positive or negative remain unknown. In any case, the chief justice on Monday sent an urgent telegram to Buonconto's prison asking for his medical records.[13]

In the meantime, the men of power who had been out campaigning returned to Rome. They began to pick up the scent that something was happening beyond the perimeter of the executive branch and the parties.

Zaccagnini, who had made an electoral speech in Pavia speaking of the state's handling of the Moro case in the past tense, had a long talk with Cossiga on Monday. Both men surmised what Fanfani was up to and they agreed that it had to be rigorously opposed.[14] Berlinguer, looking for votes in Viterbo, had said that "weakness and errors" had to be met head on with "intransigence at every sign of subversion . . . and tolerance," and now the Communists were beginning to speak with disdain of proposals that had already been declared "unproposable and infeasible" and were still making the rounds.[15] These were signals, too.

The family had given up on Justice Minister Bonifacio, and pressure was being exerted from all quarters directly on Leone to sign the decree. Leone continued to say that he would, and by now this had drawn Andreotti's attention.

Andreotti had spent part of the weekend writing or authorizing a memorandum of reply to February '74 as to why the Geneva Convention could not be applied. Calling in the International Red Cross, in Andreotti's opinion, would acknowledge that a state of civil war existed in Italy, and while the "killings, woundings, and taking of hostages constitute serious fragmentary conflicts," that would not be true.[16]

Now he would deal with Leone.

Fanfani, his great bald head fringed with white hair, went home to Arezzo, where in the outlying parish of St. Stephen he was born when the century was young. He, too, made a campaign speech to his constituency. Not that he needed their votes. In 1972, after the so-called snipers in his party had, promoting Leone, sabotaged his bid for the presidency, the new Chief of State had used his constitutional power, making Fanfani a senator for life.

This evening, Fanfani spoke not for his own good but for the good of Aldo Moro. Fanfani spoke the language of Dante, but in a haggard and ponderous form that was uniquely Fanfanian. As he had promised, he attacked the government's shortcomings and defended a man's right to live. It sounded like this:

> Those who have been struck by the harshness of the particular consequences of past negligence, and they are many, must not forget that the moral limits cannot be determined by the individual painful cases that happen, without first defining a strategic and tactical framework. Its definition indicates what, respecting law and the Constitution, can be done without yielding, but without negligence, in the defense of the life and liberty of every citizen and therefore of Aldo Moro, too.[17]

Only wide-awake Talmudists of the political class in Rome could distill meaning from Fanfani's address in Arezzo. It was plain enough to them that he was accusing Andreotti of neglect and advocating the acceptance of the Socialist line. But why? And where was his leverage? Had the Fanfanians succeeded where other factions had failed in making that elusive, temptress alliance with the

Socialists to smash the new majority, drive the Communists back, and replace the Andreotti government with a reempowered center-left coalition?

These were the questions being asked on the evening of May 8 while Fanfani was on his way back to Rome. Their only connections with Aldo Moro were that both the center-left and the new majority were the creatures of his mind, and that his life and his death were the spears and the shields in a war between one and the other.

Fanfani had taken only an old man's plunge, or, rather, had dipped one toe into hostile waters. Tomorrow, at the meeting of the party directorate, he would live up to his obligation in full, he said to those who worried that his signal, too, had been short of loud and clear. After explaining himself in the privacy of the Square of Jesus, he would issue a public statement. He had made no deal with the Socialists. All he wanted was Leone's signature, which would rectify the government's negligence and save Aldo Moro.[18]

Leone wanted the same thing. He had said it that evening once more, and an aide had repeated it to a friend of the family. But Leone, after having spoken with Andreotti, Cossiga, and Zaccagnini, knew now he was helpless alone.[19]

"Only by tiring myself out," Giovanni Moro told a friend on the phone that night, "can I convince myself that there are still some ways to save my father."[20]

Aldo Moro had stopped eating. He had stopped shaving. Once in a while, he took some tea. He made a request. He hoped that when it would all be done, his wife would be among the very first to know, and that she would be told, not by the blare of a radio or a hypocrite's voice on the phone, but by someone she knew to be true.

He did not want his body to fall into the hands of the state.

His request was granted. He waited.

The anonymous selector of articles from the morning newspapers for the press review prepared by Parliament for the men of power was at work at first light on Tuesday in the palace built by Bernini. He or she would have a good briefing ready for that time of day when *cappuccino* and all kinds of brioche sell best.

A piece clipped from the *Corriere della Sera* set the tone. After Fanfani's speech in Arezzo, it said, "all eyes are pointed at the Square of Jesus." Fanfani was going to call the government to action, said the paper's political correspondent in a forecast of what would transpire that morning, and Craxi would back him despite open dissent in his party. "But the idea of granting a pardon to one of the imprisoned terrorists has been shelved. The government considers it unrealizable and the Demo-Christian leaders are in agreement." Would there be any news? Christian Democratic spokesmen excluded it. Zaccagnini had returned from his campaign travels "more convinced than ever that he has chosen the right road."

Craxi's paper, *Avanti!*, came out with strong support for Fanfani along the lines of government and police ineptitude, but the chief editorial writer of *La Repubblica* was relieved to note that the Socialists had denied having made any deal with the powerful senator. Though the new majority walked on a thin sheet of ice, he said, it did not appear likely that Fanfani's grand entrance, without a Socialist pact, could alter the power equilibrium in Rome. "So one can only welcome the incitements of the Fanfanians," it said wryly, "as a contribution to the will to do better and more."

From the Street of the Dark Shops, *L'Unità* wondered in the press review "how anyone could continue to speak of who knows what new initiatives." The silence of the Red Brigades since "that gerund" last Friday was nothing but a tactic to force the republic to cede. If the Andreotti government had any failing, it could be corrected by "clear ideas, a firm hand, and a strong will."

The selector gave the first page of his review to Christian Democracy's *Il Popolo* so that when the men of power would open their copy of the digest they would begin their workday with the following headline:

STILL ANGUISH AND HOPE
FOR THE FATE OF ALDO MORO[21]

He had bathed or showered. He did not shave. He had no breakfast. He had been given all the clothing he had arrived in, freshly laundered, cleaned, and pressed.

He dressed. He put on two layers of underclothing, the outer longer and fuller than the inner. He put on a pair of midnight-blue socks. He put on a blue-lined white shirt made by Ninarelli of

Bologna and bearing the initials A.M. He clipped cufflinks into
place. He knotted a blue-and-white tie, carefully, as always. He
put on a dark-blue suit, the cuffed trousers held up by white sus-
penders, and the matching vest and jacket. He slipped his feet
into a pair of black moccasins. Everything fit loosely. They were
winter's clothes, not spring's.

He stood. He had dressed himself completely, closed all of the
twenty-odd buttons on his clothing correctly. He had made only
one error. His socks were on inside out.

In Naples, Chief Justice Longo received the medical history of
parole candidate Alberto Buonconto. It confirmed that for the past
two years Buonconto had been suffering from "hepatic disorders."
There was no mention of depression. The judge withdrew to the
chambers of his mind.

He left the prison where he had spent the past fifty-four days. A
few of those days, he had said when he used to think and speak of
such things, had been passed in "intellectual idleness."[22] Now he
went outside, walking. Everything he had arrived with had been returned except for the briefcase filled with papers that once, even as
late as ten days ago, had importance to him. Now it had none. He
did not actually have on him his wristwatch, wallet, and the
woman's bracelet of sentimental value. Someone else was holding
these things. They were in a plastic bag.

The meeting in the Square of Jesus had been scheduled for 10:00
A.M., but it would not begin punctually. In Rome, the time
established for an appointment is, by custom, more often an indication of when to set out than when to arrive. But the seats of
power are contained in a tiny baroque quadrant of the city.
Andreotti, for example, would have to travel less than half a mile
from the Prime Minister's palace to the Square of Jesus.

Only two men were expected to speak in behalf of a softer line,
Riccardo Misasi and Fanfani. Misasi would address the group before Fanfani, who being the senior man would speak last.

The person with the plastic bag and at least one other person, a
man and a woman, it seems, walked with him to a car. The car had

a hatchback. Someone opened it and asked him to get inside. He was over five feet, ten inches tall. The space in the hatchback was only about half that in width. He could think of no reasoning that would persuade the persons to offer him a more adequate place, and he most certainly would not resort to any physical force. He was almost as powerless as a man can get.

Bending, folding, twisting, he squeezed inside the hatchback. In the least uncomfortable way, he reclined on an orange blanket. The car was red.

Only the men and women who attended the meeting in the second-floor salon in the Square of Jesus know what was actually said that morning, and they no longer care to speak of it to others. Of Misasi's intervention, he later said laconically, "I began to explain my thoughts. Then Fanfani took the floor."[23]

Presumably, Misasi's thoughts were the same as the ones that had inspired Aldo Moro to rally him on publicly and privately. Thus, even as he came home from the people's prison, riding along in a red hatchback car, men still argued the case for the life of Aldo Moro.

27.

"Dr. Nikolai" walked through the huge piazza outside Termini train station in central Rome. He was heading toward a phone booth. It was a little past noon. A light haze had painted out all the blue in the sky and had made a smear of the sun. The piazza, named for five hundred Italians slain in a battle lost and forgotten, was alive with the arrivals and departures of people with things to do. Yellow cabs made drops and pickups. Buses, roaring, did the same. The square was filled with a tinny cacophony coming from cassette recordings up for sale on the cheap. Coarse-looking men and women hawked contraband cigarettes and other items of dubious origins. Policemen, more concerned with the overall security of the train station, paid them no mind, just as Dr. Nikolai, as he stepped into the phone booth, cared little about the omnipresence of police. He knew he had three whole minutes before the law would come to get him.

Dr. Nikolai put a token in the slot and dialed the home number of Professor Franco Tritto. At exactly 12:10 P.M., his call was answered.

"Hello," said Dr. Nikolai without waiting for voice contact from the other side. "Is this Professor Franco Tritto?"

"Who's speaking?"

"Nikolai."

"Nikolai who?"

"Are you Professor Franco Tritto?"

"Yes, this is he."

"All right. I thought I recognized your voice. Listen, even though your phone is tapped, you have to bring a last message to the family—"

"But who is this?" Tritto asked in spite of having spoken several times in the past weeks to the man on the other end of the line.

"But are you really Professor Franco Tritto?"

"Yes, but I want to know who's speaking."

Dr. Nikolai gave a sigh of exasperation. Then he said, "Red Brigades. Understand?"

"Yes."

"All right. I can't stay on the phone very long. So here's what you should tell the family. You should go there personally. It doesn't matter that your phone is tapped. You should go there personally and tell them this: We are respecting the last wishes of the president by informing the family where to find Honorable Aldo Moro's body."

Moro's university assistant did not reply at first. It was as though he had not heard any of the words that had crossed Rome and the Tiber to his ear.

"But what should I do?" he asked with a note of disorientation in his voice.

"Do you hear me?" said the man who called himself Dr. Nikolai. The train-station sounds came through. He was using up his time, and he seemed to sense that he was running into difficulty.

"No," said Tritto, "if you can repeat it, please."

"No, I can't repeat it. Well, look, you must tell the family that they can find Honorable Moro's body in Via Caetani. That's the second cross street to the right on Via delle Botteghe Oscure. Have you got that?"

"Yes," said Tritto, but he sounded impenetrable.

"There, there's a red Renault-4. The first two numbers on the license plate are N 5."

"N 5?" Tritto began to sob. "Do I have to telephone?"

"No, you have to go there personally," the *brigatista* said slowly, as if to shore up the courage of a child.

"I can't," Tritto said, weeping uncontrollably now.

"You can't? You have to."

"Yes, of course, yes—"

"I'm sorry," said the *brigatista*. "I mean, if you telephone, you wouldn't—it wouldn't be carrying out fully the request that the president asked of us—"

Tritto broke down. "I beg you," he murmured, "speak to my father—"

"All right."

More than two of his three minutes had been used. The police, Dr. Nikolai knew, had heard every word. By now, they had electronically plotted the location of the phone booth, and the Flying Squad was on its way.

The elder Tritto, who was at his son's side, got on the phone at once. "Hello? What is it?"

"You should go to Honorable Moro's family, or else send your son. At the very least telephone."

"Yes," said the older man.

"As long as it gets done. Your son already has the message. All right?"

"Can't I go?"

"You? Yes, you can go." The *brigatista's* voice was growing edgy.

"Because my son is feeling ill."

"You can go instead. That's just fine. Certainly. As long as you do it urgently, because the wish, the last wish of the president, was to inform the family, I mean, because the family has to get back his body. All right? Good-bye."[1]

He hung up. He had come within thirty seconds of his margin of security. Now he slipped into the shuffling crowd. The police "Panther" was stuck in the noonday traffic.

Aldo Moro was home, taken up in an interstice of time where pettiness and pain never pass. But his body was only temporarily at rest. His last will was yet to be administered by men, and some of them would attach more worth to his body dead than they had alive. For the body in this form, they would be prepared to negotiate. Now, however, they lived a moment of restive ignorance.

The intercepted message from the Red Brigades did not reach the men of power for more than an hour. This was the hour in which Fanfani, his turn having come in the Square of Jesus, threw his weight at last against the hard line, as Andreotti, Zaccagnini, and all the others listened. Their midday meals were already on the fire, but they would have neither the time nor the appetite to eat them. Not only would they soon be aware that Aldo Moro was dead, they would learn at the same time that the Red Brigades had succeeded in committing their highest act of mockery against the state and its institutions.

In a Trojan horse of an old red Renault, they had brought the body to the very quick of fortress Rome, and had left it in the shadow of the Capitol. As though measured by tape, it was precisely equidistant from the headquarters of Christian Democracy and the doorstep of the Communists in the Street of the Dark Shops. While Fanfani spoke, the body lay cooling no more than a hundred yards away from him, Andreotti, and Zaccagnini, as well as Enrico Berlinguer.

The red Renault stood unobserved directly across from a Renaissance palace, Palazzo Mattei, owned in the last century by a nobleman for whom the cobblestone street was named, Michelangelo Caetani. It was parked in a bad spot. The building alongside it was being refurbished, and scaffolding extended a car's length away from the wall, which placed the Renault halfway into a traffic lane. But in Rome any space is fair game, and the Renault was just one of a long line of cars.

Although Via Caetani lay in a congested area, between the Street of the Dark Shops and the edge of the old Jewish ghetto, it was somewhat off the beaten track for pedestrians. There were no sidewalks, and the few stores were mostly wholesale outlets for commerce in fabrics and mattress fillings—traditional occupations for the ghetto Jews. The Palazzo Mattei, however, housed three specialized libraries and was a tourist attraction in itself, but mainly to connoisseurs. There was a small café on the corner. Normally, during the time the Renault was left unattended, two whole hours, it seems, there was a steady but light flow of people passing by. Had they looked inside, in the rear section of the car, they would have seen an overcoat lain across a blanket that covered a large bulge, from which a tuft of gray hair stuck out.

From where the red Renault had come only the survivors knew. The car when recovered had been driven only fifteen kilometers since it had been stolen ten weeks earlier some three kilometers from Via Caetani, so it could not have come from much beyond the city center. A host of tall tales would enjoy varying degrees of popularity, but Aldo Moro was killed in Rome at about ten o'clock on the morning of May 9 in the rear of the car before the hatchback was closed. As the circumstance makes it all but inconceivable that the murder took place oudoors, he was probably killed in some lonely small garage.

When he had nestled himself into that distressing enclosure in the rear of the car, two persons opened fire as he looked into their eyes. An instant before the first shot, doubtless when he sensed the trigger was about to be pulled, his right hand jerked instinctively to protect his vital organs. The bullet nicked his thumb, uprooting the fingernail, driving through bone and flesh into his left lung. He was still very much alive, but bleeding violently, as nine more rounds were pumped from an extended barrel .32-caliber Scorpion machine pistol equipped with a silencer. They were fired by an unsteady "light hand," ballistics experts said later, suggesting that the killer was a woman. Still another round, perhaps a *coup de grâce*, came from a 9-millimeter (.38) automatic, probably a Beretta.

The bullets entered the body in the same thoracic region, a surprisingly large area about the size of an outspread hand held over the left breast. The heart was unscathed. All the bullets penetrated the lung. Three, including the one from the second weapon, exited and ended up buried in the side panel of the Renault, behind the victim. Seven were lodged in the back of the lung, flattened under the skin, and one, deflected, was under the left collarbone.

Moro died of a massive internal hemorrhage. In this case, it was a relatively slow but not exceptionally painful passage through shock and unconsciousness to death some minutes later.[2]

The killers placed four large handkerchiefs over the mortal wounds to absorb some of the blood. They put the plastic bag containing the dead man's watch and the other objects beside the body, and without moving it appreciably, they covered it with part of the orange blanket. They lay an overcoat on top.

How they brought the car so brazenly close to the Square of Jesus and the Street of the Dark Shops remains a mystery. The testimonies of persons who claimed to have seen the Renault at various times and places on its way to Via Caetani are too conflicting to be of any value. The only one in accord with the postmortem facts was a negative report of a trained observer. A television newsman happened to be in Via Caetani that morning, and as of ten minutes past eleven, he said, the Renault was not yet in the spot where it was left. In its place was a young man on a stationary motorcycle.[3] As it is almost impossible to find a parking spot at that hour in Via Caetani, the man on the motorcycle undoubtedly was a member of the Red Brigades taking part in a more complex operation.

To reserve the space for their spectacular finale, which would be felt to the grated ganglions of all Rome, it would have been necessary to keep another car parked in that spot, placed there during the night, or perhaps nights before. At least one other person besides the motorcyclist would have been required to receive the Renault—one to remove the advance car and one to hold the spot— and if they had not come directly from the people's prison they would have to have been otherwise in touch with the killers.

In any event, the Renault could hardly have been parked any closer. The next street over was within the heavily patrolled range of the Communists' closed-circuit television scanner, and the Square of Jesus and environs teemed with contingents of the riot squad.

The first part of Aldo Moro's final request was fulfilled when the message was brought gently to his wife and children by Franco Tritto's father.[4] Except for the oldest daughter, who was in a hospital recovering from minor surgery, they were all at home, the "little one," too. They had of course been waiting for word from Fanfani, but he was still speaking. Later, Eleonora Moro would reveal her true feelings, but now there was not a moment to be lost. A new struggle, she knew, had to be faced, the struggle for Aldo Moro's body. She began to telephone, more conscious than ever that her line was tapped.[5]

In his slow, circumfluous, and measured way, Senator Fanfani continued to speak. Sirens wailed outside. On the floor above the meeting salon, the telephone was ringing in Zaccagnini's office. The call was taken by Zaccagnini's press secretary, Umberto Cavina. It was from police headquarters.

· "You know," the hesitant voice at the other end informed, "I think they've found him, near you."

Cavina, given few further details, called Cossiga. The minister said that the matter was at that moment being investigated. Two minutes later, Cossiga called back. It was true.

The press secretary went downstairs to the meeting. Fanfani was still speaking. Cavina moved quietly to Zaccagnini, who was seated beside Andreotti, and Cavina whispered to them.

"Cossiga is on the telephone," he said, "and he wants to speak to both of you."

Cavina did not say why, but he knew they had understood. Zaccagnini interrupted Fanfani. Zaccagnini suspended the meeting until his return. He went out to speak with Cossiga. The men and women of Christian Democracy understood, too. The sirens continued.

When Zaccagnini got back, he remained standing. Everyone else rose to their feet. The chairs stopped scraping, and a silence fell, except for the sirens.

"I have spoken with Cossiga," Zaccagnini said. "The murder is done. The whole complex of initiatives was of no value in saving the life of our friend Aldo Moro."

After the first shock, the second.

"The body of Aldo Moro is only a few meters away from us."

Christian Democracy wept. It prayed. Zaccagnini had to lie down. Some of the leaders went to Via Caetani to see their president's body with their own eyes. Others remained behind. The meeting was reconvened. There was much to be discussed, much more to be done.[6]

Across the street, the switchboard at the Dark Shops was overloaded. Sketchy reports were moving quickly now in official circles, and some callers wished to know if it were true that Aldo Moro's body had been left at the Communists' front door. At first, such inquiries were taken as a prank of exceedingly poor taste, but the noisy activity on the street outside gave cause for alarm.

Word reached the third floor. Berlinguer, recklessly, went to the window of a balcony that overlooked the busy thoroughfare below. He could see Via Caetani on his left. It was being closed off by police. He turned away in silence.

Shadow minister Pecchioli received confirmation from Cossiga.

They agreed to meet in Via Caetani. Berlinguer stayed behind. He ordered the hammer-and-sickle red flag lowered to half mast.[7]

Choked with police, Via Caetani was sealed at both ends. The lawmen had been ordered not to touch the red Renault and to keep everyone else away from it. It could have been rigged as a bomb, it was thought, set to go off when the hatchback was lifted. Nevertheless, while waiting for the bomb squad, someone had opened the right front door and had peeled back the blanket, permitting the first, tentative identification of the body.

When Cossiga and Pecchioli arrived, the bomb squad proceeded to open the hatchback. From over their shoulder, both men could see through the rear window only that there was a corpse inside; a folded hand, a profile that lay in shadow. Not that anyone doubted who it was. Cossiga continually ran his fingers through his hair.

The bomb squad cut through the rear panel and made a rectangular opening between the window and the license plate almost as wide as the door itself. The metal was bent back, widening the hole, and the door was tested down to its moorings for the presence of explosive devices. The Renault was clean.

The chrome latch was opened and the door was raised. Cossiga, Pecchioli, and a crowd of officials and policemen around them strained and pressed forward on their toes to look inside.

Aldo Moro lay with his legs bent behind him on the orange blanket beside two sets of rusty snow chains. His jacket hung open. His wounded right hand was half clenched above the pocket of his trousers. His head rested on his left shoulder, and that rested on the spare tire. His blue-yellow face had two days' growth of beard. His cheeks were sunken. His eyes were three quarters closed. He did not look asleep.

Senator Pecchioli, as a former Resistance fighter, was familiar with the sight of death, but he was "deeply moved," he said later. In front of all those people, he recalled, "Cossiga had to keep a straight face, but it was terrible for him because between Moro and Cossiga there had been a master-and-disciple relationship."[8]

A priest pushed his way forward. He had known the dead man well. He had come from the Jesuit church in the Square of Jesus. He relieved Aldo Moro's spirit of its mortal sins.

28.

Aldo Moro went back to the University of Rome, to the morgue. His body was transferred from a stretcher to a marble slab and covered to the head with a sheet.

Almost at the same time, three-twenty or so in the afternoon, Eleonora Moro and her children arrived, as well as two Christian Democrats who could make an official identification. Here, Mrs. Moro shed no tears. Only Anna began to sob quietly. The family stared at Papà in silence for a few minutes, then returned to Via Forte Trionfale.

At home, Mrs. Moro went into her bedroom. She removed a small crucifix from above the bed, and looking at it, she said to her children, "Prayer is the only way left for us to be close to your father."[1] She then dictated a brief statement to the men of power:

The family desires that the authorities of state and of the parties fully respect the precise will of Aldo Moro. That means: no public demonstrations or ceremonies or speeches; no national mourning, no state funeral or commemorative medals. The family closes itself in silence and asks for silence. Of the life and death of Aldo Moro, history will be the judge.[2]

History is a slow horse. It comes around when everyone else has gone home. The world, least of all Rome, had no time for history. The death ritual had already begun. The news, in words and images, had whipped through the public domain, circling the planet. It had arrived, and in most cases departed, like distant lightning, which is ever an affair of others. In Rome, the long-studied plans of the government and party apparatuses had gone operational, and if the speed of poster plastering, filling public squares, and turning out printed and oral incantations was the measure of efficiency, Italy would be Japan.

In spite of tears and tribulation, nobody shirked the call to duty. Everything Aldo Moro had done in the past fifty-four days to sunder the front of unity in Rome was, if not forgiven, instantly forgotten. Instant, too, was the resanctification of a man who, it was thought at the time, could no longer speak from the people's prison. Everyone sought to be first with the highest reverence for the life and miracles of Aldo Moro minus fifty-four days.* Not so suddenly —since all the hagiographies had been prepared during the many false alarms back to Lake Duchessa and before—Moro in death became a man who in life had been unflawed. And just as there was nothing wrong with Aldo Moro, there was nothing wrong in Italy that could not be put aright with more and more unity—a unity as undefined and, in the end, it seems, as tight as a black hole in the universe. The panegyrics of Andreotti, Zaccagnini, Berlinguer, and everyone else of a nerve to write one were as embarrassing to their readers as they surely were to their authors. They endure purely as anthropological curiosities.

A few spontaneous, honest human acts of significance were recorded on both sides of the hard line. In the only unorganized demonstration, somehow an angry mob fell together in the Square of Jesus and shouted its wrath at the men of power. Men and women shook their fists at Christian Democracy for having abandoned Aldo Moro. They wanted Curcio dead, but Berlinguer, they cried, was a hangman.[3]

On a higher plane was the immediate resignation and withdrawal from public life of Minister Cossiga, an extremely rare gesture in Italy. In a letter to Andreotti, Cossiga assumed "full political and moral responsibility" for his role in formulating and executing the government's position and for the police operations. He said that

* By an early counting error exhaustively repeated, it became a commonplace to refer to the *fifty-five* days of Aldo Moro, and it is a rarity now to see the correct figure. No matter how it may be calculated, however, the number of twenty-four-hour periods between the mornings of March 16 and May 9 are only fifty-four.

he was convinced that terrorism and political violence in Italy were "above all, political problems" related to the country's economic, social, and educational development.[4] His master would have agreed with that.

Of stainless outrage was the first reaction of ex-Chief of State Saragat. Momentarily throwing empty ceremony to damnation, Saragat, to the everlasting consternation of the other men of power, declared: "Alongside the corpse of the president of Christian Democracy there lies the corpse of the first republic, which did not know how to defend the life of the most generous political man in our country."[5]

But the corpse of the first republic was metaphor; the corpse of Aldo Moro was the order of the day. While it was being inspected and prepared for autopsy the following day, the family laid plans to carry out the final part of Papà's last will: There had to be no men of power at his funeral.

Eleonora Moro's request, made public at six o'clock that evening, meant exactly what it said, and as such had no more force than any of the previous family statements. By the evening, it was clear that the government had no intention of adhering to any of the family's wishes, not to mention Aldo Moro's. The predictable demonstrators were already in the streets by the hundreds of thousands. The national mourning had been proclaimed. The state funeral was to be held on Saturday. There was not to be a moment's silence.

The one faculty left to the family, however, was its right to take possession of the body. Naming Socialist Giuliano Vassalli as her lawyer, Eleonora Moro proceeded to take the necessary legal steps to guarantee her rights. The government, the Square of Jesus, and the men in the Dark Shops were caught off guard and shaken. A hundred nations would be represented at the state funeral, and if the state did not have the body, a hundred nations would wonder why.

The Communists solicited the government and the Christian Democrats to try "every means of delicate persuasion" to alter the family's decision. The Communist argument ran that the family had to respect the needs of the collectivity and popular sentiment. Moro belonged to Italy, and his burial was not a private matter [6] This was not an example of persuasive delicacy coming with the body still supple, but the Christian Democrats needed neither urging nor instructions from their political partners. When it came to certain things delicate, they knew where to turn. Skyward.

That evening Cardinal Poletti came to call at Via Forte Trionfale. He wished to convey Pope Paul's and his own condolences. The cardinal had also been entrusted by the Christian Democrats, and by proxy the Communists, too, with the mission of reconciliation. It was not that there was any lack of comprehension and sympathy downtown, but everyone, including the Holy Father, agreed that the tragedy would only be deepened if it were to end in a small good-bye. No one would say it, but the feeling was among the responsible people in Rome that the family would be paying yet another price; a show of disunity before the eyes of the world would be a further triumph for the Red Brigades. Of such temporal reasoning are many last wills broken, but the cardinal was sent away empty-handed, though not yet convinced that he had failed.[7]

Among the hundreds of messages and telegrams of condolence Eleonora Moro had received, a letter from the President of the United States had been left with her concierge. "Rosalynn and I," he wrote, ". . . hope you will find comfort in the knowledge that so many share your sorrow."[8] She did not and could not—not until she had Papà safely underground.

With the attendance of a medical consultant representing the family, Aldo Moro's body was autopsied in the early afternoon of May 10. The family had to file legal documents to assure this presence, and that they did so was an act of wisdom. The first reports of the results of the autopsy were filtered through government sources, and, as might be expected, came out the other end as support for its political position.

The picture projected was one of a victim who if he had not been tortured in the old style had been treated abominably and broken down. He had lost twenty-two pounds, his kidneys and liver were wrecked, and his digestive system was in a state of atony, brought on apparently by having hardly been fed at all, and what he had actually eaten was of scarce nutritious value. There were signs on his wrists, it was said, that he had been kept bound for long periods, freed only, it seemed, whenever he had been forced to take dictation for his otherwise unascribable letters. The toxicological studies to learn whether he had been drugged were still to be done, but a partially healed wound on one buttock, thought at first to be an injury received in Via Fani, was now described as an infection coming from a dirty syringe. Thus it was less a matter of if he had been doped than which stuff he was on. Since the bullets that had killed him had been fired from a Scorpion, which was made in Czechoslovakia, the suspicion that the Red Brigades were really an arm of Moscow found reinforcement—though the weapon can be purchased in Italian gun stores. For those who preferred the CIA, the bullets were .38 Brownings made by Winchester, U.S.A.

Finally, and most macabre, was the widely reported assertion that the postmortem examination had revealed Aldo Moro to be suffering from cancer of the thyroid, or "a tumor of the worst kind," as the disease is euphemistically called in Italy. The implication was that he would have shortly been dead *anyway,* but few reports left anything implicit.[9] Thus whoever may have harbored doubts about the hard line had no longer to overly burden himself with alien thoughts in his conscience.†

The truth of the autopsy, the tissue and ballistic studies, like most truths, came out later in small print. The examiners had been struck by the unusual cleanliness of the body. The nails had been recently trimmed, and the victim had bathed within twenty-four hours of death. At no time had the ankles or wrists been bound. Apart from the mortal wounds, there were no injuries or skin punctures. The body was free of any toxic substance or any form of drug or medicine. Moro had not ingested anything but liquids in the forty-eight hours prior to death. Compared with the reported weight of the body before the kidnapping, it had decreased by about fifteen pounds, but the organs were in excellent condition for a man of Moro's age, and their tone confirmed that he had been adequately nourished during his imprisonment. Moro had an enlarged left kidney and a pea-sized adenoma, a benign nodule on the left lobe of the thyroid gland, which his physician had dis-

† Enemy-circulated allegations of tumors of the worst kind had been a political fact of life that Moro had grown accustomed to (see above, p. 8). Persisting after the kidnapping, they became deadly, and the family had issued a denial.[10] Now the latest "scientific" version was a comfort to both the old and the new believers.

covered twenty years earlier.[11] Alive, at sixty-one, he had a life expectancy of fifteen, perhaps twenty years, and his health and habits were such that he probably would have lived every minute of it.

In the morning, Zaccagnini, who had been declared unwelcome in the mourner's home, had sent a letter by messenger to Eleonora Moro. He had pleaded with her to reconsider the funeral plans, but she refused to even answer. At noon, Cardinal Poletti showed up once more. He had a new message from the Pope, a gift. The Holy Father had wanted her to have his rosary. She was extremely moved, but when the cardinal left this time he knew that the family's bereavement, much of it inextinguishable anger, could not be consoled, not even by the Vicar of Christ.[12]

The funeral arrangements had been made clandestinely, an almost ghoulish undercover operation in hostile territory. Calls were made from sidewalk phone booths to foil the electronic eavesdroppers. Cover stories were issued to the press as to where and when the funeral would take place, and people who telephoned the Moro home to ask about the burial, even those whose presence was welcome, were told, "I don't know" or "I can't say," and the closest friends knew why.[13]

Months back, when death seemed only a normal problem of old age, Eleonora Moro had made some cursory plans for a burial place. The Moros owned a modest farmhouse north of Rome, which they had turned into a weekend retreat. It was situated in one of those jewel-like medieval hill towns that glorify the Tiber Valley, and this one, called Torrita Tiberina, took its name from its several stone towers. They had bought the place in 1953 for the equivalent of about five thousand dollars, had fitted it with a simple elegance it had never known, and though their family ties were to more distant regions, they had come to think of Torrita as their final home. Mrs. Moro, at the time, had made some inquiries about building a mausoleum in the village cemetery, but the work had never begun and not even the space had been set aside.[14]

On the morning of May 10, she called the parish priest to ask if on that very day she could entomb Papà. The entire village, population seven hundred, was put to work; none of the children went to school. The floors of the tiny church were scrubbed, the saints were dusted, the twenty hand-carved pews were polished, and a purple carpet was rolled down the center aisle. A temporary resting place was found in the *campo santo,* an as yet unneeded crypt reserved for a friend of the family.

In Rome, at about 4 P.M., while the men of power were in Parliament paying grandiloquent tribute to the fallen statesman, the family moved with stealth to get back Papà. They had had word that everything was ready at Torrita Tiberina, and the autopsy would soon be completed. A family spokesman came downstairs from the penthouse and told the press corps that nothing had been decided and it was useless for the newsmen to wait around. The funeral would take place no sooner than tomorrow, he said.[15] As soon as the way was relatively clear,‡ the family drove across Rome to lay hasty claim to the body.

The remains had barely been prepared when Mrs. Moro placed the papal rosary in Aldo Moro's hands and the body was sealed in an oaken casket. Asked by the taken-by-storm officials at the morgue if the family wanted a police escort, Mrs. Moro pointedly said no. The hearse and only three cars full of mourners—those who truly loved him—stole out of Rome.

It was a funeral fit for a lately common man. The coffin was carried on thick, rural shoulders. There was no organ music, no choir sang, no bell pealed from the simple campanile of St. Thomas the Apostle. An old priest said something about Aldo Moro having been a good man, "one of us." Someone recited the Lord's Prayer. Black clouds covered the Sabine hills. Vapor rose from the Tiber. It rained on black umbrellas. It hailed. The graveyard was muddy. The casket did not fit well in the crypt and was left at an awkward angle. There were flowers, broom, the free flowers of the country people.

Eleonora Moro's eyes were dry. She spoke to no one, not a word, but before she turned away from the coffin, someone heard her say, slowly and softly, "Goodbye, Aldo."

They had come and they were gone in forty minutes. The dead man's will was done.[16]

‡ A few sharper-eyed reporters who had noticed Mrs. Moro's chauffeur checking out and filling the tank of her Alfa 2000 had remained behind and were now rewarded.

29.

This Godforsaken season still had more of the bizarre up its sleeve.

The Red Brigades were striking almost daily now, crippling middle-ranking men who like everyone else would never know why. The trial in Turin resumed on Thursday, May 11, and Renato Curcio read a collective statement saying that the execution of Aldo Moro was the highest form of proletarian justice possible in a class society.[1] What it would be like in a classless society was left to the imagination.

On Saturday, the day before the elections, the state went ahead with its "funeral" anyway. If the men of power could not have the body, they certainly got the very next best thing. In a gesture of magnanimity that seemed the act of someone who had the original Sermon on the Mount still ringing in his ears, Pope Paul, who looked old enough for that to be true, had offered to conduct the ceremony.

Nobody could remember any Pope ever leaving the Vatican for such an earthly event, all the less for a man who at the time of his death held no other office of state than a simple membership in Parliament. Once again, Paul VI had astonished even the Curia, thoroughly delighting the men of power. They had been cringing since Wednesday at the prospect of a glaring emptiness where a bier ought to be. The announcement had come only twenty-four hours before, and according to Vatican sources, Paul had deliberated at length because he knew the family would not be there.[2] Now he had hoped to use his spiritual powers not only to relieve the malaise in Rome, but also to reconcile the family with the state and Christian Democracy. In this he failed anew. Mrs. Moro publicly thanked him for his kindnesses and stayed home.

Neither did he succeed in lifting the pall of a ceremony cursed by the dead man. To see the Holy Father on satellite TV in the magnificent basilica of St. John in Lateran—at the wooden table where tradition says Peter himself celebrated Mass—was more awesome than a lunar landing to many, but where the lens never pried was where terrible truths lay rawly exposed. The great church was empty except for the men of power. They sat down front, their faces completely covered with their hands much of the time. One needed only to remember broken phrases from the letters of Aldo Moro to see among these men and women a huddling of his enemies. With all the hidden faces, few took note that one man was missing. Retired, relieved of the call of office, Francesco Cossiga spent those very hours at the master's crypt in Torrita Tiberina.

Outside St. John's, the security forces had cut off the surrounding area from the rest of the world. They watched from the ground, from the roofs, and from the sky with a finger on the trigger. A "public" consisting of party faithfuls and plainclothesmen was in the restricted zone. Some waved the red-and-white flags of communism and Christian Democracy, intermingling by force of arms that improbable unity. Karl Marx surely rolled in his Highgate tomb, not to speak of the other half's Inspirer.

The Pope could barely stand unaided. Yet he seemed infused with a cosmic energy as he raised his mottled head and all but bellowed in anger to God.

"Lord, listen to us!" he cried with more than papal authority in the prayer he had written that very morning. "You did not hear our plea for the safety of Aldo Moro, for this good, gentle, wise, and innocent man, for this friend; but You, Oh Lord, have not abandoned his immortal spirit. . . . For him, for him, Lord, listen to us!"[3]

Sometimes, it seemed on a cold and livid day in May, God, too, needed reminding.

There being nothing more to do or not to do for the life and death of Aldo Moro, the state, as states must, went on to other business. But the family remained behind, frozen in a spring that had promised so much so early in March and had gotten strangely stuck in gray skies, trapped in the same time void as Papà; mourners, as mourners must, do not go on to other business until their grief has been purged. Thus to the family was the last word left on the matter of Aldo Moro's funerals.

By the Eighth-day Mass, a Catholic rite for the dead, the family had begun to receive the silence they had demanded. A ceremony was held, the antithesis of a state funeral, in the modern nondescript Church of Christ the King near the Moro home. It was a counterculture Mass organized by Giovanni Moro and the old scouts of February '74. A thousand people came on invitations passed by word of mouth. Many were youths dressed in jeans. They arrived on motorcycles and tiny, unescorted cars, and they carried the guitars, the flutes, and bongo drums for the "Luba," an African Mass evolved from the liturgy of Catholic missionaries. Only Craxi and Fanfani were permitted to cross the brawny line held by thickly bearded young men posted outside. The press was unwelcomed. The state, the government, the whole new majority preferred to stay downtown.

Eleonora Moro sat with her children and the "little one" among the families of the men who had been killed in Via Fani, the very persons whose sensibilities had been used—and in some instances manipulated—in justification of the hard line. Perhaps that was the final chafing irony, for though the ceremony was meant to be "not of mourning but of joy," the gnashing bitterness of it all could not be contained.[4]

A string was plucked, a drum was beat, a woodwind hooted; a priest, more angry than the Pope had been with God, read a prayer composed by Eleonora Moro:

> For those who ordered,
> carried out and supported
> this horrible crime,
> let us pray

> For those who by their jealousy,
> their cowardice or fear or stupidity
> ratified the death sentence of
> an innocent man,
> let us pray

For me and my children
so that this sense of
despair and anger we feel
be transformed into tears
of forgiveness,
let us pray[5]

They prayed. Another metal-cold night was falling. Primitive, forest sounds rippled the air. They went no farther than the Church of Christ the King. Such was Rome's last good-bye to this man who wore a suit and tie to the beach, this pillar of bourgeois society, removed.

Yes, these were days of wrath.

VII

DELIVERANCE

How can it be that a country like Italy, rich in sentiment, capable of understanding suffering in all its forms, was in this instance so hard, pitiless, myopic, and one-sided? . . . Is it a sign of an impoverishment of our democratic way of life, as though we now must fight for our salvation with arms and arms only?[1]

30.

The whole world praised the hard line.

Jimmy Carter wrote to Andreotti, "You have shown courage and wisdom in renewing your own commitment to the democratic principles and values that are the shared heritage of our two peoples."[1]

The New York *Times* said that Moro's friends in government had made "a hard decision—but they had little choice." The only thing reassuring to be found in this episode, "is that Italy, for all its troubles, held fast."[2] Said the Washington *Post:* "To its great credit, the Italian Government remained absolutely firm in its refusal to bargain with the terrorists. Despite the bloody outcome, that decision was right."[3]

In Europe, the house of modern terrorism, Rome was seen for the first time in memory as an exemplar. The government was "undoubtedly right," the London *Times* averred, commiserating with the unbearably strained Christian Democratic leaders—friend or foe of Aldo Moro—who "did not allow their nerves to snap."[4] The Germans, according to one authoritative voice, found in Italy "a lesson in democracy,"[5] and the *Financial Times,* of London, wrote that if other governments would only follow Italy's lead, "Aldo Moro may not have died in vain."[6]

Not since Sarah Bernhardt did *Lady of the Camellias* at the Teatro Valle had Rome read such good reviews.

The election results were startling, a solitary mirror of reality flashing sunlight in the eye. The issues were parochial, and only 10 per cent of the electorate was called to the polls. But coming when it did—the day after the state "funeral"—the voting was seen quite correctly in Rome as a valid sampling of public opinion on how the new majority had handled the Moro affair.

Christian Democracy, which had always been the party of law and order and now had showed its capacity to undergo supreme sacrifice on that very altar, was rewarded abundantly, returned for the first time in many years to the 40 per cent bracket. The Communists, in their first test as full participants in a democratic majority, were repulsed with a vengeance. They registered a near 25 per cent loss from the high point of 1976, when it had been thought they might even overtake the Christian Democrats.

This turnabout was explained by a rather plausible theory. Communist power in Italy had been founded on the party's opposition to a complacent and not always above-board establishment. Now that the Christian Democrats could be relied on to defend with their blood the shibboleths of state, who needed the Communist Party and all their liabilities on the nation's shoulders? For that matter, needed even less were the nominally more conservative parties to the right of the Christian Democrats. The gains in the Square of Jesus were amassed at their expense as well as from those who used to vote Communist to protest Christian Democracy's tergiversations. In the after-Moro there was a great coming home of the prodigals.

As for the Communist voters who felt that the party with the clean hands had perhaps washed them once too often over Aldo Moro's plight, they cast their ballot for the Socialists or the tiny opposition leftist parties. Craxi's gamble on a separate identity paid enormous returns. With an almost 50 per cent leap from the 1976 debacle, he brought his party from below the 10 per cent threshold to within striking distance of 15 per cent, stilling all the factions and backbiting within.

The outcome of the elections had no direct effect on the balance of power in Rome, but the omens were unmistakable. Craxi could strut if he cared to, but his party could never be more than a gadfly. Berlinguer had wounds for the licking. Eurocommunism had tripped. The "historic compromise" was in a cast. Christian Democracy alone, as Moro had foretold in the people's prison, had turned woe into virtue. It had all been a *buon affare,* a good deal, after all, and Andreotti, his power enhanced by megatonnage, needed only to do as he had lately urged others: work so that this ugly season might be forgotten.

And so he labored. On May 18 and 19, Parliament, which had been scheduled to debate the ways that Aldo Moro might be rescued, rubber-stamped a resolution saying that there never was and never would be an alternative to the hard line. The resolution, expressly approving the government's intransigence and recommending that it be maintained *permanently,* was written by Andreotti. The Socialists stung at it in good gadfly fashion, then voted it in like everyone else. A no-opposition situation is self-reinforcing.

Pleased with Parliament's near-unanimous support, Andreotti addressed the chamber, commending the responsible men and women of government and the parties for not bending. They had adopted a "courageous and disinterested line in defense of freedom." To anyone who did not agree, he had this to say: "The State could not but have been firm. And to no one is it permissible to assert that in being so it co-operated in not saving Moro."[7]

As if to help the rubber-stamp days get started, on May 18 the Court of Appeals in Naples finally had handed down its decision on whether or not to parole Alberto Buonconto, so ardently solicited by the negotiations party. Buonconto's health, it was judged, was in no way prejudiced by the regimen of his Neapolitan prison, where he was duly returned.[8]

Spring, of course, came; Rome without spring was as unthinkable as Rome without *gnocchi* on Thursday. Roses of every color cocked their heads at an unblinking sun. Pergolas at last made smooth shade. Suddenly, the brown on the palm leaves was gone. Mayors of big cities and small began to talk of naming streets and piazzas after Aldo Moro. Normally, there were local laws requiring that five or ten years pass before such a step can be taken, but to commemorate Aldo Moro there would be ways to get around the law. Books appeared on the "fifty-five" days. The family, locked up in silence and in that silence disconsolate, was simply not heard from anymore. The *Azzurri*—that national soccer team—went to Argentina. It almost seemed that five or ten years had gone by. The passing of an era was in the air. Someone melancholy wrote poetry on a Trastevere wall:

> Moro is dead
> Pope Paul is sick
> And I myself
> Don't feel very well

In many ways, the first republic *did* die, or at least got deathly ill, alongside the body of Aldo Moro. A very new kind of republic, for Italy, was in the founding when on June 11 a national referendum made an institution of mindless law and order. Laws that had been called liberticide by civil libertarians and had been vigorously denounced by the Communists when they were in the opposition, now obtained the sanction of not only the Communists but also a whole people yearning for what the legislators promised but could not possibly deliver. Of dubious constitutionality, these so-called antiterrorist laws were nothing but an expansion of the state's powers to restrict the freedom and rights of individuals—the oldest and least effective folk medicine dispensed for all manner of social ailments. Yet, where is the nation that has found a better elixir for the price? A society that could satisfy its discontents would have to be a very rich society, indeed, and so Italy, threatened by a problem whose vast dimensions had only now become visible, saw its salvation, for the time being, in arms and arms only.

In the "second" republic, merit was measured by how one had stood on the hard line during the fifty-four days, and the spoils of the first were so divided. From the people's prison, Rome had drained and recalled every last drop of Moro's power, and now it was all in a political jug awaiting redistribution.

Foremost was his claim on the presidency of the republic, and unexpectedly that became the first order of business when on June 15 Giovanni Leone resigned. The scandal-tainted Chief of State had been hoping to slip into oblivion by treading softly through the last six months of his seven-year term. But his troubles had mounted in the past few days with new allegations, and nine hours after the Communists called for his departure, he was gone—packed and on his way from the Quirinal Palace to his villa outside of Rome. It was during those frantic, humiliating hours that Andreotti and Zaccagnini informed him that Christian Democracy was leaving him in the lurch, and there are good sources who say that his doveish willingness to sign that crucial pardon was the reason why.[9]

Be that as it may, there was to be no doubts about his successor. The choice belonged to the two houses of Parliament. By the early balloting, in which, incidentally, Eleonora Moro on three occasions received the secret votes of some electors, it became clear that no Christian Democrat could muster a majority. Since a Communist President of Italy was out of the question, the Socialists put forth the candidacy of Giuliano Vassalli. Both the Communists and Christian Democrats had raised no objections against a Socialist Chief of State in principle, thus assuring the acceptable candidate's victory, but when Vassalli's name was advanced, Berlinguer reminded Zaccagnini of the lawyer's role in the Moro affair, and Vassalli was forced to withdraw.[10]* Some, but not many, have missed their nation's highest office by less.

The man finally elected as Italy's seventh President, by a better than 80 per cent majority, was a popular political iconoclast, eighty-two-year-old Sandro Pertini. A hero of the Resistance (and a member of the clandestine urban guerrilla military junta during the Occupation of Rome), Pertini, it was happily remembered, was the first Socialist to speak out against Craxi after the party chief broke with the hard line.

Now, in his inaugural address, Pertini paid tribute to Aldo Moro: "What a void he has left in his party and in this assembly! If he had not been cruelly assassinated, he, not I, would today be speaking to you from this chair."

But worship of Aldo Moro—minus fifty-four days—was what the new republic was all about. To which Pertini vowed "not one concession" to its enemies, and "firmness at any cost."[12]

Three weeks later, Flaminio Piccoli, the man ready to negotiate with the Red Brigades had Craxi come up with the right offer, got Moro's presidency of the party. "It's not a question of succession," he said humbly, as he moved into his predecessor's office. "One does

---

* The official reason for the Communists' rejection of Vassalli was even more outrageous. They suggested that since one of his clients was the principal defendant in the Lockheed bribery case he was in some way connected to the scandal.[11] This brought a wave of protest from every quarter, but the Vassalli affair came and went like a comet. About Vassalli's other controversial client, Eleonora Moro, the Communists did no more than whisper.

not succeed an Aldo Moro."[13] On that occasion—the meeting of the National Council, three months to the day from when Moro had ordered it convoked—Zaccagnini, speaking in front of a gigantic poster of the murdered president, called him "the man who better than anyone else understood our times."[14]

And so it went. Everyone staked his claim as Moro's political heir, and the inheritance was large enough for everyone who was *someone* to get his or her piece of the estate.

This kind of theocratic, single-minded republic might have gone on until Rome became Aldo Moro City had not a saving grace, a redeeming Shakespearean guilt, crept in and waxed from the very beginning. It was not easy to make a hero of Aldo Moro and remain comfortable, too. One could build a statue to the stars but by that measure would the accusing finger be lengthened. "I will not absolve or justify anyone," the slain man had twice repeated, and those were the stains that could never be washed out.

On the other hand, not that anyone considered it, he could not be simply forgotten. An abominable crime that had made Italy stand still and the world look up for fifty-four days, that had taken the lives of six men and had failed to leave a single clue behind, had to be prosecuted without respite by a state with ethical pretensions. If the prisoner had thrown all his power at Rome, the Red Brigades had sacked him of his prestige. Now they wore it in infamy, but the infamous are no less famous than anyone else who commands the attention of others. Finally, Aldo Moro looking out from the people's prison with a thousand mysteries in his eyes was unforgettable. Everyone knew he would one day speak from the grave, and none knew what he would say.

A survey unrelated to the Moro case but made late in May to learn what Italians dream, revealed that Moro's ghost haunted the nation by night as well as by day.[15] The keepers of the state could declare and declaim whatever their conscience allowed, and the whole world could wink back in approval, but whichever way the heads were counted somebody in Italy was missing, and Italians, to begin with, wished and had a right to know why.

It was not enough to say to adults that the hard line was the right line when it brought not one positive result. Even less satisfying was casting all the blame on an enemy as invisible as some heinous strain of the swine flu. The gullible nations are extinct or live in camps or on reservations.

Moreover, many people—the press first of all—began to emerge from the communal nightmare. To them, it suddenly seemed no longer imperative to stamp out dissent; indeed, they awoke with a postintoxication thirst for fresh opinions. With embarrassing receptiveness, the kind that seeks to make amends, the pages of the mass-circulation dailies were thrown wide open to anyone who had something critical to say. To be sure, the old conformists had much to defend, and they redoubled their efforts to make their case, but the bugaboos of the negotiations party slowly became "understandable" and once in a while "respectable." Before long, an almost healthy debate was on, the topic being: Why did Aldo Moro die?

At first, those among the men of power who felt obliged to explain tended to project all guilt as far away from Rome as was geographically possible. Much was made of alleged contacts between the Red Brigades and so-called international terrorism, meaning the Baader-Meinhof Red Army Fraction, which was the switching station for both the Palestinian and Japanese connections. Theories that Aldo Moro was a victim of some terrorist international† were jerry-built. They simply could not stand in the absence of any known motive, particularly with Moro having long been regarded by the Palestinians as sympathetic to their cause. The Palestine Liberation Organization and its chief, Yasser Arafat, had in fact made public appeals to the Red Brigades for Moro's release. Furthermore, it was later learned from Arab sources that Arafat, working with George Habash's extremist wing of the PLO, had tried for weeks to make underground contact with the Red Brigades to convince them to spare their prisoner. They had, however, found the

---

† The popular idea of a terrorist international, with Carlos the Jackal in the role of Dr. No, is a dangerous myth. Political terrorism, on the left or the right, is national by definition. When it goes transnational, as it has on aberrant occasions (Entebbe, Mogadishu, etc.), it has always been to further nationalist causes (Palestinian liberation, German revolution, etc.). These limited episodes, however spectacular, have become the case histories for terrorists of what *not* to do. They represent the tiniest fraction of the problem, and the belief that they *are* the problem is often a pretext for avoiding it. Their origin can almost always be traced to support for the Palestinians, particularly from West German terrorists and Arab Soviet-bloc governments.

Red Brigades impenetrable, "an organization closed to any external relations."[16]

The Red Brigades, according to Arafat aide Ibrahim Ayad, are "a special squad that brings to mind the CIA and the Israeli secret services."[17] And at the time Arafat himself said, "The Moro kidnapping is also an attack on the Palestinians."[18]

Were the Red Brigades really the Mossad of Tel Aviv or an undercover task force from Langley, Virginia? The question would be unworthy of an answer were it not for the fact that when the terrorist-international theory was found to have no bite, the men of power in Rome put forth the International Plot.

To his credit, Andreotti denied that there was any evidence implicating foreign intelligence agencies in the Moro case, and no one paid any attention to the notion of Israeli interference. But several highly placed political figures in Rome, particularly among the Christian Democrats, began to give credence publicly and privately to charges that the United States had conspired—perhaps with NATO and even with the Soviet Union—to engineer the kidnapping and murder of Italy's leading statesman. Unfortunately, the record of the U. S. Government and especially CIA meddling in Italian affairs, not to speak of other countries, was so well documented that anyone lacking thorough knowledge of the Red Brigades could easily believe that Moro's fate had been made in the United States.

Here, the motives were strikingly clear. The United States was adamantly opposed to Moro's political design, which was seen as abetting Eurocommunist power. In this it had the full accord of NATO and Moscow. There was no one else in Italy of Moro's stature, and he was expected to become Chief of State. His elimination would slow, if not reverse, the advance of Eurocommunism.

The "evidence," too, was highly suggestive. Moro had been treated roughly by Washington, notably by Kissinger, and between the two men there was a well-known enmity.[19] Complaints about this to his friends in Rome were now repeated by men who maintained that Moro had been warned to get out of politics. In February 1978, a Washington-emanated rumor sought to link Moro to the Lockheed case, and in March, two weeks prior to the kidnapping, the U.S. ambassador to Rome, Richard Gardner, allegedly told a conference at Columbia University that "Aldo Moro is the most dangerous and ambiguous personality on the Italian political scene."[20]‡ The chief of the CIA Rome station, identified by the Italians as Mike Seydenhower, was reported to have been very active during the Moro affair, especially at the Ministry of Interior, having come alive after a long period of noninterference. The mystery of the undiscoverable people's prison was suddenly solved by placing it in "an embassy," which of course is immune to police search and investigation. A Christian Democratic Under Secretary in the Foreign Office told Zaccagnini that the U.S. diplomats in Rome had behaved "coldly" and otherwise suspiciously throughout the fifty-four days.[22]

"Is there someone who does not want the Italians to make their own policies?" asked the new president of Christian Democracy, Flaminio Piccoli. Maybe that was the reason, he said archly, "for the kidnapping one day in March and then the killing of the most independent politician in Italy."[23]

Moro's murder, Zaccagnini declared, was a "plot still obscure, but surely aimed against the Italian people."[24]

The Communists and everyone else, including the Socialists, joined in, and the men in the Dark Shops, with no sense of irony, urged a careful rereading of the Moro letters. They were now believed to contain the key, in a secret code, perhaps, to "far-off mysteries,"[25] said *L'Unità*.

Backing of sorts came from the "plotters" themselves. Beyond the exchange of accusations between the New York *Times* and *Pravda* while Moro was in captivity, the Soviets now released a long "documented" report that began, "Italy is at the center of a perfidious international plot . . ." The strings that were maneuvering the Red Brigades were in the hands of the CIA and NATO. It quoted a former CIA official as admitting that the agency used organizations like the Red Brigades as a cover, and that the idea was "to destabilize the governments and convince the population to accept the emergence of a strong police state." Moro had been one of Moscow's favorites, the Soviet report said, and contrary to Reston's ac-

‡ This was vehemently denied by Gardner and the American embassy in Rome, and in any case is almost certainly a misquote. It is most unlikely that an ambassador would make such a comment at a public meeting. In his interrogation, Moro praised Gardner and said Gardner was mainly interested in promoting Carter's global policies, in which Italian politics "must appear to him as a mere detail."[21]

cusations, the KGB never had, or would have, anything to do with the likes of the Red Brigades.[26]

All this was played very widely by the Italian press and fostered by a surprising, but not very surprising, number of leading Christian Democrats. Ambassador Gardner and his staff at the U.S. embassy had to devote much of their time to indignant repudiations.[27]

Apart from its rather obvious psycho-origins in the heart of a guilt-struck party, the CIA-plot theory was troubled by absurdity. If Langley had wanted Moro neutralized and had been willing to violate new congressional controls and take the enormous risk of sabotaging the United States' credibility at home and abroad, the Italian would never have gotten past Via Fani. It is simply inconceivable that the CIA, or for that matter the KGB or any other foreign service, would involve itself in a protracted and complex operation whose outcome would grow more and more unpredictable from day one onward. Had the CIA by some untraceable method* taken control of the Red Brigades, it certainly would not have used them to create a situation in Italy that could have thrown it into total chaos in which the unfavorable scenarios would far outnumber any of the schemes Washington could possibly think of. The same is true for Moscow and any other country. The United States as culpable of having destabilized a strategic NATO country, which would be absolutely ruinous to American foreign policy, sounds like one of Jimmy Carter's most frightful nightmares and nothing else.

Washington's contribution to the annihilation of Aldo Moro, as will be seen, was made in quite a different way.

* The most novel was imagined by the Catholic review *Studi Cattolici* in an article that was widely circulated in the Square of Jesus at the time. The Red Brigades, it said, had been created artificially out of the "state of effervescence" in 1968 by "discreet manipulators" seeking to control the future of postindustrial society. These manipulators, or neocapitalists, had been trained by the Massachusetts Institute of Technology, the Rockefeller Foundation, and the Trilateral Commission.[28]

31.

The Red Brigades went about their bloody business of killing and crippling, and, secretly, reappraising the results of the Moro affair. They moved up and down the peninsula with customary impunity. The police and Carabinieri, under many atmospheres of pressure to break the Moro case, made several arrests, uncovered five or six Red Brigades' bases, and impounded carloads of weapons and documents. But it brought them not a shred of proof closer to Moro's kidnappers or killers. True to their handbooks, the captured *brigatisti* declared themselves political prisoners and refused to answer any questions, and the other arrested men and women protested their innocence.

The Curcio trial ended in June. The fifteen were found guilty of among various other offenses, participating in an illegal armed organization, and so were fourteen other minor defendants. Curcio got fifteen years, the others decreasingly less. Participation, unless caught in a worse act, was more or less the most serious charge that could be proved against nonco-operative political prisoners. Some law-and-order advocates called for making the very self-declaration as a political prisoner a mandatory life sentence.

As a result of the crackdown, the antiterrorist-special-prison population rose to more than 300. But terrorism itself, despite all the brand-new "preventives," continued to expand drastically. By the end of the year, the nation had counted 2,365 acts of political terrorism, a 10 per cent growth over 1977 and 400 per cent over 1974, the year the killings began. Deaths were up 20 per cent in 1978 as compared with 1977, and the rate of action was more than 6 attacks and more than 1 dead or wounded each day. The Red Brigades led the field by far, but the number of terrorist groups claiming separate political identities was up from 147 in 1977 to 209, of which 181 were on the left and 28 on the right.[1] Moreover, inside the special prisons, the Red Brigades, led by Curcio and comrades, were fomenting riots against the conditions, and this was backed on the outside by assassinations of penologists and others held responsible for the treatment of self-declared political prisoners. There was plenty of law that year but not much order.

In the final communiqué from the people's prison, the Red Brigades had promised to release Moro's interrogation and other information about the episode to the Movement through underground channels. Months went by without further word, yet this was not unusual. The so-called collegial decision-making practiced by the organization was nothing more than their own version of the slow and fastidious above-ground bureaucracy. The process required long discussion and self-criticism, the drafting of a final report, and its approval by each of the four columns.

The Movement, however, did not wait for any reports to express its opinion. One by one the multiform groups and grouplets of the ultraleft, armed or not, issued a unanimously negative judgment against the murderers of Aldo Moro. Not that there was an ounce of sympathy for the dead man, but in the eyes of many, the organization that had set out to unite the extreme left and divide the establishment had succeeded only in accomplishing the exact opposite. Others saw the Red Brigades as having made an attempt to capture and dominate the Movement, and therefore they had to be shunned, if not denounced as militarists. Some remained neutral, but it was impossible to find an expression of support at least for the way the Moro affair ended.[2]

In the meantime, news of the internal debate among the Red Brigades began to seep through the far left. A split had developed in the organization, principally over the matter of whether or not the prisoner should have been killed, but also about how the entire operation was handled. The Italian Secret Service learned from a German terrorist arrested in Yugoslavia two days after Moro's death that the decision to carry out the execution had been made in

Milan. The German, Brigitte Monhaupt, claimed to have been present and she intimated that the Red Brigades had been almost equally divided, but the hawks had prevailed. Monhaupt's alleged presence and the cited meeting place are strong reasons to doubt the complete authenticity of this report, but more reliable sources agree that Moro's fate was decided by the slimmest majority. That event, it seems, took place far from Milan, on Sunday, May 7. The execution was then delayed forty-eight hours to allow Fanfani his move. Apparently the slow-plodding senator's signals were not regarded as promising or were unraveled incorrectly.[3]

The divisions within the organization, however, never reached serious proportions, and a unitary document was drawn up in which lingering dissent was stifled ("Regarding the considerations of the comrades in Milan, who in a certain sense were very removed from the decisions, it must be noted that these are the same comrades who in another place expressed themselves favorable."[4]). The final draft contained an analysis of the entire event, and the Red Brigades criticized themselves for a lack of flexibility, inefficiency, and a failure to communicate the operation's "revolutionary possibilities" to the Movement. The strategic command adopted another long resolution redefining objectives and targets for the future (industry and the Communist Party high among them).[5]

Copies of this material, and a great deal more, were circulated for approval among the four columns in September, prior to printing and distribution. It contained the forty-nine-page transcript of Moro's interrogation, fifteen letters whose existence was either unknown or unconfirmed, and much if not all of the prisoner's notes.

Toward the end of the month the timing of its release suddenly became important. The silly season of plot and counterplot was coming to an end, and the fear of the truth was subsiding. On the contrary, a great cry was being raised for a parliamentary inquest, the formation of a credibly impartial commission to uncover all the half-buried and buried truths. The government and the leaders of the two superparties were opposed to this, but attitudes, especially those of the press, had come full circle, and even they paid lip service to the idea. The Socialists, who were in possession of a large store of information that had not yet come out (since their moves during Moro's imprisonment had been distortedly reported when not covered up), were using it now as political ammunition. The Red Brigades were beginning to look more astute politically than many had believed. Those who had earlier either condemned or in a sense thanked them for uniting rather than dividing Rome were making reassessments. Six months had passed since the attack in Via Fani, and in spite of the presidential election, the death of two Popes, and the *Azzurri* placing fourth in the World Cup, a willing nation had been unable to forget Aldo Moro, and the time of recriminations had set in.

The government was in serious difficulty, Rome was at a breast-beating standstill, and the Red Brigades' project to destabilize the new majority seemed the one aspect of the Moro operation that had after all succeeded. A Parliament that appeared very much more uncertain than it had been in May was scheduled to reopen the debate in mid-October, and the Red Brigades were the sole proprietors of sensitive documents that could agonize Rome. Carefully handled and purveyed, they had the potential of bringing down the new majority and plunging a tired political class into an extended crisis.

It was in this situation that on October 1, as a result of an incredible breach of security, a well-known *brigatista* under surveillance led the Carabinieri directly to members of the Milan column. With much promptitude, they made three arrests, closed down what may have been the column's headquarters, and among five thousand captured documents, they had seized a copy of the Red Brigades' entire Moro file.*

A large part of the truth was now not in the hands of the Movement or the public but in those of the Andreotti government.

At first it was thought that Andreotti would use the power of his office to declare the material a state secret. Parts that began at once to be leaked suggested that Moro had told all, rattling every skeleton in Christian Democracy's closet in hopes of winning his freedom. But this was slanderously untrue, and the idea that the file

---

* The blunderer was twenty-six-year-old Nadia Mantovani. She had been convicted with Curcio among the Turin Fifteen, but was immediately released for having served most of her time awaiting trial. Breaking parole, she had gone underground, where a cooling-off period of up to a year is *de rigueur* before "reinsertion" in the organization. Mantovani was especially familiar in Milan. Three years earlier her trial had brought the Carabinieri to Curcio, but the slipup here—an undeveloped negative of the two together left in Sossi's people's prison—appears to have been his, not hers.

could remain classified was both impractical and foolish. It would only hand back the initiative as to when and how to release it to the Red Brigades, who still held all the original papers.

Andreotti in September had shown skill, if not grace, in managing the publication of eight Moro letters and other documents held secret by the government. They had been leaked to head off the Socialists, who were pressing their advantages in the new climate. When the letters appeared and Andreotti was asked where he thought they had come from, he implicated Socialist Vassalli and the family, but only the politically uninitiated took him seriously.[6]

Now, after seventeen days of infighting and media clamor, the government released what it claimed to be the full text of Moro's interrogation. This was readily discovered as not completely true and hotly disputed by a press suddenly trying to be fierce and fearless. But the expurgated portion—a reference to foreign intelligence operations in Italy that might have embarrassed Tel Aviv and some NATO countries—and the withholding of the new Moro letters still left it the most voluminous document by far to come out of the people's prison.[7]

To everyone's relief, the Red Brigades' admission in Communiqué VI that the prisoner had made no sensational disclosures proved to be true. Also true, however, was their contention that he had illuminated the dark and dirty side of the daily struggle for power in Rome. This bothered no one. He had revealed nothing that was not already known, though only a political man hopelessly abandoned by his own kind would ever have spoken so candidly. Those who still felt a need or were ordered to time-serve the myth of Moro's madness unwrapped the old clichés about forgeries and psychic torture; others who had been their vociferous proponents last spring preferred silence, but neither tactic had much effect.

The *Corriere della Sera*, in a front-page editorial, spoke of the "balance and lucidness with which the prisoner responded to the questioning of the Red Brigades about some of the most dramatic and controversial issues of [Italian] political life."[8] Moro's voice— his rankling posthumous voice, full of ire, caustic irony, incredulity, regrets, and unsettling insight—was at last heard unpolluted by fear and listened to with the respect reserved for the loved one safely dead. In return, the living, or those among them by whom the prisoner felt betrayed, had now to suffer, without recourse to self-defense, Aldo Moro's unforgiving worst.

In a long, singular passage bursting with choler and vexation and a pathetic hatred made of all things unrequited, Moro from the tomb took final leave of his party:

> You, my ex-Demo-Christian friends, were all there in that moment we were negotiating the government, when my word was decisive. I feel an immense pleasure to have lost you and I hope that everyone loses you with the same joy I felt in having lost you. With or without you, Christian Democracy won't go very far. The few serious and honest men and women that there are [in the party] won't be much help, as long as you are there.

But he saved his venom for the two "partners" of his demise. First, for the man who lived "without a moment of human pity":

> Getting back to you, Hon. Andreotti, head of government to our misfortune and the misfortune of the country (which won't take long in finding that out), it is not my intention to speak of your lackluster career. That's not a fault. One can be lackluster but honest, lackluster but kind, lackluster but filled with fervor. Well, Hon. Andreotti, these are just the things you lack. . . . You lack that combination of good will, wisdom, flexibility, and sincerity that are the qualities of the few democratic Christians there are in the world. You are not one of them. You will last a little more or a little less, but you will pass on leaving no trace. . . . That's all. I have nothing that I must thank you for and I do not even feel resentment for what you are. I wish you well in your work, with your inimitable group of fellow leaders, and may God spare you from the experience that I have known . . .

Second, for "the new tenant in the house of power":

> And also many good wishes to Hon. Berlinguer, who will have a versatile partner in any task of great value. Think of how little he risked in inaugurating the new political phase by letting the strategist . . . and sole originator of the entente between the Demo-Christians and the Communists go to his death.

Finally, in October, it seemed his faith had been rewarded and that he was as he had hoped to be watching it all from above, when with a dose of heavenly sarcasm he said, "It's true that order is established, and there isn't any indulgence, but a little bit of Christian Democracy is gone."[9]

For a while, it looked as if the Andreotti government would fall. The campaign for the parliamentary inquest was reaching its peak. Eleonora Moro, who like everyone else in the family had maintained the strictest silence, let it be known privately that she wished to testify before such a commission.[10] French Socialist François Mitterand revealed Craxi's confidences to him about the one-for-one exchange and the cold and scheming hearts in Rome. The superparties pretended they were hearing the one-for-one thesis for the first time, and sanctimoniously called for the proof that such a possibility ever existed.

Red Brigades' lawyer Giannino Guiso declared flatly that Moro would have been freed had one prisoner been paroled. In a mordant editorial, the Rizzoli-owned mass-circulation weekly L'Europeo wrote that Moro not only could have, but should have, been saved. It said that Andreotti, Zaccagnini, and Berlinguer—"the theoreticians of the so-called intransigence"—"cannot legitimately think of constructing the political future of the country on this man's cadaver. . . . Now, it is no longer the time of commemorations but of taking responsibility."[11]

The Socialists were preparing a heavily publicized "white paper," in which they planned to demonstrate how little was needed to save Aldo Moro and how great was the will to do nothing. They promised to present this at the parliamentary debate, and as the Communists were demanding yet another reiteration of the hard line and a unanimous resolution by the new majority re-commending the government's behavior as having been necessary and just, the inevitable showdown had a time, place, and date.

With the publication of Moro's interrogation, Andreotti asked for and received a brief postponement of the debate, which was moved up to October 24. This allowed seven days for the digestion and cooling of the Moro papers, and those were the seven days in which Andreotti moved with some of the fanciest political footwork seen since Moro himself covered up the 1964 attempted *coup*.† Meeting separately with Craxi and Berlinguer, Andreotti, by means still to be told, convinced both men to back down. The Communist agreed to settle for a watered resolution against terrorism in general if the Socialists would sign, and vice versa. The white paper was put back in Craxi's arsenal, the parliamentary inquest on the shelf. It was to be rubber stamps once more.[13]

And so it ended. In frustrating, tantalizing anticlimax—not unusual in the land of *omertà*, yet Italy is nearer the rule than the exception. Only rarely is the truth, not to speak of justice, accessible to the survivors, who need it most. The fortunes of the guardians of special interests rise and fall on how well the truth is handled when hot. Between October 24 and 28, in a thinly attended parliamentary "debate," the hot truth, or the quest for it, was bottled up for storage, stuffed back into the corners of timid men's minds, and returned with a thousand unanswered questions to the collective unconscious. There it was left to burn down alongside a host of other darkening embers. The press hissed and stamped its feet for a time, but the news market is like the fruit market; only under unusual conditions can a story be kept longer than a banana.

In November, two investigative reporters disclosed fresh details about the efforts to free one harmless political prisoner, and in December, a series of new Moro letters were acquired and published by an Italian newsweekly. The case was anything but closed. The investigation, although hampered by political maneuvering to control it, continued—without success, but a multitude of leads were still pending. No one was deliberately trying to impede the accumulation of facts. There was only one sacred cow in the Rome of the new majority: the hard line. Any testimony that supported the belief that Aldo Moro could have been legally rescued by a slightly softer heart in Rome was flattened by the full weight of the government and the superparties.

The official truth, repeated to this day like a catechism, is that

† The means Moro used to persuade the Socialists to accept the coverup are indicative of the power game. He told Socialist Party chief and vice premier Pietro Nenni that he was being blackmailed by the plotters of the *coup* against his government. The chief conspirator was in possession of compromising documents that showed that Socialist politicians and journalists had been receiving subsidies from the Secret Service, which was the force that had sought to overthrow Moro's center-left government.[12]

the Red Brigades never showed any sign that they were prepared to free Aldo Moro. The proof is in their request for the release of thirteen prisoners, which they knew in advance was unacceptable. As for the one-for-one exchange, the prevailing version goes, no hard evidence has been produced to substantiate this contention. And besides, even if the state could have legally released a prisoner, it would have committed an immoral act of indulgence. The only thing certain was the Red Brigades' objective to humiliate the state and split the new majority. As this did not happen, the hard line was the just line. The sacrifice of one man, if indeed his fate was not already determined by his capture, was the price the community had to pay to protect the lives of many. Terrorists do not kidnap when they are convinced that the state will not yield.

The only thing that can be said in favor of the validity of this otherwise specious argument is that if it were really true that Aldo Moro's life was contingent solely on the freeing of the thirteen prisoners, the government behaved impeccably. No state can survive very long when a knife at someone's throat can empty out its prisons. On the other hand, the more the demands can be lowered, the more the future threat is lessened. If, then, the truth lies with Aldo Moro's claim that the long and the short of the matter was a one-for-one exchange, the future threat is practically nonexistent. There is no organization in the world, guerrilla or not, that would embark on a program risking the lives and safety of more than fifty of its members for a full year in the planning and execution and exposing them permanently to life imprisonment merely to obtain, at a further cost of about two million dollars, the release of one incurably ill comrade.

This reason alone assured that a one-for-one exchange offered no incentive for future actions of the same kind, and can in no way be regarded as an indulgence. The Red Brigades, as was seen in the Sossi case, needed no convincing that kidnapping was an unprofitable venture insofar as freeing prisoners. They had reached that conclusion on their own four years before they set out for the Via Fani.

Nevertheless, in spite of the testimony of Aldo Moro, his family, the Socialists, and the lawyers of the Red Brigades, the "unanswered" question of whether the prisoner could have been brought back on terms that represented no clear and present danger to the state remains as the ultimate comfort for the advocates of the hard line and other skeptics. It is a comfort bound to wither with time.

I have no illusions about reducing the level of pious surety felt by men and women who made vital decisions in the case of Aldo Moro, but I am in a position to offer additional information that may interest others who are less convinced of the wisdom of the hard line. When I proposed to write this book, I believed, as I had since April 30, 1978—the day the final Moro letter to his party appeared in print—that he had given the formula for his release. I considered that this had been abundantly supported by all the known facts in the case. The only missing element, not that it was essential, was direct evidence from the Red Brigades themselves. It was most unrealistic to expect such a proof, since they had gone to extremes to insist on the differences between their position and the prisoner's on the question of the exchange, and, in words, they had not been heard from since.

In the course of my research, however, I continually sought to make contact with the Red Brigades. I hoped to get a clarification not only of the matter of the one-for-one exchange, but also of the decision to kill Aldo Moro.

Such contact took place in Milan on October 12, 1978. What follows is *everything* concerning the case that I am at liberty to report.

The connection was made through a go-between (Y). Y is a person of high repute, with political leanings on the far left. I did not personally speak to the contact (X), though I saw X from a distance. X is a member with unimpeachable credentials of the highest level of the Red Brigades. As far as I know, however, X took no direct part in any stage of the Moro affair.

Earlier in the day, I wrote two questions in Italian for X and gave them to Y. The exact text, in translation, was:

Would it have been possible to obtain Moro's release with the one-for-one exchange? If not, how?

What was the political reasoning behind the decision to execute the sentence against Moro?

Shortly after I saw X and Y together, Y was alone with X for about two hours. I knew I would see, or make an appointment to see, Y on the following day, but by chance we were trying to catch the same flight out of fogbound Milan, and I ran into Y at the airport bus terminal in the center of the city. This happened immediately after Y had left X.

Y and I rode out to Linate International Airport together. Y is not the sort of person who initiates conversation or volunteers information. After a long silence and a few monosyllabic responses to my uneasy attempts to warm my interlocutor with light banter, I finally got to the point, and as we crept through the early-evening traffic, Y speaking in a soft monotone, gave me X's answers to my questions. Some hours later I summarized in my notebook what Y said. I wrote:

This is [X's] answer according to [Y]: The Red Brigades had no initial interest in an exchange of one, or two, or three for one. What they wanted was getting some kind of political recognition, recognition as a political force (e.g., armed revolutionaries as opposed to common criminals). If in the dynamic of the operation an exchange of one-for-one would have been acceptable, just as *any other sign* would have been, the Red Brigades were predisposed to release Moro. "It's one thing to kill someone in an attack," [Y] said, "and quite another after holding him for so many days. After all, they were killing a prisoner of war."

As for the decision to kill him, they had been left with no alternative. If he had been released, he was the kind of man who could recompose, or patch up, all that had been done, and in the end, the kidnapping would have appeared as a "joke," or something of little consequence. On the other hand, if they had released him after obtaining what they wanted (recognition of some sort), nothing could be done to deny it no matter how much patching up Moro might have done.

The impression I got from [Y], who had discussed these matters before with [X], was that the decision had been very weighty, and when I brought up the reports that there was much dissent in the Red Brigades about the decision [Y] didn't deny it.

Riscontro. That is the most expressive Italian word for corroboration. In the admittedly filtered but still authoritative voice of X, we find *riscontro* for all the affirmations of the negotiations party. *Riscontro* for the claims of the Red Brigades' lawyers about that elusive recognition; for the Socialist insistence on the release of one political prisoner (what better recognition than arbiter of a comrade's freedom?); for the family's belief that even a mere willingness would suffice for the "*predisposed*"; and when set jaw-to-jaw with X's "*any other sign*," in Aldo Moro's message to Zaccagnini stressing the importance of "any opening, however problematical the position, any immediate sign of awareness of the magnitude of the problem," more than *riscontro*, we find vindication. For the arguments and the platitudes of the hard line, there is only utter contradiction.

32.

The hard line, as it was practiced in Rome, is the wrong line, the line of escalation, the blood line. As a preventive against kidnapping, it is a most unsatisfactory measure. It is not true that political terrorists do not kidnap when it is clear their demands will not be met. In the first place, this message can never be made completely clear, since it is by nature ambiguous. That Aldo Moro was not ransomed only proves, to speak bluntly, that he was not regarded as worth the price. If, say, the President of the United States visiting Italy were kidnapped by the Red Brigades, the price for his return might also be considered too high, but it is inconceivable that no attempt would be made to negotiate. The same applies, as the Socialists pointed out, to policemen and prison guards, as well as, one hopes, kindergartners, and perhaps in Italy, some soccer teams.

Second, most of the persons kidnapped by the Red Brigades were not captured for blackmail purposes but solely to obtain information and for propaganda. There is nothing to believe that this practice will not be continued, with the fate of the victim beyond the reach of reason.

Finally, to the extent that the hard line acts as a deterrent for Moro-type kidnappings, the state, not its enemies, is the loser. Considering the outcome, it is difficult to imagine a less-efficient expenditure of terrorist resources than that of the fifty-four days. For an urban guerrilla organization the only place to attempt to go when sensational kidnappings are confronted by the hard line and nothing else is up. If the same planning, risk, and energy that went into the Moro operation had provided for multiple assassinations rather than a single kidnapping, the Red Brigades would have achieved much the same effect killing Moro on the first day as they had on the last, and they would have had eight weeks free to do all sorts of destabilizing mischief besides.

This is precisely the pattern that has emerged. There have been no political kidnappings in Italy since the Moro affair; every major incident afterward, with the exception of one or two kneecappings, has been an assassination, which has therefore quickened the kill rate. Kidnapping may have had its day, but the scenarios in a country that hosts nuclear missiles, the U. S. Seventh Fleet, and the Pope are endless.

Moreover, as the rest of us advance deeper and deeper into technological society, so do the terrorists. Who would bother with an Aldo Moro when a captured barrel of nuclear wastes can hold a whole nation for ransom? Security systems, as every terrorologist knows, are no answer. As long as there is one person without an armed bodyguard, there will always be a target, and the first nation to aspire to the bulletproof society will be the first to self-destruct. There are already more than enough incentives for more efficient terrorism; the hard line is nothing but a heartless redundancy.

For these reasons and many more, until Italy, of all countries, became the singular exception, no state in the world had adopted a policy of total intransigence. Even commando-minded Israel has and will negotiate with terrorists when there is no possibility of counterattack. The United States, too, will negotiate, and its general approach of no concessions is regarded as a guideline and not a fixed response.[1] Harsh U.S. policy not to ransom American diplomats captured by foreign terrorists is somewhat alleviated by advance notice to the civil servants in question and theoretically adequate security measures. Aldo Moro in his own country had neither, not to speak of the chances of a raid to set him free.

According to terrorologist Brian Jenkins of the RAND Corporation, it makes no difference whether a government yields to terrorists or not. "In reality," he told an Italian interviewer early in the Moro affair, "the course of each episode is so unique, the sequence of events so unforeseeable, that when a government discards its options in advance it nullifies its own capacity to react to a situation. More important than the fact that a government gives in or decides not to give in to the demands, whatever kind they may be, is that it appears competent and in a position to control the situation."

The line adopted, says Jenkins, who is no partisan of pussyfooting, is the lesser factor "because if the government were to appear incompetent, if it were to appear inert, if in short it were to appear that the incident has thrown the government into total chaos, then the alarm the terrorists seek to arouse cannot but augment. At the same time, this would increase public indignation and the pressure for the adoption of draconian measures."[2]

This is precisely the upward spiral foreseen by Moro in the people's prison. It leads ineluctably and painfully to either failure or Pyrrhic victory. Failure—much to be preferred—when the cycle of restriction of civil rights and liberties turns the tide against its perpetrators, if not on the side of the guerrillas. "Victory" when the last freedom is gone.

The hard line's only success story is the famous case of Uruguay. In a battle to the death between the Tupamaros, the model of an urban guerrilla organization, and a republic considered the most democratic in South America, Uruguay was turned into a police state and the Tupamaros were crushed. All that survives is a "terror free" military dictatorship.

"Part of the price we pay for the survival of democracy," says scholar Paul Wilkinson in a paper for the Institute for the Study of Conflict, "is the freedom of ideas. Hence in a working liberal democracy it is both dangerous and naïve to hope to destroy a subversive movement utterly."[3]

How, then, the case of Aldo Moro can be applauded as a victory for democracy demands an explanation. In the black book of the more than one thousand major terrorist incidents that took place worldwide in the 1970s and how they were confronted, the universal abandonment of Aldo Moro stands alone, a frightening portent of the 1980s.

It would be slightly less disconcerting if the decisions to leave Moro stranded, transform him into a nonperson, and maintain that the three-monkey response to evil is the highest form of civilization were purely Italian. We could then either clack our tongues complacently or say with Luigi Barzini that the *real* Italy "is a smile on a waiter's face." To be sure, those decisions, as has been seen, were made exclusively in Rome, determined rather less by the spirit of democracy than because of the passing exigencies of domestic power politics. Nevertheless, the interests of powers far bigger than Italy were hot breaths on Rome's neck. Nowhere along the line were the men in the Street of the Dark Shops unaware that Eurocommunism was on trial both in Moscow and in Washington,* and not for a moment did Christian Democracy forget the United States and West Germany.

After the 1977 Schleyer affair—a landmark in the development of the hard line—West German Chancellor Helmut Schmidt declared his belief that in the future no other Western European government "would act very differently from the way we acted."⁴ Bonn's presence in Rome, notably at the Ministry of Interior, represented prophecy in the act of self-fulfillment. As for the United States, Washington was still under the sway of the 1973 Nixon doctrine that America "cannot and will not pay blackmail."⁵ More important, since the United States does not consider itself as having a terrorist problem, it was pursuing a policy of backing Bonn as the strongest currency of antiterrorism.

Significantly, it was not the advice of Brian Jenkins that was sought and followed in Rome (although Jenkins is probably the world's most consulted terrorologist), but that of State Department crisis manager Steve Pieczenik. Unlike Jenkins's flexible-line theory, Pieczenik's, as we saw, advanced the thesis that it was essential to demonstrate "that no man is indispensable to the viability of the nation-state." This demonstration was particularly crucial because Moro, according to Pieczenik, "was an extremely important member of the system." In other words, the idea, it seems, was to prove that *even* Aldo Moro was dispensable.

---

* The party seems to have fared well in both capitals. Washington has since eased its less-power-not-more position, and the American ambassador has lifted his ban on Communist attendance at U.S. diplomatic functions in Rome. The Kremlin, during the fifty-four days, simply mimicked Berlinguer's stance against the Red Brigades and the Socialist proposals. For his part, Berlinguer has gone out of his way to please, chastened by his May 14 defeat at the polls. No one seems to have noticed, however, that Eurocommunism's first participation in the exercise of state power, under the crisis conditions of the Moro case, unfortunately, confirmed the worst fears of its most strident critics by completely reverting to Stalinist tactics. Whether this is an irremedial feature of Eurocommunism remains to be seen (many Italian Communists admit privately that they "overreacted" or were "a little hysterical").

In his letter of resignation, Interior Minister Cossiga wrote that he had consented and had made his contribution to the government's line because he was convinced that it had been uniquely imposed by his duty to serve the state, its "concrete needs" of the moment, and its "permanent interests." Cossiga, in fact, in the style but not the substance of his mentor, was the true architect of that line. The stuff of which it was made was a blend of the immediate, or the concrete needs of the Communists and the Christian Democrats, and we now know that the part expressing Italy's "permanent interests" came directly from young Dr. Pieczenik.

In the fluid period immediately after the attack in Via Fani, the government, after hearing the superparties and its foreign allies, opted for what the *Corriere della Sera* has called, without guile, "the strategy of inactivity." This was Cossiga's strategy, and the principal strategist behind it was Dr. Pieczenik. The British and the West Germans appear to fit in on the technological side; Pieczenik in Rome made no note of their presence in the planning of the Italian response.

The philosophy shaping this response, according to an authoritative report in the *Corriere*, was that "the more the behavior of the state apparatus remains calm, phlegmatic, almost indifferent, the more were the possibilities to save the life of the hostage."[6]

This strategy of inactivity, or as the case may be, indifference, was backed at every critical turn by the highest officials of the Carter administration. Two House resolutions of "solid support" and "full confidence" for Rome brought Congress into the picture.[7] Whatever part of this was based on uninformed sympathy should be doubly criticized. The American President's public messages to Rome, unsparing in explicit support of the Andreotti government's handling of the affair, were almost as numerous as Aldo Moro's public assaults against it. On May 4, while Andreotti was elaborating his "not even the minimum departure" from the hard line, then U. S. Cabinet member Joseph Califano was praising Italy as "an example for all countries that seek to follow the democratic way of life."[8]

By then, Califano's remark was an embarrassment of riches for the Italian Government, but the personal letter from Carter to Andreotti in mid-April was a thumb on the scale of events. Pieczenik had returned to Washington, declaring Rome's course of action "commendable," but someone, if not Pieczenik himself, felt that the Italians needed still more encouragement. Carter's April 14 letter to Andreotti ("You and your government can count on my unswerving support") was just that.[9] It arrived in Rome on the fifteenth—the day the Red Brigades announced that Moro had been sentenced to death. This was a moment when the pressure on the strategy of inactivity was mounting to unbearable levels, and lest anyone think that Washington was weakening, too, the State Department on the seventeenth, addressing itself specifically to the authorities in Rome and the Italian nation, declared, "The Italian Government has our full support."[10]

Inactivity, intransigence, and insufferable indifference prevailed, but, as the *Corriere* commented when it was all over, this "philosophy" may have brought results with Pieczenik's management of ethnic and religious terrorist incidents in the United States, but "against the Red Brigades, it did not work."[11]

Pieczenik, who calls the *Corriere's* description of his counsel "just nonsense," insists that the Italian response consisted of highly sophisticated tactics and strategies, though he refuses to reveal what they might have been,[12] and they are certainly not apparent. He prefers to emphasize that what did not work was the strongest attempt in the Western world to destabilize a democracy. Of Aldo Moro, he said, "He was not sacrificed for a policy." That was three weeks before the Italian's death, which is about as good a time as any to fix the moment when Moro's cause was lost. Oddly, it was at about that time or some days earlier that Moro, perplexed to the end that Italy could be so unbending, wondered in a note from the people's prison, "Is there, perhaps, in all the holding hard against me, a suggestion from the Germans and the Americans?"[13]

In big-power diplomacy it is not plots but suggestions that are mighty. To what extent they tipped the balance in Rome, with its age-old yearning to gain credit in the disciplined societies, seems an enigma as vexing as trying to measure the killing force of the Red Brigades' foreknowledge of the spectacular finale that called like the wild from Via Caetani.

In the wind of the hard line the disappearance of Aldo Moro comes as a beginning, not an end. Its implications reach beyond the time and place of Italy and the 1970s. We, or the men of power on whom we lavish the we-ness of democracy, appear to be grossly miscalculating the damage being done to our societies, not as much by political terrorism, but by the one-dimensional reaction to it.

As Brian Jenkins has shown, all the world's terrorism of the seventies, from Belfast to Buenos Aires and back to Beirut by east route or west, barely adds up, in terms of dead and wounded, to one tenth of 1 per cent of the dead only, in the thirteen wars of the same decade. Yet the smaller threat has produced the less-measured response—along with the ugly, self-terrorizing, bulletproof, mini-fortress, *Berufsverbot* syndrome.

When a single political kidnapping, apart from the social expulsion of the victim by the whole of the international community, can bring about a general curtailment of freedom, months of power instability, and, worst of all, a state of mind characterized by fear, intolerance, and a desire to cover up the truth, any claim of victory for democracy would in the most generous instance be cause to ask what kind of democracy the claimant has in mind. Somewhere, somehow, berth must be assigned to balance and reason. Murderers and maimers must be tracked down and called to account for their crimes, but a society that is deaf to the authentic voices of despair, which is what most political terrorism really is, will cast aside its prophets and see blood and fury in its streets; it will know terror in its heart.

POSTSCRIPT

The Moro tragedy continues. The prophecies of the dead man are coming true. The new majority collapsed in 1979. Andreotti is out, though very much backstage. He has been replaced by Cossiga, who evidently felt himself recalled to public life. Cossiga heads a minority government whose sole *raison d'etre*, it surely seems, is to administer the latest set of anti-terrorist measures it itself decreed. Among them: arrest without charges, interrogation without counsel, long detention without trial. They are not merely on the books; they are being practiced.

Terrorism—more violent than ever—is rampant. Hit-and-run slaying is the rule rather than the exception; the recent capture in Turin of 190 hostages and the kneecapping of ten of them attests more to scope than to style. Italy, the majority of Italians feel, is ungovernable, and their leaders who say otherwise speak the language of the defensive.

The specter of Aldo Moro still haunts the nation. A parliamentary inquest has at last been sanctioned. Unfortunately, a commission weighted by the same power balance as that which assured Moro's demise is bound to have difficulty in getting at the truth. But some truths have a way of surfacing of their own accord, and these are the hardest to abide. Moro's preoccupations about his family, for example, have lately been seen to have been more than justified. The family has known no quietude since the fifty-four days, fallen prey to fears and isolation. Their unhappiness grates on the national conscience. A senior columnist of the *Corriere della Sera*, commenting recently on a rather sorrowful family squabble concerning the Aldo Moro Foundation, found it necessary to redefine what was once conveniently called Eleonora Moro's "dignified silence" as her "arrogant solitude"— "arrogant" because he sees in it a pointing finger that refuses to relent. Some solitudes are too damning for others to bear.

Events, too, are chafing. Ironically, in December 1979, Alberto Buonconto, the convicted terrorist proposed as an exchange prisoner for Aldo Moro, was released from his Naples prison on the very grounds for which his candidacy had been put forward: "serious physical infirmities." In the same month, the last four known letters of Aldo Moro came to light. They were all to Eleonora Moro. They included his very last words.

To his family: "A kiss and a caress for everyone, face by face, eye by eye, hair by hair."

To his wife: "Be strong, my sweet, in this absurd and incomprehensible ordeal. Such are the ways of the Lord."

To posterity: "Nothing is possible when you refuse to open a door."

In the last moments of this decade, Aldo Moro's message seems meant for all the world.

R.K.
Los Angeles
December 31, 1979

SOURCE NOTES

The principal sources of this book were the letters of Aldo Moro, the transcript of his interrogation, the nine communiqués of the Red Brigades, other published and unpublished documents (particularly those associated with investigations and trials of Italian terrorists), reports in the Italian press, and personal interviews.

The forty known letters of Aldo Moro, currently in possession of the Aldo Moro Foundation, Via Savoia 88, Rome, are now conveniently collected in an appendix to a foundation-sponsored work: A. Moro, *L'intelligenza e gli avvenimenti*, Milan: Garzanti, 1980. They are divisible into two significant categories:

a) those unpublished while he was alive (9)
b) those published after his death (31)

The authenticity of these letters is beyond question and by now is rarely if ever disputed. The same is true of the 25,000-word transcript of Moro's "trial," though here the original material has not been recovered. A study of this document, however, made by the Aldo Moro Foundation, demonstrates that the copy released by the Italian government contains two small deletions and a major transposition in the sequence of the text (see p. 271).

ABBREVIATIONS USED

L	Aldo Moro letter (L-a signifies category (a), etc.).
Int.	Aldo Moro's interrogation.
C	Red Brigades communiqué (C-I signifies first communiqué, etc.).
WP	"Libro bianco sul caso Moro," *L'Espresso*, October 15, 1978 (a white paper on the Moro case).
M	*Il Messaggero.*
Cds	*Corriere della Sera.*
R	*La Repubblica.*
P	*Il Popolo.*
U	*L'Unità.*
Adn	*Moro: il diario di un dramma*, Rome, 1978 (a "dossier" on the Moro case prepared by the news wire ADN Kronos).
Pers. Int.	Personal interview (followed by name of person interviewed).
FS	Close family source (FS-I signifies first source, etc.).
PD	*Rassegna stampa* (Press digest issued daily by the Chamber of Deputies for Members of Parliament).
ES	U. S. Embassy spokesman (Rome).
SDS	U. S. State Department spokesman (Washington).
UNS	United Nations spokesman (world headquarters, New York).
AIS	Amnesty International spokesman (London).
SPS	Socialist Party spokesman (Rome).

FOREWORD

1. Washington *Post,* May 10, 1978.
2. C. Bocca, ed., *Moro, una tragedia italiana* (Rome, 1978), p. 27.

1 ARREST

1. Quoted in *Panorama*, Milan, June 15, 1978.

Chapter 1

1. My reconstruction of the kidnapping is based on investigation documents (e.g., eyewitness testimony, ballistic and autopsy reports, etc.). These have been best pursued and analyzed by R. Martinelli and A. Padellaro, two investigative reporters for *Cds*. See their book *Il delitto Moro* (Milan, 1979). Another important reconstruction is that of Derisi in *M*, March 26, April 2, August 6. See also *L'Europeo;* April 5, 1979, pp. 11–15.
2. Martinelli and Padellaro differ with Derisi on the movements of the car, as do the eyewitness versions. I have followed the most logical sequence.
3. *Aldo Moro* (Rome, 1960), p. 10.
4. Photographs published in *Epoca*, Milan, May 17, 1978 (special supplement, pp. iv, vi).
5. Quoted in *Cds*, August 31, 1978, p. 2.
6. FS-I.
7. Address by Aldo Moro, February 28, 1978; quoted in G. Selva and E. Marcucci, *Il Martirio di Aldo Moro* (Bologna, 1978), p. 187.
8. See Martinelli and Padellaro, op. cit., pp. 7–9.
9. *P*, March 16, 1978, p. 1.

Chapter 2

1. Text in Selva and Marcucci, op. cit., p. 11.
2. R. Guerrini, "Una Grande caccia fallita," in *Epoca*, May 17, 1978, p. 40.
3. *M*, March 17, 1978.
4. Press release, U. S. Embassy, Rome.
5. *International Herald Tribune*, February 7, 1978.
6. *M*, March 17, 1978. See also Martinelli and Padellaro, op. cit., pp. 52–58.
7. *M*, March 17, 1978.
8. Pers. Int., Ugo Pecchioli, Rome, August 1, 1978.
9. Ibid.
10. Ibid.
11. *M*, March 17, 1978.
12. Ibid.
13. Ibid.
14. Quoted in A. Coppola, *Moro* (Rome, 1976), p. 72.

15.   Statement by Poletti in radio broadcast, GR2, August 7, 1978.
16.   ES.
17.   *M*, March 17, 1978.
18.   Pers. Int., Ugo Pecchioli.
19.   White House press release, March 16, 1978.
20.   *M*, March 17, 1978.

Chapter 3
1.   Quoted in Coppola, op. cit., p. 38.
2.   *M*, March 17, 1978.
3.   Guerrini, op. cit., p. 40.
4.   FS-I: Cf. Martinelli and Padellaro, op. cit., pp. 12–16.
5.   See G. Galli, *Storia della D.C.*, Bari, 1978, pp. 361–78.
6.   Ibid., p. 429.
7.   Quoted in *M*, March 17, 1978.

II PRISON

1.   Int.

Chapter 4
1.   Quoted in V. Tessandori, *Br Imputazione: banda armata* (Milan, 1977).
2.   Document in WP, pp. 13–14.
3.   *M*, March 18, 1978.
4.   Quoted in L. Sciascia, *L'Affaire Moro* (Palermo, 1978), p. 37.
5.   Ibid., p. 37.
6.   Quoted in Tessandori, op. cit., p. 147. The best account of the Sossi case is in Soccorso Rosso, *Brigate Rosse*, 2nd ed. (Milan, 1967), pp. 185–253.

Chapter 5
1.   Quoted in V. Goresio, "Moro: una politica pensata sempre in anticipo sui tempi," in *Epoca*, May 17, 1978 (special supplement, p. x).
2.   *M*, March 19, 1978.
3.   The following biographical material is based on C. Pizzinelli, *Moro* (Milan, 1969), Coppola, op. cit., and FS-I.
4.   Quoted in Coppola, op. cit., p. 115.
5.   Quoted in Galli, op. cit., p. 233.
6.   C. Cederna, *Giovanni Leone* (Milan, 1978).
7.   Speech of February 28, 1978, in Selva and Marcucci, op. cit., p. 18.

8. Coppola, op. cit., p. 119.
9. C-I, released March 18, 1978.
10. Coppola, op. cit., p. 120.

Chapter 6
1. *Cds*, May 12, 1978.
2. C-I, released March 18, 1978.
3. *Panorama*, October 17, 1978, pp. 50–51.
4. U. S. Embassy, Rome, Document April 24, 1978 (text of an article scheduled to appear in the New York *Times* of April 29, 1978 article was slightly cut when actually published on that date); also ES, SDS-1, and Pers. Int. (telephone) Steve Pieczenik, New York–Washington, February 23, 1979.
5. Red Brigades communiqué of April 26, 1974, published in Soccorso Rosso, op. cit., pp. 199–202.
6. Ibid., pp. 243–44.
7. Stendhal, *A Roman Journal* (New York, 1961), p. 301.
8. See A. Silj, *Mai piu senza fucile,* 3rd ed. (Florence, 1977), pp. 33–79. Also Soccorso Rosso, op. cit., pp. 217–18.
9. Silj, op. cit., p. 37.
10. Ibid., p. 70.
11. Ibid. Silj is probably the most objective observer of the Red Brigades' formational history.
12. See Tessandori, op. cit., pp. 236–40.
13. *Risoluzione della direzione strategica delle Brigate Rosse.* Text in op. cit., p. 93.
14. Silj, op. cit., p. 78.
15. Tessandori, op. cit., p. 303.
16. *Risoluzione della direzione strategica delle Brigate Rosse;* text in Bocca, op. cit., p. 95.
17. Ibid.
18. See Martinelli and Padellaro, op. cit., pp. 23–26.
19. Quoted in C. Dobson and R. Payne, *The Carlos Complex,* rev. ed. (London, 1978), p. 247.
20. Cf. T. Fazzolari, "Brigatisti, postino e vivandiere scelto," in *L'Espresso,* May 21, 1978.
21. R. Chiodo, "Il Manuale delle BR," in *L'Europeo,* January 11, 1979, p. 15. See also "Norme di sicurezza e stile di lavoro," (another Red Brigades handbook); text in Tessandori, op. cit., pp. 395–400.
22. R. Chiodi, op. cit., p. 15.

III TRIAL

1.   Int.

Chapter 7
1.   *R,* March 29, 1978.
2.   *Il Tempo,* March 29, 1978.
3.   Adn, p. 12.
4.   C-II, released March 25, 1978.
5.   "Le lettere nascoste" in *Panorama,* December 5, 1978; see also "Quelle lettere sparite," *Panorama,* December 12, 1978.
6.   L-b, received March 29, 1978.
7.   C-II, released March 25, 1978.
8.   *L'Espresso,* April 25, 1978.
9.   L-a, released March 29, 1978.

Chapter 8
1.   FS-I.
2.   L-b, received March 29, 1978.
3.   *L'Espresso,* April 23, 1978.
4.   Ibid.
5.   L-a, released March 29, 1978.
6.   C-III, released March 29, 1978.
7.   WP, p. 14.
8.   *Cds,* May 12, 1978.
9.   Ibid.

Chapter 9
1.   A. Silj, *Brigate Rosse-Stato* (Florence, 1978), p. 163.
2.   *Cds,* March 30, 1978.
3.   *R,* March 30, 1978.
4.   *Paese Sera,* March 30, 1978.
5.   *M,* March 30, 1978.
6.   *P,* March 31, 1978.
7.   *U,* March 31, 1978.
8.   Ibid.
9.   Ibid.
10.   *L'Osservatore Romano,* March 31, 1978.
11.   *Cds,* March 31, 1978.
12.   P. Buongiorno and C. S. Fioretti, "Quelle lettere di Moro," in *Panorama,* June 13, 1978.
13.   *Paese Sera,* March 31, 1978.
14.   *La Stampa,* March 31, 1978.
15.   *Cds,* March 31, 1978.

16. *L'Osservatore Romano,* March 31, 1978.
17. *P,* April 1, 1978.
18. Int.
19. *Cds,* May 12, 1978; see partial "denial" in *P,* May 13.
20. *M,* April 3.
21. P. Mielli, "Quel Craxi, però, che giocatore," in *L'Espresso,* May 21, 1978; see also WP, pp. 11–13; and G. Guiso, *La Condanna de Aldo Moro* (Milan, 1979).
22. Adn, p. 13.

Chapter 10
1. *Cds.*
2. Galli, op. cit., p. 429.
3. See ibid., pp. 361–63, 368–71.
4. Document in WP, p. 14.
5. *M,* April 4, 1978.
6. Selva and Marcucci, op. cit., p. 43.
7. Galli, op. cit., p. 421.
8. Int.
9. L-a, released April 4, 1978.
10. Selva and Marcucci, op. cit., p. 44.
11. *Cds,* April 6, 1978.
12. *P,* April 5, 1978.
13. Selva and Marcucci, op. cit., p. 41.
14. A. Moro, *Il Diritto* (Bari, 1978), p. 175; also FS-I and FS-II.
15. *Cds,* June 15, 1978.
16. *Paese Sera,* April 11, 1978.
17. See L-a, released April 10, 1978, and *Paese Sera,* April 11, 1978.
18. *Cds,* April 5, 1978.
19. *U,* April 5, 1978.
20. New York *Times* April 6, 1978.
21. New York *Times* April 9, 1978.
22. C-IV, released April 4, 1978.
23. Trial Communiqué thirteen, April 4, 1978. This unpublished document may be found in the records of the trial.

Chapter 11
1. See P. Mielli, op. cit.; WP.
2. L-b, received April 4, 1978.
3. *Il Giorno,* April 7, 1978.
4. Transcript in *Cds,* October 27, 1978.
5. Adn, p. 16.

6. Transcript in *Cds,* October 27, 1978.
7. *L'Osservatore Romano,* April 7, 1978.
8. L-b, received April 8, 1978.
9. FS-II.
10. G. Quaranta, *La Politica della Cultura* (Rome, 1978), privately published, p. 27.
11. Ibid., p. 28.
12. See WP, p. 9; also FS-II.
13. A. Rossi, *La Cicala* (Milan, 1978).
14. Pers. Int., Ugo Pecchioli, August 1, 1978.

Chapter 12
1. Red Brigades' internal document in Soccorso Rosso, op. cit., pp. 202–6.
2. *Cds,* April 12, 1979.
3. L-a, released April 10, 1978.
4. C-V, released April 10, 1978.
5. Int.

IV *SENTENCE*

1. L-b (Letter to Freato, received April 24 or 25, 1978).

Chapter 13
1. See *L'Espresso,* April 23, 1978, p. 27; also *Cds,* October 17, 1978.
2. Ibid.
3. C-VI, released April 15, 1978.
4. *L'Espresso,* April 23, 1978, p. 22.
5. Unpublished letter from Carter to Andreotti, April 14, 1978. (White House file number 7807478.)
6. C. Cederna, op. cit., pp. 201–3; also *L'Espresso,* April 23, 1978, p. 27.
7. *L'Espresso,* April 23, 1978, p. 27.
8. Int.
9. WP, p. 11.
10. Photograph in Adn.
11. FS-I.
12. Leone's statement in *M,* April 17, 1978.
13. *M,* April 17, 1978.
14. Pers. Int., Ugo Pecchioli; cf. WP, p. 11.
15. See Amnesty International News Release, NWS 02/22/78, of April 17, 1978.
16. *Cds,* April 18, 1978.

Chapter 14
1. Text in *Cds,* April 19, 1978.
2. Ibid.
3. See Martinelli and Padellaro, op. cit., pp. 118–24.
4. *Paese Sera,* April 19, 1978.
5. PD, April 19, 1978.
6. *M,* April 19, 1978.
7. Pers. Int., Ugo Pecchioli, August 1, 1979.
8. *M,* April 19, 1978.
9. See, for example, PD, April 19, 1978.
10. New York *Times,* April 18, 1978.
11. *M,* April 19, 1978.
12. Ibid.
13. *Il Giorno,* April 20, 1978.
14. FS-II.
15. *Lotta Continua,* April 18, 1978.
16. *Panorama,* September 21, 1978, p. 45.
17. Text in *Lotta Continua,* April 19, 1978.
18. *U,* April 20, 1978.

Chapter 15
1. *M,* April 21, 1978.
2. Ibid.
3. C-VII, released April 20, 1978.
4. *L'Espresso,* April 27, 1979, p. 28.
5. Selva and Marcucci, op. cit., p. 72.
6. *R,* April 21, 1978.
7. Pers. Int., Eduardo Di Giovanni, Rome, July 26, 1978.

Chapter 16
1. L-b, received April 20, 1978.
2. *Avanti!* April 21, 1978.
3. Text in *Cds,* April 21, 1978.
4. *Cds,* April 21, 1978.
5. *Cds,* April 21, 1978.
6. L-a, released April 21, 1978.
7. *Lotta Continua,* April 21, 1978.

Chapter 17
1. *Paese Sera,* April 21, 1978.
2. Text in *Avanti!* April 22, 1978.
3. *R,* April 22, 1978.
4. *U,* April 21, 1978.

5.   *R*, April 22, 1978.
6.   Text in *Cds*, April 22, 1978.
7.   Ibid.
8.   Text in *P*, April 22, 1978.

Chapter 18
1.   Text in *L'Osservatore Romano*, April 30, 1978. Text in Bocca, op. cit., pp. 129–30.
2.   Pers. Int., Eduardo Di Giovanni. July 26, 1978.
3.   *Cds*, April 23, 1978.
4.   *Cds*, April 24, 1978.

V APPEAL

1.   L-b, undated letter to Cossiga.

Chapter 19
1.   L-b, received April 24 or 25, 1978.
2.   FS-I.
3.   L-b, received April 24 or 25, 1978.
4.   L-b, received April 24 or 25.
5.   L-a, released April 24, 1978.
6.   L-b, April 22, 1978.
7.   L-b, received April 22, 1978.
8.   L-b, received April 23, 1978.
9.   L-b.
10.   *Panorama*, December 12, 1978, p. 53.
11.   L-b to Corrado Guerzoni, received April 24 or 25, 1978.
12.   Ibid.
13.   L-b, to Mennini, received April 24 or 25, 1978.
14.   C-VIII, released April 24, 1978.

Chapter 20
1.   See various reactions in PD, April 25.
2.   L-a, released April 24, 1978.
3.   L. Sciascia, op. cit., p. 33.
4.   Text in *P*, April 25, 1978.
5.   L-a, released April 29, 1978.
6.   United National Press Release SG/SN/2565, April 25, 1978. See also note 7, below.
7.   Waldheim's thoughts and actions recounted by UNS, February 23, 1978.
8.   United National Press Release SG/SN/2565, April 25, 1978.
9.   *U*, April 26, 1978.

10.   UNS, February 23, 1979.
11.   *Cds,* April 26, 1978.
12.   See Mielli, op. cit., WP, pp. 11–12; Barberi, op. cit.; also SPS, July 30, 1978.
13.   Barberi, op. cit., p. 44.
14.   Ibid., p. 43.
15.   WP, p. 11, and also FS-II.
16.   *Il Giorno,* April 26, 1978.
17.   FS-II.
18.   *Cds,* April 27, 1978.

Chapter 21
1.   L-a, released April 24, 1978.
2.   L-a.
3.   L-b, to Eleonora Moro, received May 5, 1978.
4.   *Panorama,* September 26, 1978, pp. 44–45.
5.   Ibid.
6.   R.
7.   L-b to Pennacchini, received April 27, 1978.
8.   L-bs to Piccoli and Renato Dell'Andro, received April 27, 1978.
9.   L-b to Mennini, received April 27, 1978.
10.   L-a to Craxi, released April 30, and L-a to Leone, released May 3, 1978; L-bs to Andreotti, Fanfani, Ingrao, and Misasi, received April 29 and 30, 1978.
11.   L-b to Misasi, received April 29 or 30, 1978.
12.   L-b to Andreotti, received April 29 or 30, 1978.
13.   L-a to Craxi, released April 30, 1978.
14.   See *P,* April 26, 27, 28, 1978.
15.   *L'Umanità,* April 27, 1978.
16.   *U,* April 27, 1978.
17.   *La Voce Repubblicana,* April 27, 1978.
18.   *L'Osservatore Romano,* April 27, 1978.
19.   FS-II; see also *Panorama,* October 10, 1978, p. 66.
20.   *M,* May 7, 1978; see also New York *Post,* May 6, 1978. Buckley's column is also widely syndicated in the U.S. and abroad.
21.   *M,* April 30, 1978.
22.   F. Mitterand, "L'abeille et l'architecte" Paris 1978; This political diary by the French Socialist Leader was excerpted in *L'Europeo,* September 22, 1978.
23.   *M,* April 29, 1978.
24.   *M,* April 29, 1978.
25.   Ibid.

Chapter 22
1. L-a.
2. L. Sciascia, op. cit., p. 39.

Chapter 23
1. See *Panorama*, September 26, 1978, pp. 40–41.
2. *M,* April 30, 1978.
3. *Avanti!* April 30, 1978.
4. See account by G. Guiso in op. cit., pp. 223–31.
5. *La Voce Repubblicana,* April 30, 1978.
6. *L'Umanità,* April 30, 1978.
7. *M,* April 30, 1978.
8. Ibid.
9. Ibid.
10. WP, p. 11, also FS-II.
11. *M,* April 30, 1978.
12. Transcript in *Cds,* October 27, 1978.
13. *Cds,* May 1, 1978.
14. Text in *Cds,* May 1, 1978.
15. F. Mitterand, op. cit., quoted in *L'Europeo,* September 22, 1978, p. 17.

VI *IL GRAN RIFIUTO*

1. Int.

Chapter 24
1. See Tessandori, op. cit., pp. 275–76.
2. Guiso, op. cit., p. 119.
3. *Panorama,* September 26, 1978, p. 44.
4. Guiso, op. cit., p. 120.
5. L-b to Ancora, received May 2, 1978.
6. Ibid.
7. WP, p. 15.
8. *Cds,* April 27, 1979.
9. Statement of Pasquale Balzammo on television program "Primo Piano," RAI TV 2, November 23, 1978.
10. WP, p. 15.
11. *Lotta Continua,* September 26, 1978. Piccoli denies this (*Cds,* September 26, 1978); however when the matter was disclosed in Parliament by left-wing deputy Mimmo Pinto, threatened action against him by Piccoli and others was soon afterward quietly dropped (see *Cds,* November 27, 1979).
12. WP, p. 15.

Chapter 25
1. *Paese Sera,* May 3, 1978.
2. Ibid.
3. *U,* May 3, 1978.
4. *P,* May 4, 1978.
5. *Cds,* May 4, 1978.
6. *Paese Sera,* May 4, 1978.
7. C-IX, released May 5, 1978.
8. L-b to Eleonora Moro, received May 5, 1978.
9. See Mielli, op. cit.; also SPS.
10. *Cds,* May 6, 1978.
11. Pers. Int., Eduardo Di Giovanni; see also *Panorama,* May 29, 1978.
12. *Cds,* May 6, 1978.

Chapter 26
1. Int.
2. Mielli, op. cit., WP, p. 12.
3. Reaction in *U* and *La Voce Repubblicana,* May 6, 1978. Amnesty "welcomed" Andreotti's action (Amnesty Press Release, May 9, 1978) but according to AIS that was the last they heard of it.
4. *M,* May 6, 1978.
5. WP, p. 13; also FS-I.
6. Statement by Mimmo Pinto in the Chamber of Deputies, October 26, 1978; text in *Lotta Continua,* October 27, 1978. (Pinto's speech was based for the most part on sources close to the Moro family.)
7. Martinelli and Padellaro, op. cit., pp. 204–9; also FS-I and II.
8. Mielli, op. cit.
9. *M,* May 8, 1978; see also statement by Mimmo Pinto in the Chamber of Deputies, October 26, 1978; text in *Lotta Continua,* October 27, 1978.
10. *Cds,* May 8, 1978.
11. *M,* May 8, 1978.
12. WP, p. 13; cf. Mielli, op. cit.
13. Martinelli and Padellaro, op. cit., pp. 204–8.
14. *Cds,* May 8, 1978.
15. *U,* May 8, 1978.
16. Letter from Prime Minister's office to Giancarlo Quaranta, May 6, 1978, text in *Lotta Continua,* October 28, 1978.
17. *Cds,* May 9, 1978.
18. Mielli, op. cit., also WP, p. 13.

19.   WP, p. 13.
20.   *Epoca,* May 17, 1978, p. 38.
21.   PD, May 9, 1978.
22.   Int.
23.   *Panorama,* September 26, 1978, p. 41.

Chapter 27
1.   Text in *Cds,* July 2, 1978.
2.   The most accurate report on the autopsy is in *Panorama,* June 13, 1978, pp. 55–57. Unique and grisly photographic documentation appears in *L'Europeo,* April 5, 1979.
3.   *M,* May 10, 1978.
4.   FS-I.
5.   Ibid.
6.   See especially accounts in *M* and *P,* May 10, 1978.
7.   Pers. Int., Ugo Pecchioli, August 1, 1978.
8.   Ibid.

Chapter 28
1.   *Epoca,* May 17, 1978, p. 39.
2.   *Cds,* May 10, 1978.
3.   *M,* May 11, 1978; cf. *Epoca,* May 17, 1978, p. 39.
4.   *Cds,* May 11, 1978.
5.   *M,* May 10, 1978.
6.   *Cds,* May 10, 1978.
7.   Ibid.
8.   U. S. Embassy, Rome Press Release, May 10, 1978.
9.   See especially *M,* May 10 and 11, 1978.
10.   *M,* May 11, 1978; also FS-I.
11.   *R,* May 12, 1978.
12.   Ibid.
13.   FS-I.
14.   Ibid.
15.   *M,* May 11, 1978.
16.   See accounts in *M* and *R,* May 11, 1978; also cover stories in *Time* and *Newsweek* (European editions), May 17, 1978.

Chapter 29
1.   Red Brigades' Trial Communiqué N. 15, May 11, 1978.
2.   Statement of Papal Secretary Monsignor Pasquale Macchi, RAI Radio II, May 8, 1979.
3.   *L'Osservatore Romano,* May 14, 1979.
4.   See *M,* May 17, 1978.
5.   Ibid.

VII DELIVERANCE

1. Int.

Chapter 30
1. U. S. Embassy, Rome Press Release, May 10, 1979.
2. New York *Times*, May 10, 1978.
3. Washington *Post*, May 10, 1978.
4. *The Times* (London), May 10, 1978.
5. PD, May 10, 1978.
6. *Financial Times*, May 10, 1978.
7. *Cds*, May 20, 1978.
8. Martinelli and Padellaro, op. cit., p. 209.
9. *Cds*, May 23, 1979.
10. *La Nazione*, July 27, 1978.
11. *Cds*, July 27, 1978.
12. *Cds*, July 9, 1978.
13. *M*, July 30, 1978.
14. Ibid., July 30, 1978.
15. *L'Europeo*, May 28, 1978.
16. *Panorama*, October 10, 1978, pp. 61–65.
17. Ibid.
18. *M*, May 28, 1978.
19. See Int., FS-I.
20. *L'Europeo*, August 18, 1978, p. 18.
21. *L'Europeo*, September 29, 1978, p. 9.
22. *Panorama*, December 23, 1978, p. 32.
23. *Cds*, December 24, 1978.
24. *Panorama*, December 23, 1978, p. 32.
25. *U*, December 24, 1978.
26. S. Giannella, "Un dossier da Mosca" in *L'Europeo*, September 29, 1978.
27. ES, Rome.
28. *Studi Cattolici*, December 1978.

Chapter 31
1. *Cds*, December 31, 1978.
2. See *Controinformazione*, Summer 1978, and *Praxis*, July 1978.
3. WP, p. 17. See also special issues of *Panorama*, October 17 and 24, 1978.
4. *Panorama*, October 17, 1978, p. 50.
5. WP, pp. 17–18, and special issues of *Panorama*, October 17 and 24, 1978.
6. *Quotidiano dei Lavoriatori*, September 17, 1978.

7.   *L'Espresso,* April 29, 1979, p. 42.
8.   *Cds,* October 18, 1978.
9.   Int.
10.   FS-I.
11.   *L'Europeo,* November 3, 1978, p. 3.
12.   Galli, op. cit., p. 230.
13.   *Cds,* October 27, 1978; see also *Lotta Continua,* October 26 and 27, 1978.

Chapter 32
1.   Pers. Int., Ambassador Anthony Quainton. Director Office for Combating Terrorism, U. S. State Department, Washington, February 22, 1979.
2.   *Il Tempo,* March 21, 1978.
3.   C. Dobson and R. Payne, op. cit., p. 313.
4.   Ibid., p. 317.
5.   Ibid., p. 318.
6.   *Cds,* May 12, 1978.
7.   See House Congressional Resolution 616, May 9, 1978.
8.   Adn, p. 35.
9.   SDS.
10.   *Il Tempo,* April 18, 1978.
11.   *Cds,* May 12, 1978.
12.   Pers. Int., Steve Pieczenik (telephone, Washington, New York), February 23, 1979.
13.   L-a, released April 10, 1978.

APPENDIX

Chronology of the Fifty-four Days

CHRONOLOGY

MARCH

Thurs. 16: Aldo Moro, president of Christian Democracy, Italy's ruling party, is kidnapped in Rome; his five bodyguards are slain. The Red Brigades announce that Moro is in their hands. Parliament, in an overwhelming vote of confidence, empowers the government of Christian Democrat Giulio Andreotti, backed by the "new majority," a five-party coalition including for the first time the nation's second most powerful political force, the long-ostracized Communist Party. It is the world's first experiment with "Eurocommunism." The Communists decide immediately to adopt an intransigent position against the communist Red Brigades and "prevent negotiations."

Fri. 17: Andreotti meets with the party chiefs of the new majority. They agree on stern measures against political terrorism.

Sat. 18: Red Brigades issue Communiqué I, declaring that Moro is being held in a "people's prison" and is to be tried as a political prisoner. They also release a photograph of Moro.

Mon. 20:   The state's trial of Red Brigade's chief, Renato Curcio,
            and fourteen other *brigatisti* resumes in Turin after a
            series of delays imposed by terrorist actions.

Tues. 21:   The Andreotti government promulgates decree laws
            limiting civil liberties and increasing police powers, as
            the nation's most massive manhunt extends throughout
            Italy. The press, urged by the government to exercise
            "caution," debates the wisdom of self-censorship, which
            it is already practicing and will practice throughout.
            U. S. House of Representatives passes unanimous reso-
            lution giving "solid support" to Andreotti government.

Fri. 24:   Christian Democrat ex-mayor of Turin is shot and
            wounded in the legs (kneecapped) by Red Brigades.

Sat. 25:   Communiqué II released; Moro's "indictment," it de-
            clares that his interrogation is under way by a "people's
            tribunal."

Wed. 29:   Three confidential letters written by Moro (to his wife,
            his secretary, and Interior Minister Cossiga) are de-
            livered by the Red Brigades in an attempt to set up a
            two-way secret hot line. Red Brigades, along with
            Communiqué III, make public the letter to Cossiga, in
            which Moro speaks of a prisoner exchange to be nego-
            tiated by the Vatican.

Thurs. 30: Andreotti, spurred by the Communists and the other
            parties of the new majority, assumes a no-negotiations
            stance. The Moro letters, present and future, are to be
            regarded as extorted and "not morally imputable" to
            their author. The mass-circulation press and the state-
            controlled television networks back the hard line un-
            critically, portraying Moro as a man under torture and
            mind-altering drugs.

Fri. 31:   Vatican announces its availability as a mediator, but
            backs down when this creates "difficulties" for the
            hard line.

APRIL

Sun. 2:   Pope Paul VI, appealing publicly for Moro's life, begins to develop a position independent of and in contrast to the Vatican.

Tues. 4:   Communiqué IV distributed with letter from Moro to Christian Democratic Party chief executive Zaccagnini, citing evidence that Moro's position on prisoner exchanges predates his capture and thus cannot be considered as forced on him by the Red Brigades.

Thurs. 6:   Moro writes secret letter to family asking for a situation report.

Fri. 7:   Family replies in coded letter to the editor of Milan daily *Il Giorno*, saying it has not had "any sign" of the hard line weakening.

Sat. 8:   Moro writes back outlining his "war plans" to break the "fictitious unity" in Rome, which he sees as mainly determined by the Communists being in an experimental situation. This message is intercepted by the police, but is kept secret by both the government and the family.

Mon. 10:   Communiqué V arrives containing a handwritten note by Moro attacking his ex-Interior Minister who denied his precapture advocacy of soft line (one of the ministers cited by Moro; the other confirmed it).

Tues. 11:   Red Brigades assassinate Turin prison guard branded as "torturer"; guard wounds one assailant, later left by his comrades at a hospital.

Fri. 14:   Jimmy Carter sends Andreotti personal letter with full backing for the Italian Government's line.

Sat. 15:   Communiqué VI proclaims Moro's "guilt"; people's tribunal sentences him to death.

Mon. 17:   U. S. State Department reaffirms Washington's complete support of Rome's stance. Amnesty International
appeals to Red Brigades seeking to discuss terms of
Moro's release. Communists warn Amnesty not to inter-
fere politically. Christian Democrats and government
reiterate hard line.

Tues. 18: An unauthenticated "Communiqué VII" announces
Moro's execution, giving highly improbable particulars
about the body being submerged in a frozen mountain
lake. Nevertheless, the government mounts a spectacular "recovery" operation, lending credibility to the
death notice. In Rome, police discover an abandoned
Red Brigades base used for the Moro kidnapping.

Wed. 19:   Family disregards "Communiqué VII" in petition to
open negotiations signed by internationally renowned
personalities and Church figures.

Thurs. 20: Red Brigades assassinate head of Milan prison guards.
Verified Communiqué VII released with photo of Moro
reading news of his death. Christian Democrats given
forty-eight-hour ultimatum to indicate willingness to
negotiate prisoner exchange. Socialist Party defects
from the new majority's position of intransigence and
seeks a negotiated solution. The Conference of Italian
Bishops, outflanking the hard-liners in the Vatican, calls
on the intransigents to "desist" and pursue a more
reasonable path.

Fri. 21:   New Moro letter to Zaccagnini accuses party of immo-
bility, urging him to break with the hard line.

Sat. 22:   Pope Paul writes open letter "to the men of the Red
Brigades," hoping that by this recognition of their
political identity they will release Moro uncondition-
ally. Hortatory appeals are made also by U. S. Ambassador Andrew Young and UN Secretary General Kurt
Waldheim. Ultimatum expires at 3 P.M.

Mon. 24:   Red Brigades break silence with Communiqué VIII, giving list of thirteen communist prisoners whose freedom is asked in exchange for Moro. They insist on negotiations with the Christian Democrats, inviting the appealers to address themselves to the party. Moro sends third letter to Zaccagnini, trying to exert maximum pressure on the "weak link" in the hard line.

Tues. 25:   Secretary General Waldheim goes over the heads of the Italian Government, speaking directly, by satellite TV, to the Red Brigades as a political entity. This infuriates the hard-liners. Christian Democracy releases a statement signed by Moro's "friends" who dispute the authenticity of his letter to Zaccagnini.

Wed. 26:   Christian Democratic Rome regional leader kneecapped by Red Brigades. *Il Giorno* publishes letter from the family to Moro—reassuring him of support.

Thurs. 27:   FIAT executive kneecapped by Red Brigades in Turin. Socialists propose release of some political prisoners and improvements of conditions in antiterrorist "special prisons" as inducement for Moro's release.

Fri. 28:   Andreotti reaffirms hard line.

Sat. 29:   Moro, in an outpouring of letters to key persons in power, makes a final attempt to bring about a grassroots revolt against the leadership of his party; he convokes by right of his presidency the party's highest governing body to review his case. He declares that his release is contingent on a one-for-one exchange and he backs the Socialist position. He bars the men of power from his funeral.

Sun. 30:   Family breaks with Christian Democratic Party leadership, charging them by name with obstructing all initiatives to free Moro and thereby ratifying his death sentence; the leaders are accused as seeking to depict Moro as "substantially mad."

MAY

Mon. 1:   Socialists meet with Red Brigades contact and are con-
            vinced their plan for a one-for-one exchange will ob-
            tain Moro's release.

Tues. 2:   Socialists meet with Christian Democrats to gain sup-
            port, after rejection by the Communists; meeting aborts
            when Christian Democrats demand further guarantees.

Wed. 3:   Andreotti repudiates one-for-one proposal.

Fri. 5:   Communiqué IX announces the conclusion of the affair
            by "executing the sentence," but falls short of a defini-
            tive statement. Moro sends a nonpolitical, farewell
            letter to his wife.

Sat. 6:   Family joins with Socialists to bring all pressure to bear
            on Chief of State Leone to pardon one incurably ill
            brigatista; Leone agrees but stalls. Senator Fanfani
            agrees to attack hard line.

Sun. 7:   Fanfani forces speak out publicly but cautiously, hop-
            ing to signal Red Brigades that new moves are on the
            way without tipping their hand.

Mon. 8:   Fanfani himself attempts signal but holds back his
            main thrust for private talks with party and Andreotti
            the following morning. Family again reassured by
            Leone that he will sign pardon, but he buckles under
            pressure applied by Andreotti.

Tues. 9:   While Fanfani argues his case against the hard line,
            news arrives that Moro has been found dead in the
            back of an old Renault parked "a few meters away"—
            in a street midway between the party headquarters of
            Christian Democracy and the Communists.

Wed. 10:   Autopsy proves Moro was never drugged or mistreated.
            Family takes possession of body to forestall planned
            state funeral and adhere to last wishes of the victim.
            Aldo Moro is buried in a peasant village north of Rome.

INDEX

NOTE: Moro's married daughters and grandson are indexed under *Moro* rather than their last names.